A PILGRIM'S GUIDE TO THE

Camino

Lisboa · Santiago

John Brierley

*A Practical & Mystical Manual
for the Modern Day Pilgrim*

3rd edition

© John Brierley 2011

First published in 2005. This new, totally revised and updated edition, published in 2011.

ISBN 978-1-84409-530-8

All rights reserved. The contents of this book may not be reproduced in any form, except for short extracts for quotation or review, without the written permission of the publisher.

British Library Cataloguing-in-Publication Data.
A catalogue record for this book is available from the British Library.

All maps © John Brierley 2011

All photographs © John Brierley 2011

Printed and bound in the European Union

Published by
CAMINO GUIDES
An imprint of Findhorn Press Ltd.
117-121 High Street
Forres IV36 1AB
Scotland
Tel: +44(0)1309-690582
Fax: +44(0)131-777-2711

Email: info@findhornpress.com
www.findhornpress.com
www.caminoguides.com

Pontesampaio – *Part of the modern camino and the original Roman Road Via XVI*

CONTENTS:

Foreword		5
Introduction		7
Historical sketch		13
Preparation		19
Check-list:		23
Map Legend		25

• *Portugal* —

Lisbon City – Arrival / Departure		31
1. Lisbon – Alverca do Ribatejo	31.1 km	34
2. Alverca do Ribatejo – Azambuja	30.8 km	40
3. Azambuja – Santarém	32.3 km	46
4. Santarém – Golegã	31.2 km	52
5. Golegã – Tomar	29.7 km	56
6. Tomar – Alvaiázere	31.3 km	66
7. Alvaiázere – Rabaçal	32.5 km	70
8. Rabaçal – Coimbra	29.5 km	74
9. Coimbra – Mealhada	22.4 km	82
10. Mealhada – Águeda	25.4 km	86
11. Águeda – Albergaria	16.3 km	90
12. Albergaria – São João da Madeira	29.2 km	94
13. São João da Madeira – Porto	<u>34.3 km</u>	100
Total distance Lisbon – Porto	376.0 km	
Porto City – Arrival / Departure		107
14. Porto (Maia) – Vilarinho (Rates)	25.9 km	114
15. Vilarinho (Rates) – Barcelos (Portela)	27.3 km	126
16. Barcelos (Portela) – Ponte de Lima	33.6 km	136
17. Ponte de Lima – Rubiães	18.1 km	148
18. Rubiães – Tui (Valença)	19.3 km	154

• *Spain* —

19. Tui (Valença) – Redondela	31.1 km	162
20. Redondela – Pontevedra	18.2 km	168
21. Pontevedra – Caldas de Reis	23.1 km	176
22. Caldas de Reis – Padrón	18.1 km	182
23. Padrón – Santiago	<u>24.9 km</u>	190
Total distance Porto – Santiago	<u>239.6 km</u>	
Total distance Lisbon – Santiago	615.6 km	
Santiago – Arrival / Departure		198
Bibliography & Useful Contacts		203
Returning home – Stay in Touch		204

"We walk to God. Pause and reflect on this.
Could any way be holier, or more deserving of your
effort, of your love and of your full intent?...
Look not to ways that seem to lead you elsewhere."

A Course in Miracles.
Workbook for Students Part 1, lesson 155.12

Notes to the 3rd Edition:

Several improvements have been incorporated in this latest guide. Firstly the size and layout has been changed to make it easier to fit in your pocket. The maps now have additional information that makes it easier to identify pilgrim hostels and other accommodation along the way and to spot cafés, bars and restaurants for refreshment. But the biggest change is the addition of route finding information from Lisbon to Porto, which has now been fully waymarked. However, facilities for pilgrims along this section are still limited and, until infrastructure is improved, should only be undertaken by seasoned pilgrims with a flexible approach and a reasonable ability to speak Portuguese.

Contrary to popular belief the Portuguese Way is one third by earthen tracks and woodland pathways. This is true for both the Lisbon (33.2%) and Porto (32.5%) sections. While over half the first stage out of Lisbon is on pathways (much of it along the rio Tejo estuary) the waymarked route out of Porto has no natural pathways. Accordingly detailed options are given as to how to avoid the busy road network around Porto city.

Acknowledgements:

I would like to thank *Joana Castro, Antonio Martins Ferreira, José Figueiras, Fernanda* and *Jacinto Gomes Rodrigues* and their families, all of whom have welcomed me into their hearts and homes and provided me with a sound basis for my love and deep appreciation for Portugal and her people. Gratitude is also due to all those pilgrims who have walked this path over the centuries. Each one has helped to shape and make this path what it is today. From St. James himself who risked life and limb to carry the message of love and forgiveness to the Iberian peninsular and now — some two thousand years later, the Friends of the Way in Portugal who voluntarily give of their time to waymark the route so that we might find our way safely to Santiago de Compostela. In particular I would like to acknowledge *Ilídio Silva, Nuno Ribeiro, João Moreiro, Ana Castro, Alison Raju, Paul Crocker* and *Rodney Asher* who offered valuable feedback. And let us not forget all those people who live along the camino and offer welcome and shelter to us as we pass by. *Muito Obrigado.*

John Brierley

< Sao Pedro de Rates – *Corpus Christi*

Foreword:

In the beginning was the Word, and the Word was with God, and the Word was God. John 1.1

We live in a dualistic world of past and future, left and right, right and wrong. This world of time and space, of judgment and condemnation often feels contradictory and threatening. How do we honour our worldly commitments and make time to go on pilgrimage? How do we balance work and play and still find time to pray? How do we resolve a world of seeming opposites and our prejudice and judgement of others?

Perhaps pilgrimage, the Path of Enquiry, will lead us to that point of understanding where there is no longer any separation between path and goal, where life itself is pilgrimage and every step a prayer. In the meantime, we stumble along in dark clouds of unknowing and that is, perhaps, the essential beginning place; to have the courage to admit we are lost and the humility to ask directions.

When I was stumbling around wondering how best to start this guide, a neighbour appeared with a newspaper cutting with the heading, *what is the best guide to the camino?* The instant I asked for help I was handed the answer. The words and timing were perfect: *The best guide to* **what** *camino?* There are many guides to the physical path but if we attend only to the practical we miss the mystical and perhaps we miss the whole point. We walk down a cul-de-sac called despair with only our own mortality waiting for us at the end. There is no way out of our conundrum but in — through the inner landscape of soul.

So suddenly I was prompted to write a foreword, a beginning. And it occurred to me that unless I put God first in everything I do, I will not find my way out. If I look on the world through my lower self with my physical eyes alone I see an image of divisiveness and chaos with the only certainty being death and decay. From the perspective of lower mind the world itself is already half way through its biological life — even the sun will die. I find these thoughts wonderfully liberating because it frees me from my bondage to the material and opens a way to knowledge of Higher Worlds.

Synchronicity was also working when, after walking for five days in perfect weather along the peaceful pathways that make up the Camino Portugués, I arrived in town and was confronted with a television image of three Western kidnap victims in Iraq with their Islamic guards standing ominously in the background and the imminent threat of beheading. It was a dreadful image of intense pain and suffering that left me feeling shocked and nauseous. I wandered out into the sunlight in a vain effort to erase the terrifying image. An hour later, I found myself in a chapel before an image of St. James the Slayer of the Moors *Santiago Matamoros* occupying the central position over the altar. This was a place of modern Christian worship and the nausea returned as I realised that I was kneeling before an image of St. James with sword raised decapitating Islamic 'Infidels'. The way to forge peace can never be achieved through jihad and crusade.

There are many gods, but one God and whatever term we use to describe what cannot be described seems immaterial. God or Allah will do just fine, provided we direct our prayers towards an image of Love and Light. Words are powerful symbols and we need to be careful how we frame them. We may need to alter our images and think twice before we ask our questions and to whom we direct them. A loving God may provide a very different answer to a vengeful one. We need to watch our terminology, mindful that those who look for separation and dissent will find it, but those who seek the truth and a unified purpose will find that also.

Along every Path of Enquiry there comes a point that requires a leap of faith. A point where we have to abandon the security of outdated dogma handed down to us over millennia. To let go of the familiar story taught to us by our tribe and develop the courage to dive instead into the mysteries – this is the story of the Grail Knights and the heart of modern day pilgrimage too. When we meet that void no one else can cross it for us. We have to let go the safety of the familiar and dive into the unknown, with nothing but our faith in God to support us.

That is why I call these guides A Practical *and* Mystical Manual for the Modern Day Pilgrim. That we might find a place to eat and sleep at the end of a long days walking – but also, and crucially, that we might support each other to dive into the mysteries of our individual soul awakenings, without which all journeying is purposeless. We have a sacred contract, a divine function, and a reason why we came here. Perhaps your calling to go on pilgrimage will be the opportunity to find out what that purpose is and to provide the necessary space to re-orientate your life towards its fulfilment. Maybe this is the point in your life where all your neat and tightly held beliefs get shattered so that you can begin to piece together Who you really are and what your part in God's plan for salvation really is. We don't really have a choice, except to delay. Why wait for the inevitable and eternal?

So I end this foreword by giving the last word to the great mystic poet, Kabir.

Friend, hope for the truth while you are alive.
Jump into experience while you are alive!
Think... and   think... while you are alive.
What you call 'salvation' belongs to the time before death.
If you don't break your ropes while you are alive,
Do you think ghosts will do it after?

The idea that the soul will join with the ecstatic
Just because the body is rotten —
That is all fantasy.
What is found now is found then.

If you find nothing now,
You will simply end up with an apartment in the city of death.
If you make love with the divine now, in the next life
You will have the face of satisfied desire.
So plunge into the truth, find out Who the Teacher is,
Believe in the Great Sound!

The Portuguese Way *Camino Portugués* Caminho Português

The Towers of the West *Torres del Oeste*

Along this route lies Monte Santiaguiño where St. James first preached Christ's great lesson of unconditional love and forgiveness thus helping to write the first pages of Christian history. This pivotal event is represented on the front cover. Santiago returns to Jerusalem to face martyrdom and his body is returned to this self-same spot – the boat carrying his mortal remains sailing up past the Towers of the West *Torres del Oeste* at Catoira to fetch land again at Padrón, his body finally being transported to Libredon – now renamed Santiago de Compostela. The Camino Portugués is thus both a starting point and an end point in the legendary Santiago story.

Much of the route follows the original Roman military road that connected Portugal with Spain and then France via the major 'crossroads' town of Astorga *Asturica Augusta*. You will pass by Roman milestones *miliários* to confirm that you are, indeed, directly on this ancient way. We will cross Roman bridges built 2,000 years ago, but this period, which marks St. James life and teaching, was to fade into obscurity for 800 years until the discovery of his tomb in the Roman town of *Liberum Donum*. The legend of the 'Field of Stars' *Compo-Stellae* was born just in time for the Christian re-conquest *reconquista* of the Iberian peninsular from the Moors and the renaming of Libredon to *Santiago de Compostela* was to follow. And here we also see the emergence of the terrible image of St. James the Slayer of the Moors *Santiago Matamoros*. This was an ideal image to spearhead the re-conquest but one far removed from the message of love of God, self, and stranger that is portrayed in the image of St. James the Pilgrim *Santiago Peregrino*. It is this latter figure that was to lead the revival of Christian pilgrimage as early as the 10th century and was to make Santiago de Compostela the third greatest pilgrim destination after Jerusalem and Rome. Most of the bridges that we walk over today were built during this medieval period, sometimes using the earlier Roman foundations. But it is at the dawn of the 21st century that we witness an extraordinary revival of pilgrimage that now places the Camino de Santiago at the forefront of this extraordinary modern phenomena and the most popular Christian pilgrimage route in the world today.

However, this brief overview is only part of the story, for there is not one camino – but many (see map on back cover). Today the Camino Francés accounts for 80% (down from 95% 5 years ago) and the Camino Portugués has now become the second most popular route but this only comprises 7% of the total arriving at Santiago, still leaving the Portuguese Way relatively uncrowded. Here you follow in the footsteps of Celtic, Roman, Islamic and Christian wayfarers going back over millennia. Today we seek the very same treasures they looked for – to find and embrace that loving Presence that offers us the gifts of joy and peace. In this fearful and war-torn world our mission has never been clearer and more urgent – every step now becomes a prayer for peace. The Way is open again for everyone, irrespective of gender or generation, colour, class or creed and from every religion, or none. This inclusivity marks it apart from virtually every other pilgrim itinerary around the world.

Alternative routes: Before setting off you should at least hold an overview of the alternative routes that come under the general heading *Camino Portugués*. Not all of these are waymarked but enough have been painted with the familiar yellow arrows to cause possible confusion at certain points where they merge and branch off again. What follows is not an exhaustive list but it contains the major routes that have been used over the centuries and which are still in existence today, in some form or another. It is an indication of the popularity of the cult of St. James in Portugal during the Middle Ages that so many routes were available at that time. There are, perhaps, two contrasting reasons for its decline – the arrival of the industrial revolution in the 19th century and the apparition at Fátima in the early 20th century. The early 21st century witnesses a marvellous awakening and renewal. Gratitude is due directly to you for being part of its re-emergence and I trust that it will feed and nourish you to the extent that you feed and nurture it.

[1] The Central Way *Caminho Central* via Barcelos (The recommended route described in this guide book).

[2] The Interior Way *Caminho do Interior* via Braga. Braga was, and remains, the ecclesiastical heart of Portugal and is rich in religious monuments. Churches abound and there are several museums displaying religious artefacts and iconography. The most widely visited 'tourist' site in Portugal is the intriguing church of Bom Jesus, which lies on a hill overlooking the city. The extent and wealth of its historical

Braga – *Hospital São Marcos*

monuments is, perhaps, one of its biggest drawbacks for the modern day pilgrim. Its popularity as a tourist destination means that the roads into and out of Braga are busy and accommodation is relatively expensive. While 'officially' this route is promoted as an alternative to the Central Way through Barcelos, it is very hard going and waymarks are sporadic in comparison. But the biggest detraction is the road work; almost the entire route from Porto to Braga is on asphalt or granite road ways, many of them quite hazardous. Also accommodation at convenient intervals is difficult to secure. Finally, Braga can be visited relatively easily by bus from Barcelos. So if you want to experience the sites and sounds of Braga, you can do so as a day's detour (see Barcelos for details).

[3] The Coastal Way *Caminho da Costa* via Viana do Castelo. In many respects this is one of the easiest routes to follow as it basically hugs the coast to rejoin the main routes in Valença. It is difficult to get lost and perhaps for this reason it was a popular route in medieval times, although it required pilgrims of yore to take a ferry across the major river mouths or detour inland to cross the bridges further upstream. The

Viana do Castelo – *Centro*

current tourist office in Viana do Castelo bears graphic witness to its popularity; it was built in 1468 as a pilgrim Inn or hospice to house the increasing numbers of pilgrims on their way to Santiago using this route. The main drawbacks to the coastal route are; [a] there is often a strong westerly breeze off the sea (especially at the shoulder seasons of early spring and late autumn with the equinoctial gales). This can make walking along the beaches difficult and walking along the coastal roads isn't much better and has the added hazard of traffic to contend with. [b] This coastal stretch is very popular in the summer months, which reduces the contemplative aspect and increases the demand (and therefore availability and cost) for accommodation. [c] Few pilgrims choose this route and it lacks the familiarity of waymarks and friendships that build along the other caminos. Notwithstanding these drawbacks it is being slowly rediscovered.

[4] The Northern Way *Caminho do Norte* via Lanheses. This route is not well waymarked and the lack of accommodation makes it difficult to negotiate. It combines the early stages of the Coastal route and then swings eastwards to connect with the Central route at Rates before branching off again at Barcelos. It comes close to the Central route again around Aborim. We need to be careful in this area to avoid confusing these separate routes. The Northern Way then climbs steeply through the Serra de Padela *Parque de Valinhas* to descend sharply to cross the Rio Lima into Lanheses. From here it is another steep climb up through the Serra de Arga before dropping down to join the Coastal route at Vila Nova de Cerveira and thence to Valença. While this way passes through some lovely countryside, and is arguably the quietest route, it also takes in much road work. While many of the roads have little or no traffic they are tiring underfoot and it is the most arduous route, taking in the steep mountains of the Serra de Arga.

[5] The Lamego Way *Caminho Português de Lamego* from Coimbra to Chaves. This route continues northwards to connect up with the Vía de la Plata at Verín. It starts in Coimbra and goes via Viseu, Lamego, Vila Real and Chaves before crossing over the border into Spain to Verín.

[6] The Way of the Star *Caminho de Via de Estrela* from Caceres to Braga. Not to be confused with the Vía Lactea or Milky Way. This route follows the line of a Roman road that branched off from the Vía de la Plata. While it has ancient roots it is only now re-emerging as a possible viable alternative pilgrim route to Santiago. It crosses the remote and beautiful Monte Estrela before entering Viseu and connecting with the Caminho de Santiago in Braga. Waymarking commenced in November 2008 and the first 16 kilometres was laid out between the Roman bridge at Alcantara and Brozas.

[7] Fátima: *Caminho de Tejo* This route follows the camino de Santiago from Lisbon as far as Santarém where it branches off to the west. To pilgrimage in Portugal we need to understand that Fátima and Portugal are virtually synonymous. Since the vision of the Blessed Virgin appeared to three young shepherd children (Lucia, Francesco and Jacinta) in Fátima in 1917, it has become a major pilgrimage centre and place of veneration in its own right and one of the great Marian Shrines in the Catholic world. While the thousands who travel there every year do so mostly by bus, you may well come across happy bands of walking pilgrims, sometimes as many as 100 in a group. Lucia was the only one to survive the flu epidemic that ravaged Europe after the First World war and the one to whom the *Three Secrets* were revealed. The first was a horrifying vision of hell and a call for repentance. The second was similar and concerned the threat of world war and persecution. The third was the most prophetic but has never been fully revealed. The Vatican has suggested it concerns the attempted assassination and death of Pope John Paul II *(A bishop dressed in white who falls to the ground as if dead)* but others suggest it prophesies the fall of the Church itself *(due to scandals at the heart of the hierarchy)*. Lucia died near Coimbra in 2005 and the Congregation of the Doctrine of the Faith will publish the text of the message that was revealed to her – in due course and after suitable preparation.

However we might individually interpret such prophecies, the fact remains that in order to breakthrough to a new reality we have to allow old thought-forms and dogma to die. The death of the old is generally experienced as painful, but the emergence of the new often brings elation. As we begin to shift from an imperfect outer authority to our innate inner wisdom we might experience an intensity of both anxiety and a sense of freedom. Fátima struggles with this self-same acceleration of both negative and positive forces. A headline in a Portuguese newspaper declared: *'Another Interfaith Outrage Blessed by Fátima Shrine Rector. Appearing on Portuguese television, Msgr. Guerra regurgitated the long-discredited ecumenical slogan that different religions should concentrate on what we have in common and not on what separates us.'* Pilgrimages of reparation still take place to atone for this outrage – and what, pray, is this defilement? A Hindu priest was permitted by Msgr. Guerra to offer a prayer for peace and reconciliation at the Catholic altar in the Little Chapel of the Apparitions.

Fátima clearly struggles with both traditional and a more progressive faith. This snapshot of Fátima will hopefully provide a context to understand the general lack of interest, even suspicion within Portugal, towards Santiago. The town of Tomar on the historic Santiago route lies 35 km east of Fátima and represents the Gnostic perspective held by the Order of the Knights Templar. This is no less threatening today as it was in 1312

Fátima – *Basilica*

when the Order was outlawed by the Vatican for it proclaims the sanctity of the God that lies within every individual and is less dependent on external authority. It is, perhaps, one of the reasons why no official pilgrim hostel is available on the Lisbon section, although they were everywhere in the medieval period. However, this lack of any single authority trying to take sole responsibility for the camino permits a more open and eclectic orientation. It might also help us understand why the familiar yellow arrow pointing to Santiago is often accompanied by a blue arrow pointing in the *opposite* direction – to Fátima. If you intend to detour to Fátima contact the tourist office in the town ***Turismo*** © 249 531 139. It can be walked in 2 days from Santarém. Alternatively it can be easily reached by bus from either Santarém (55 km) or Tomar (35 km).

Pilgrimage is experienced on many different levels. At one end is the physical challenge of walking a long distance route with a group of friends in a limited time frame, always with an eye on the calendar. Perhaps now is an opportunity for you to experience pilgrimage at the other end, at a pace that allows for the inner alchemy of introspection. How deep you choose to make the experience is, of course, up to you. Nevertheless the basic counsel is to go on foot, alone. The extended periods of silence will open up space to reflect on your life and its direction. Go alone and you may find that you are never alone and that may prove a pivotal turning point.

The Camino Portugués is shaking off centuries of slumber and ready to play its part in the great flowering of human imagination, cooperation and consciousness. In the oft-repeated words of Christopher Frye from *A Sleep of Prisoners*, "…Affairs are now soul sized. The enterprise is exploration into God. Where are you making for? It takes so many thousand years to wake, but will you wake for pity's sake."

… And so, like a latter-day Rip Van Winkle we rise to dust off our boots and join the merry band of pilgrims making their way up through the welcoming beauty and peace of northern Portugal to the city of St. James in neighbouring Galicia. You will meet other fellow wayfarers and the native folk whose lands you pass over, but above all you may meet your Self, and that may make all the difference. Whatever you do, don't forget to begin. Journey well, *buen viaje, boa viagem!*

Historical Snapshot and Brief Chronology:

What follows is not intended as an authoritative discourse on the history of Portugal or its pilgrim routes. It merely seeks to draw together some of the innumerable strands that make the Portuguese Way central to an understanding of the Santiago story. From St. James first landing at Padrón to convert the pagan inhabitants in his guise as *Santiago Peregrino* to his re-invention to spearhead the crusades to vanquish Islam as *Santiago Matamoros* the memory of St. James is indelibly linked to these shores. The route has remained in obscurity for too long and deserves to be more widely discovered and acknowledged.

- **Palaeolithic period c. 20,000 B.C.**

1992 saw one of the great archaeological discoveries of the modern era in Vila Nova de Foz Côa, in the Douro valley 120 km due East of Porto. Here we find one of the oldest and largest displays of Palaeolithic art dating back some 22,000 years. It was declared a UNESCO World heritage site in 1998. The Douro river valley has been a cradle of civilisation long before the Age of Discoveries was launched from her harbours.

- **Megalithic period c. 4000 B.C.**

This period is best known for the building of great *mega* stone structures sometimes referred to as Dolmens or Mamoas. They generally had evidence of human remains and have been linked to prehistoric graves. They were also aligned to the winter solstice sun and so are connected to sun worship. An example lies on our route near Arcos (see stage 2 for details). Petroglyphs or rock carvings are another feature of this period. This megalithic culture was deeply religious in nature and left a powerful impact on the peoples who followed.

- **Early Celtic period c. 1,000 B.C.**

Central European Celts settled in north-western Portugal and Spain intermarrying with the Iberians and giving rise to the Celtiberian tribes. Remains of their Celtic villages *castros* or *citânias* can be seen dotted around the remote countryside especially in the Minho area. These fortified villages were built in a circular formation usually occupying some elevated ground or hillock. They are found today

Monte Tecla – Castro

in place names on maps, but one of the most striking examples can be visited just off our route at Monte de Santa Tecla overlooking the mouth of the Minho. The extensive mineral deposits of this area gave rise to a rich artistic movement and bronze and gold artefacts of Celtic design and origin can be admired in museums all across Europe. The Phoenicians established a trading centre in Lisbon around 900 B.C.

• **Early Roman period c. 200 B.C.**

Roman Foundations – Lisbon

The Roman occupation of the Iberian peninsular began around the 2nd century before the Common Era and they too were attracted by the rich mining potential of the region. In 136 B.C. the proconsul Decimus Junius Brutus led his legions across the Lima and Minho rivers where he met resistance not only from the fierce inhabitants but also from his own soldiers wary of crossing the rivers that were thought to represent one of the rivers of Hades – the river of forgetfulness *Lethe*. Brutus became the first Roman general to make it to the end of the known world at Finis Terrae. A Roman garrison was established there that would, in time, become the Roman city of Dugium – present day Duio. This early Roman settlement played host to pilgrims from many different traditions and it was to the king (governor) of Dugium that St. James' disciples were directed by queen Lupa for permission to bury his body (see *A Pilgrims Guide to the Camino Finisterre*).

While the Phoenicians are, perhaps, best known for their syllabic writing which influenced the Aramaic and Greek alphabets developed from their base at Byblos (from which comes our word Bible) they were the great merchant nation of antiquity. They also developed the sea routes to the British Isles to promote the tin trade in particular, helping to develop the Atlantic ports such as Cadiz, Lisbon and Finisterre on the way. In 61 B.C. Julius Caesar became governor of Hispania Ulterior establishing *Olisipo* (modern day Lisbon) as his base from where he conducted naval expeditions along these shores to finally win control of the Atlantic seaboard from the Phoenicians. The most significant Roman remains in Portugal are in Conimbriga which was a major military and trading post on the Via Roman XVI between Olisipo (Lisbon), Cale (Porto) and Bracara Augusta (Braga). The Roman road from Braga to Valença was known as the Via XIX also referred to as the Antonine Itinerary *Itinerario de Antonino*.

• **Early Christian Period c. 40 A.D.**

While there is little historical evidence to support the view that St. James (The Greater, Son of Zebedee to distinguish him for St. James the Just) came to the Iberian peninsular there is ample anecdotal testimony to that effect. It would appear that he sailed to Padrón and commenced his ministry there. By all accounts his mission was largely unsuccessful and after an apparition by the Virgin Mary in 40 A.D. he returned to Jerusalem where he was decapitated in the year 44 at Herod Agrippa's own hand (and sword). James thus became the first of the apostles to be martyred and his faithful disciples decided to return his body to the place of his earlier ministry at Padrón. On the instructions of the pagan queen Lupa the relics of St. James were taken to Finisterre where permission for burial was refused by the Roman legate. In the famous story of betrayal the disciples managed to escape with their sacred cargo and the body of St. James was finally laid to rest in Libredon (Liberum Donum). These remarkable events then faded from memory until…

• The Middle Ages c. 476 – 1453

The decline and fall of the Roman Empire was hastened in Portugal with the arrival of Visigoth and Suevi tribes from Germany. The Suevi settled further north around the Douro establishing headquarters at the roman port of Portucale (present day Porto and from which we get the name Portugal). The influence of the Visigoths extended further south around the Lisbon (Olisipo) area. It was from their base in Toledo that their incessant internal squabbles resulted in one group seeking support from the Muslim enclave in North Africa – the Moors duly obliged, arriving in 711. Within a decade Islam had effectively conquered the majority of the Iberian peninsular. While we are more familiar, perhaps, with the Arab influence in Spain, they occupied the entire of Portugal where their rule appears to have been much more favourable than life under the Visigoths who initiated the first expulsion of Jews from the peninsular while the Moors allowed freedom of religious expression. The last Islamic stronghold was the coastal area of southern Portugal, which they named al-Gharb (meaning the West) that today we know as the Algarve. Contrary to popular understanding, Mozarabes (Moçárabes) was the name given to freely practising Christians under Moorish rule. It was during this period, in the year 813, that a 'celestial light' led the hermit Pelayo to the Field of Stars *Compo Stellae* and the discovery of the tomb of St. James. This visionary event was immediately endorsed by the bishop of Iria Flavia in whose diocese Libredon was, and the following year King Alfonso II commenced the building of a basilica church.

Santiago Matamoros

The discovery of the tomb arrived just in time for St. James to become the figurehead for the Christian re-conquest of the Iberian peninsular from Islam. The night before the battle of Clavijo St. James appeared to the Christian troops as a knight dressed in armour astride a white charger, which was to rally the Christian army that the Arab forces were duly defeated. The re-conquest ebbed and flowed with Almanzor arriving at the door of Santiago cathedral in 997 but the relics of the saint had been removed so the Moors took the bells instead and had them carried by Christian slaves to his base in Córdoba. Al-Mansur provided a further setback in 1190 but Portugal's turning point came with Afonso Henriques and the battle of Ourique in 1139 and the taking of Lisbon in 1147. On the strength of these re-conquests he became Dom Afonso I, first King of Portugal. Dom Afonso III (1248-1249) finally providing the *coup de grâce* by winning back the al-Gharb in southern Portugal.

Pilgrimages to Santiago began around the middle of the 10th century, becoming increasingly popular and reaching something of a climax by the middle of the 15th century. While thousands of simple peasants, priests and paupers made the journey, we learn mostly of the exploits of nobility, kings and queens. By this time the main routes via Barcelos, Braga and Viana had become well established.

In 915 Dom Ordonho II granted land in Correlhã, near Ponte de Lima, to the city fathers at Santiago de Compostela. This marks the first significant recognition of Santiago as a major pilgrimage destination through Portugal. By coincidence the only chapel dedicated to Santiago (in ruins) on the route in Portugal remains in the townland of Correlhã (see stage 16). D. Henrique and Dna. Teresa ratified the gifting of these lands on their royal pilgrimage to Santiago in 1097. Other monarchs followed with Afonso II in 1219, Dom Sancho II in 1244 and then Queen Isabel (the Saintly) made her first pilgrimage in 1325.

• **The Age of Discoveries c. 1500**

This period marks Portugal's greatest achievements and the high point in its

Portuguese Caravel *(replica)*

history. Under the auspices of Manuel I, otherwise known as The Fortunate we see the navigation of the sea routes to India by Vasco da Gama in 1498 and the creation of the first viceroy to India some years later. In 1500 Pedro Alvares discovers Brazil, establishing a link that remains strong to this day. The ensuing foreign trade made Portugal one of the richest countries in the world and saw the flowering of Christianity, art and commerce with trade agreements as far flung as China, Persia, India and South America. King Manuel I became a great patron of the arts and this period and its beautiful architectural style is known as *Manueline*. Manuel I, a deeply religious man, went on pilgrimage to Santiago in 1502. Amongst other dignitaries who made the pilgrimage through Portugal was Cosme III of the Medicis in 1669. It seems that the famous Italian pilgrim, Doménico Laffi, perhaps inspired by the Medici pilgrimage, made the journey in 1691. The first detailed account of the pilgrimage was complied by a German traveller, Jeronimo Münzer in 1495 and this was followed by the better-known account of Juan Bautista Confalonieri an Italian priest who accompanied Monsignor Fabio Biondo on his pilgrimage in 1592.

• **A snapshot of modern Portugal**

In 1807 Napoleon reached Portugal and the royal family withdrew to Brazil and made their seat of government there. After Napoleon's forces were finally defeated in 1811 unrest within Portugal led to a Constitutional Monarchy in 1820 and an era of relative stability under D. Pedro V and D. Luís I. However civil strife at the turn of the century led to revolution and the establishment of a Republic in 1910 and Manuel José de Arriaga was elected as first president. Political unrest continued through the period of the first World War up to 1926 when an army coup installed General António de Fragoso Carmona to head a new government. He appointed António de Oliveira Salazar as minister of finance. Salazar was deeply religious and set about restoring the power of the church after becoming prime minister and effectively a dictator in 1932.

In 1936 Salazar supported General Francisco Franco during the Spanish civil war and both countries signed a non-aggression pact and declared neutrality during the Second World War. Salazar's rigid regime and economic policies led to low wages with poor labour rights and, inevitably, unrest. The regime resisted all opposition, crushing a revolt in 1947. The 1960's marked another difficult period for Portugal with rebellion in the overseas territories of Goa, Angola, Guinea and Mozambique. Portugal resisted these moves for independence in its African colonies receiving UN condemnation.

In 1968 Marcello Caetano succeeded Salazar as prime minister. The repressive policies continued at home and in the colonies and Portugal's economic stability was again threatened and this led to a coup by the army in 1974, which installed Gen. António de **Spinola** as president. Spinola oversaw democratic reforms at home and in the African territories and during this period General Francisco da Costa Gomes was elected president. Nationalisation of industry, the banking system and the repossession of many large agricultural estates ensued.

Over the next few years political unrest between right-wing, communist and socialist factions led to a deepening of the economic and social problems of Portugal under the administrations of Soares, Francisco Manuel de Sá Carneiro and Francisco Pinto Balsemão. Soares was re-elected prime minister in 1983 and introduced a new austerity program that led eventually to Portugal's entry into the European Community in 1986. In 1987 the Social Democrats secured a sweeping victory. In 1995 the Socialist party came to power and Jorge **Sampaio** was elected President. In 2002 the centre-right coalition elected José Manuel **Barroso** as Prime Minister. In 2004 Barroso resigned to head up the European Commission and Santana **Lopes** was sworn in as Prime Minister. And, significantly, on 24th June 2004 (St. James Day) the first new pilgrim hostel for several centuries was opened along the Camino Portugués, in São Pedro de Rates.

• A snapshot of modern Galicia

After Franco's death in 1975, King Carlos nominally succeeded and appointed political reformist Adolfo Suárez to form a government. In 1982 the socialist party (PSOE) won a sweeping victory under Felipe González who successfully steered Spain into full membership of the EEC in 1986. In 1996 the populace gave the conservative José María Aznar, leader of the right wing *Partido Popular* (PP), a narrow mandate but in November 2002 the oil tanker Prestige ran into a storm off Finisterre and the ensuing ecological catastrophe sank not only the livelihood of scores of Galician fisherman but, in due time, the right wing government as well. The disregard for the environment displayed by the President of Galicia and the Spanish environment minister of that time resulted in a popular cry up and down the country of 'never again' *nunca maís*. It only took the government's unpopular support of the invasion of Iraq coupled with the Madrid bombings in March 2004 to put the socialist's back in power under the youthful leadership of José Luis Rodríguez Zapatero. The new government set in motion an immediate change in foreign policy and, more controversially, a sudden but decisive shift from a conservative Catholic to a liberal secular society that led to one newspaper headline declaring, 'Church and State square up in struggle for the spirit of Spain.' And seemingly immune to all these social and political upheavals, the *Camino Portugués* in Galicia goes quietly about her gentle spirit of transformation.

Preparation – A Quick Guide:

[1] Practical Considerations:

• **When?** Spring is often wet and windy but the route is relatively quiet with early flowers appearing. Summer is busy and hot and hostels often full. Autumn often provides the most stable weather with harvesting adding to the colour and celebrations of the countryside. Winter is solitary and cold and many hostels will be closed.

• **How long?** Clear the decks and allow some spaciousness into your life. This entire route is divided into 23 stages so it fits (just) into a 3 week break.

[2] Preparation – Outer: what do I need to take *and* leave behind.

• Buy your boots in time to walk them in before you go.
• Pack a Poncho, Galicia is notorious for its downpours.
• Bring a hat, sunstroke is painful and can be dangerous.
• Look again if your backpack weighs more than 10 kilos.

What *not* to bring:

• Get rid of all books (except this one – all the maps you need are included.)
• Don't take 'extras', Portugal has shops if you need to replace something.
• If you want to deepen your experience, leave behind:
  – your *camera* – you'll be able to live for the moment rather than memories.
  – your *watch* – you'll be surprised how quickly you adapt to a natural clock.
  – your *mobile phone* – break the dependency and taste the freedom.

[3] Language learn it now, *before* you go.

[4] Pilgrim Passport, Protocol & Prayer

• Get a *credencial* from your local confraternity – and join it.
• Have consideration for your fellow pilgrims and gratitude for your hosts.
• 'May every step be a prayer for peace and an extension of loving kindness.'

[5] Preparation – Inner: why am I doing this?

Take time to prepare a purpose for this pilgrimage and to complete the self-assessment questionnaire (on page 29). Start from the basis that you are essentially a spiritual being on a human journey, not a human being on a spiritual one. We came to learn some lesson and this pilgrimage affords an opportunity to find out what that is. Ask for help and expect it – it's there, now, waiting for you.

Whatever you do – for heaven's sake don't forget to start.

Practical Considerations:

This guidebook provides essential information in a concise format. It is the result of several years of extensive research of the various Ways of St. James in Portugal and provides information on where to eat, sleep and points of interest along the way. The maps have been designed to show relevant information only and accurate distances between points are printed on the map and correspond with the text – they are generally spaced at around 3.5 kilometre intervals which corresponds to around one 1 hour of walking at an average pace.

Each stage begins and ends at a town or village where some suitable accommodation can be found and details and alternatives are provided in the text. Should you become lost use the 'sun compass' for orientation. To those of you who decided to leave your watches behind the sun will also become your natural clock. It is surprising how quickly we get to know the time of day by the length of our shadow. Your body will remind you when you need to eat or drink but my advice is never to pass a drinking font without using it – a minimum of 2 litres a day will help ward off injury and fatigue.

How long will it take? Allow time to complete the journey gracefully. There's already too much pressure in our lives – so clear the decks and allow some spaciousness into your life. Walking pace naturally varies between individuals and when you add in variations in weather, detours (planned and otherwise) and different motivations and time constraints all this results in a heady mix of possibilities. The route has been divided into 23 stages (13 from Lisbon to Porto and 10 from Porto to Santiago). Fit walkers could accomplish the entire route in 3 weeks but this would allow for no rest days, no detours, no injuries and little time for reflection and integration of experiences along the way. A month is ideal and this equates to an average of 25 km per day with 3 rest days, allowing time to explore historic towns such as Tomar, and 2 weekend days to travel to Lisboa and home again from Santiago. (allow 2 weeks Porto to Santiago).

The 'average' pace varies depending on the gradient and contour maps are provided to alert you to strenuous *up*hill stretches. Be mindful, however, that most injuries are sustained while going *down*hill and occur in the early days while pushing the body beyond what it has been conditioned for. It takes the body a few days to adjust to the regular walking with full backpack. Give body, mind and soul time to acclimatise. Don't push yourself at the beginning. It is always advisable to put in some physical training before you go. A full weekend walking with backpack will show up weak spots that can then be worked on to minimise injuries when away and to improve general fitness levels. Walking poles, if used properly, can greatly reduce wear and tear on the body and minimise the likelihood of injury. If you don't have a pair (one in each hand creates better balance and is twice as effective) consider buying a set. They are likely to prove a good investment for this pilgrimage – and future ones!

Remember pace will slow, often considerably, towards the end of a long day's walking. A fit (fast) walker can accomplish up to 35 kilometres in an 8 hour day (4 kph). This drops to 25 km for a more leisurely pace (3 kph). Note that 8 hours daylight would be the maximum in winter. This guide has a daily *average* of 26 km but can (and should) be adjusted to suit individual needs.

Finisterre extension? An additional week will allow time to walk to Finisterre and back to Santiago via Muxía. This waymarked route is still relatively undiscovered and, together with the Camino Portugués, makes one of the most powerful and authentic pilgrim routes available to us today (see *A Pilgrim's Guide to the Camino Fisterra*, Findhorn Press).

When to go? The summer months can be very hot and accommodation, particularly in July and August, in short supply. This problem is aggravated during Holy or Jubilee Years, any year when the feast of St. James (25th July) falls on a Sunday – following the last Holy year in 2010 the next one will not be until 2021. Temperatures as high as 40^C have been recorded in July although the average for the month is 25^C with rainfall of only 20mm. Autumn tends to be kinder than spring with an average temperature of 24^C and rainfall of 51mm in September compared to 15^C and 147mm in March.

Full travel (summer) schedules mostly operate from April through September. Outside these months schedules might be more restricted. However, costs are lower and the bulk of tourists have left, so this is a quieter time to travel. Some of the most mystical and transformative trips can be in the depths of winter. There may be fewer flights and ferries and many hotels will be closed, but I have never wanted for a bed to sleep at this time of year. Bring warm waterproof clothes and remember that daylight hours are restricted so that the daily distance that can be covered is reduced.

Travel costs vary widely but national carriers now compete with the budget airlines and the sooner you commit to going the cheaper the ticket but you can sometimes pick up a promotional fare at the last minute. Traffic from the 3 airports at A Corunna, Vigo and Santiago have fallen and a question mark now hangs over whether Galicia can justify 3 airports in such close proximity.

How to get there: In addition to the Portuguese national airline TAP, the following airlines fly into **Lisbon**: BA / EasyJet / bmi baby / Thomsonfly / Aer Lingus / Air France / Ibéria / Clickair / KLM / Lufthansa / Air Berlin / Vueling / Finnair / Egyptair and SATA International: Departure airports in the UK include London, Bristol, Birmingham, Liverpool and Manchester. All major cities throughout Europe are covered in addition to direct flights from Canada and the USA. Recent expansion at **Porto** airport offers a similar spread of opportunities. International rail and bus services into Lisbon and Porto are more limited but there are daily services direct from Paris and Madrid – check with Portuguese rail at *www.cp.pt* that has an online booking service in English as does *www.raileurope.fr/corporate/portugal*. Eurolines, the international arm of National Express has daily services from London to Lisbon via Paris *www.eurolines.com*. Bus and rail within Portugal is efficient and comprehensive

…and back: If you are **returning from Porto or Lisbon** there are 2 daily rail services from Santiago to Porto (Campanha) with frequent onward connections to Lisbon *www.renfe.es*. This is a splendid trip along the Minho river valley and the Portuguese coast that gives a flavour of the Caminho do Costa. You can stop off in Viana do Castelo and wander the old quarter next to the train station. Alsa *www.alsa.es* also have a bus leaving Santiago daily (except Saturdays) to Porto. There are 2 daily services direct from Vigo to Porto airport.

- **Air**: •*Ryanair* fly direct to Santiago from London Stansted, Frankfurt, Rome, Madrid, Malaga, Barcelona, Alicante. *Vueling* fly from Paris direct •*Air Berlin* fly from major destinations throughout Europe to Santiago via their hub in La Palma Majorca. •*Aer Lingus* fly Santiago direct from Dublin (summer schedule) and •*BA* and •*Iberia* and other major airlines offer regular services throughout the year via various connecting airports in Spain, mainly Madrid. Check other possibilities from / to nearby airports at La Corunna and Vigo

- **Rail** – you can book online through Spanish rail network RENFE (with an English site) www.renfe.es/horarios/english or Rail Europe at www.raileurope.co.uk/ •**Bus** you can book online with Alsa www.alsa.es (English language option + St. James Way page for route options).

- **Ferry** The advantage of sailing home is that you get a chance to acclimatise slowly – check with Brittany Ferries (Santander - Portsmouth) and P&O (Bilbao - Plymouth).

- **Car Hire** If you can find other passengers to share the cost then this is often a relatively cheap and convenient way to travel on to such places as Santander or Bilbao and flying or sailing home from there.

Other Costs: Allow for a basic €25 a day to include 5 euros for overnight stay at a municipal pilgrim hostel (average €10 private) and the remainder for food and drink. Some hostels provide a communal supper on occasions (dependent on the warden *hospitalero*) and most have a basic kitchen *cocina* where a meal can be prepared. Alternatively most locations have one or more restaurants to choose from. If you want to indulge in the wonderful seafood *mariscos* available in Galicia and accompany this with the delightful local *Albariño* wines you can expect to double the basic cost.

Pilgrim hostels *albergue de peregrinos* vary in what they provide but accommodation is usually in bunk beds with additional overflow space on mattresses *colchonetas*. There are still no dedicated pilgrim hostels on the stretch from Lisbon to Porto. However several new hostels were added in 2010 from Porto so all hostels on this section offer modern facilities with kitchen and basic cooking equipment and a dining / sitting area. Opening times vary depending on the time of year but are generally cleaned and open again from early afternoon to welcome pilgrims. You cannot reserve accommodation in advance and phone numbers are provided for emergency calls only or to check availability outside the normal seasons (most are open all year but can close for holidays or maintenance purposes). See next page for information on bedbugs.

If the hostels are full **alternative accommodation** is generally available in hoteles, moteles, hostales, pensiones *pensãos*, fondas, residenciales or simply camas (literally beds). If locals describe a place as 'bad' *mau/malo* they usually mean it is used as a bordello. In addition Portugal has *Quintas* or manor houses converted for tourist accommodation in the luxury bracket (€50 to €90). In Spain a similar standard of accommodation is provided in a type of up-market B&B known as a *casa rural* literally 'rural house' generally built in the traditional Galician style but also relatively expensive (upwards of €40 depending on season). Pilgrim discounts are often available – check before booking).

Equipment: Light walking boots or shoes are fine for this route. Look again if you are carrying more than 10 kilos (22 lbs) and a 55-litre pack. If you are not fluent in Portuguese or Spanish then carry a small phrase book and dictionary. Below is a pilgrim checklist with Spanish and Portuguese translations to help strengthen your vocabulary and assist you to buy or replace items along the way. This is not necessarily a recommended list; this will vary through the seasons. Highlight your essential items and then tick them off as put them into your backpack. *Note*: bedbugs have appeared in some hostels. Prevention is better than cure. Consider carrying a suitably impregnated bed cover (sleeper) *and* pillow case. Lifeventure silk treated with ex^3 (Permethrin) are lightweight.

CHECK-LIST:

	Español	*Português*
Clothes:	***Ropas:***	***Roupa:***
hat (sun)	*sombrero*	*chapéu*
sunglasses	*gafas de sol*	*óculos de sol*
shirts [ ]	*camisa*	*camisa*
travel vest	*chaqueta de viaje*	*jaqueta de viagem*
jacket -	*chaqueta -*	*casaco*
… waterproof	*… chubasquero*	*… capa de chuva*
… breathable	*… transpirable*	*… transpirável*
underpants [ ]	*calzoncillos*	*cuecas*
shorts	*pantalones cortos*	*calções / shorts*
trousers	*pantalones largos*	*calças*
handkerchief	*pañuelo*	*lenço*
socks [ ]	*calcetines*	*peúgas*
Shoes:	***Zapatos:***	***Sapatos:***
boots (mountain)	*botas (de montaña)*	*botas (de montana)*
shoes (walking)	*zapatos (de andar)*	*sapatos (de caminhar)*
sandals (leather)	*sandalias (de piel)*	*sandálias (de couro)*
Size:	***Tamaño:***	***Tamanho:***
larger	*más grande*	*maior*
smaller	*más pequeño*	*menor*
more expensive/cheaper	*más caro / barato*	*mais caro / barato*
model / number	*modelo / número*	*modelo / número*
Essential documents	***Documentos esenciales:***	***Originais essenciais:***
passport	*pasaporte*	*passaporte*
pilgrim record	*credencial de peregrino*	*credencial do peregrino*
wallet/ purse	*monedero / cartera*	*porta-moedas*
cash	*dinero en efectivo*	*dinheiro em efetivo*
credit card	*tarjeta de crédito*	*cartão de crédito*
travel tickets	*pasaje de viaje*	*passagem de viagem*
diary	*diario*	*diário*
emergency addresses	*dirección de emergencia*	*endereço de emergência*
phone numbers	*números de teléfono*	*números de telefone*
Backpack	***Mochila***	***Mochila***
rain cover	*protección de mochila*	*capa para mochila*
sleeping bag	*saco de dormir*	*saco de dormir*

towel	*toalla*	toalha
water bottle	*botella de agua*	garrafa de água
penknife	*navaja*	navalha

Toiletries: ***Artículos de tocador:***

soap	*jabón*	sabão
shampoo	*champú*	champô
tooth brush	*cepillo de dientes*	escova de dentes
toothpaste	*dentífrico*	pasta de dentes
hair brush	*cepillo de pelo*	escova de cabelo
comb	*peine*	pente
sink stopper / plug	*tapón de fregadero*	tampa de ralo
shaving cream	*espuma de afeitar*	espuma de barbear
razor (blades)	*cuchilla de afeitar*	lâminas de barbear
face cloth	*guante de aseo*	luva de asseio
sun cream (lotion)	*crema solar (loción)*	protector solar
after sun cream	*leche solar (after sun)*	loção pós-sol
moisturiser	*crema hidratante*	hidratante
toilet paper	*papel higiénico*	papel higiénico
tissues	*pañuelos de papel*	lenços de papel
sanitary pads	*salva-slips*	salva-slips
tampons	*tampones*	tampões

First Aid Kit: ***Botiquín***   *Estojo de primeiro socorros*

painkiller	*analgésico*	analgésico
aspirin/ Paracetemol	*aspirina/paracetamol*	aspirina/paracetamol
plasters	*esparadrapo*	penso rápido
blister pads	*apósito para ampollas*	penso para bolhas
compeed-*second skin*	*compeed-segunda piel*	compeed-band-aid
antiseptic cream	*crema antiséptica*	loção anti-séptica
muscular ache (ointment)	*pomada para dolores musculares*	pomada para dores musculares
homeopathic remedies	*remedios homeopáticos*	remédios homeopáticos

Medicine (prescription):   ***Medicina (prescripción):***   *Medicamentos (receita)*

asthma inhaler	*inhalador para el asma*	inalador para a asma
hay fever tablets	*medicina para las alergias*	remédio para as alergias
diarrhoea pills	*pastillas para la diarrea*	pílulas para a diarréia
other (doctor)	*otros (médico)*	outros (médico)

Accessories: (optional)   ***Accesorios: (opcional)***   *Acessórios: (opcional)*

monocular	*catalejo*	luneta
binocular	*prismáticos*	binóculos
camera	*cámara*	câmara
torch	*linterna*	lanterna
wrist watch	*reloj de pulsera*	relógio de pulso
alarm clock	*despertador*	despertador
poncho	*poncho*	poncho
sleeping mat	*esterilla*	esteira
clothes pegs	*pinzas para la ropa*	molas de roupa
clothes line (cord)	*cuerda para tender ropa*	corda para pendurar roupa

cutlery	*cubiertos*	*talheres*
knife	*cuchillo*	*faca*
fork	*tenedor*	*garfo*
spoon	*cuchara*	*colher*
mug (cup)	*taza / vaso*	*taça / copo*
sandwich box	*fiambrera*	*marmita*
Books: (limited)	***Libros: (cupo limitado)***	*Livros: quantidade limitada*
spiritual texts	*textos espirituales*	*textos espirituais*
inspirational quotations	*citas inspiradoras*	*citações inspiradoras*
poetry	*poesía*	*poesia*
phrase book -	*libro de frases*	*livro de frases*
… (Spanish)	*… (Español)*	*… (Espanhol)*
… (Portuguese)	*… (Portugués)*	*… (Português)*

Credentials *credenciales* **& Certificate of Completion** *compostela*:
In order to stay at official pilgrim hostels you need to have a pilgrim 'passport' *credencial* impressed with a rubber stamp Spanish: *sello* Portuguese: *carimbo* at hostels, churches, town halls etc. along the way. On the Spanish section of the Camino Portugués this is generally done in the official pilgrim hostels *albergues* that are reserved exclusively for pilgrims to Santiago (or Fátima if you are doing the route in reverse). This *credencial* must be presented at the pilgrim office in Santiago in order to receive a Compostela (certificate of completion of the pilgrimage to Santiago) as proof that you have walked the route (at least the last 100 kilometres). You can obtain one of these 'passports' before travelling from the Confraternity of St. James in London or possibly from a local confraternity in your country of origin (see under *useful addresses)*. If all else fails, space has been provided for this purpose at the back of this guide, or you can make up your own. However, there is no guarantee these will be accepted and, in any case, you should make every effort to join and support the work of the confraternities. An official *credencial* can also be obtained from the information desk at Porto cathedral and the Church of the Martyrs in Lisboa. (Note there are currently no official pilgrim hostels between Lisbon and Porto).

Map Legend: Take a few moments to familiarise yourself with the symbols used on the maps in this guide. Note 1: in addition to the *actual* distance an *adjusted* distance is also provided based on the cumulative height climbed during each stage. This equates to the additional effort and time necessary to walk the stage over and above that required if it were purely a level walk. Remember that your normal walking pace (the average is 1 km in 20 minutes or 3 kph) will decrease, often substantially, towards the end of a hard day's walk. Note 2: The recommended path always follows *the road less travelled* such as natural pathways and farm tracks so as to reduce the time spent on asphalt, which is both tiring and carries the extra hazard of traffic. On those stretches where the road cannot be avoided take care of the infrequent traffic, which can be fast and especially dangerous because you may not be expecting it. Alternative waymarked routes are marked in grey to symbolise the greyness of the asphalt road they follow. The route from Porto to Vila do Conde is marked in green and is not waymarked but follows the Atlantic coast (beaches) all the way. Any optional detours are shown in turquoise.

MAP LEGEND   **25**

Map symbols used in this guide:

Total km	Total distance for each day's stage
	Adjusted for climb (100m vertical = additional 0.5km)
850m **Alto** ▲	Contours / High point of each stage
< 🅐 🅗 >	Intermediate accommodation
◀ 3.5	Precise distance between points (3.5 km = ± 1 hour walking)
→150m > / ^ / <	Interim distances •150 metres turn right / straight on (s/o) / left

Path or track (*green*: earth)
Secondary road (*grey*: asphalt)
Main [N-] road (*red*: additional traffic and hazard)
Motorway (*blue*: conventional motorway colour)
Extra vigilance required / Roundabout
Main (recommended) route (*yellow*: maximising pathways)
Alternative road route (*grey*: more asphalt)
Alternative scenic route (*green*: more remote / less waymarks)
Optional detour to point of interest (*turquoise*)

[?] [X] Option or detour point / Crossroads or Junction
Railway / Station
National boundary / Provincial boundary
River / Stream
Sea or river estuary / Woodland
Church / Chapel / Wayside cross

Windmill / Radio mast
Drinking font *(Fonte, Fuente)* / Café bar / Mini-market
Tourist Office / Manor house
Hospital / Post office / Petrol station
Airport / Rail / Bus station
Viewpoint / Ancient monument / 10th Century

🅐 🅙	Pilgrim hostel *(Albergue)* / Youth hostel *(Juventude)*
🅗 🅟	Hotel / Pension
🅒 🅠	Country B&B *(Casa rural)* / Country mansion *(Quinta)*
ⒶⒽⒿ	(*off* route accommodation
ⓅⒸⓆ	also possibilities in firestations Ⓑ *bombeiros voluntários*)
[32]	Number of bed spaces (usually bunk beds)
Muni.	Municipal hostel
Xunta	Galician government *(Xunta)* hostel
Conv.	Convent or monastery hostel
Par.	Parroquial (church parish) hostel
Asoc.	Association hostel
Priv. (*)	Private hostel (private network with star *)

Town plan
'Pop. – Alt. m)   Town population and altitude in metres
City and suburbs (*grey*) with historical centre (*brown*)

Waymarks: Thanks to the efforts of the various pilgrim associations waymarking is comprehensive and should you lose your way it is more than likely you allowed your thoughts to wander and you lost your focus in the present moment. Consider re-tracing your steps until you pick up the waymarks again. On this route there are relatively few other pilgrims to follow but ideally you will have sufficient *português* and *castellano* (perhaps even some *galego*) to be able to converse with the rural community and understand simple directions etc. In all cases where there are alternative routes I have recommended 'the path less travelled'. My criterion is always to minimise the amount of time spent on asphalt. Finding your way is complicated by the fact that, within Portugal, most people will assume you are heading to Fátima and the route is often waymarked in two directions – to Santiago always with a yellow arrow and to Fátima always with a blue arrow.

A **Sun Compass** is provided on each map as an aid to orientation. Even in poor weather we can generally tell the position of the sun. The route through Portugal is invariably in a northerly direction so the sun will rise to your right in the morning. At midday it will be behind you and by afternoon will appear over your left shoulder.

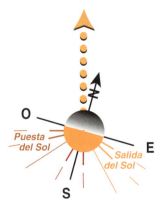

SOUL MAPS AND INNER WAYMARKS

Preparation for the inner journey: *Why am I doing this?*

Take time to prepare a purpose for this pilgrimage. Start from the basis that you are essentially a spiritual being on a human journey, not a human being on a spiritual one. We came here to learn some lesson and this may be your opportunity to find out what it is. While life maybe the classroom, pilgrimage is one way to master the curriculum. It will never be mastered by walking the physical path on its own. You will need help, so ask for it – all the help you need is here, now, awaiting but your asking. We all have a different *Way* and what is right for one may be incomprehensible to another so don't feel pressurised to follow any particular path or opinion. You will know when something rings true for you – trust your resonance. A few suggestions are listed in the bibliography.

When we go on pilgrimage we bring along our individual personality and our physical, mental, emotional and etheric bodies. We may feel a need for healing in one or all of these areas. The impetus to 'take up our bed and walk' is deeply embedded in the human psyche and soul. We do well to remember that the healing power of Love is a two-way flow. We both give and receive healing on the journey. Peter Dawkins of the Gatekeeper Trust, writing in *A Pilgrim's Handbook,* informs us:

> 'As the pilgrim moves through the landscape he or she follows certain paths. These paths become energised beyond the norm by the movement of the loving pilgrim. When Europe was given its name, taken from the myth of Europa and the Bull, it conveyed an important truth about the layout of Europe's inner landscape as a functioning pattern of energy and consciousness… There are many ancient pilgrimage routes which spread out across mainland Europe, all leading to Santiago de Compostela in northern Spain, as if all the energy within Europe is drawn up to the crown and then focused in Santiago.'

This image is mirrored in the camino as the central star route in Europe. In *Paths of the Christian Mysteries, From Compostela to the New World* Virginia Sease and Manfred Schmidt-Brabant write:

> 'Those who travelled along the star route as far as Cape Finisterre had the experience: Here is the end of the sensory world, the abyss! And If I am able to comprehend it, the spiritual world approaches me from the other side. ... Compostela was a final, decisive juncture on an inner spiritual path that was simultaneously a path of nature initiation. …Rudolf Steiner stated that people have a need to live not only with external history but also with the esoteric, hidden narrative which lies behind it: the history of "the Mysteries."'

These energy lines were well understood in earlier times and it is no coincidence that the Knights Templar set their Portuguese headquarters in Tomar. The power of the location was enhanced by the careful layout of the town and the orientation of its buildings in accordance with geomantic lore. This ancient knowledge would have been well known by St. James and his disciples and it will have been no accident of fate that they chose to enter Europe at its crown – sailing past the Towers of the West *Torres de Oeste* at Catoira to fetch land at Padrón. It is no wonder that the Camino Portugués remains such a powerful route today, its mystical allure still intact and aiding its rediscovery.

The middle path: In *A Course in Miracles* it is written: 'there is a way of living in the world that is not here, although it seems to be. You do not change appearance, though you smile more frequently. To let illusions walk ahead of truth is madness. Many have chosen to renounce the world while still believing its reality. And they have suffered from a sense of loss, and have not been released accordingly. Others have chosen nothing but the world, and they have suffered from a sense of loss still deeper. Between these paths there is another road that leads away from loss of every kind… for this road leads past illusion now. All roads will lead to this one in the end. For sacrifice and deprivation are paths that lead nowhere. Their suffering is but illusion. Yet they need a guide to lead them out of it, for they mistake illusion for the truth. Such is salvation's call. It asks that you accept the truth, and let it go before you, lighting up the path. Walk safely now, yet carefully, because this path is new to you. And you may find that you are tempted still to walk ahead of truth, and let illusions be your guide.

Step back in faith and let truth lead the way. You know not where you go. But One Who knows goes with you. Let Him lead you with the rest. This is our final journey, which we make for everyone. We walk to God. Pause and reflect on this. Could any way be holier, or more deserving of your effort, of your love and of your full intent? Look not to ways that seem to lead you elsewhere.' A.C.I.M. Workbook; lesson 155.

So let us feed the path with our loving intent and make every step a prayer for peace and reconciliation.

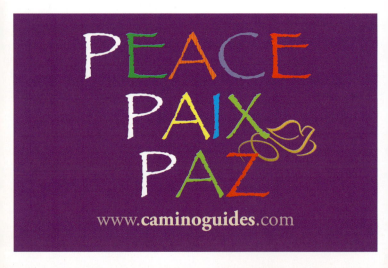

SELF-ASSESSMENT *INNER WAYMARKS*

This self-assessment questionnaire is designed to encourage you to reflect on your life and its direction. View it as a snapshot of this moment in the ongoing journey of your life. In the busyness that surrounds us we often fail to take stock of where we are headed and our changing roles in the unfolding drama of our life story.

You might find it useful to initially answer these questions in quick succession as this may allow a more intuitive response. Afterwards, you can reflect more deeply and check if your intellectual answers confirm these, change them or bring in other insights. You can download copies of this questionnaire from the *Camino Guides* website – make some extra copies so you can repeat the exercise on your return and again in (say) 3 months time. This way you can compare results and ensure you continue to follow through on any insights that came to you while walking the camino.

- ❏ How do you differentiate pilgrimage from a long distance walk?
- ❏ How do you define spirituality – what does it mean to you?
- ❏ How is your spirituality expressed at home and at work?

- ❏ What do you see as the primary purpose of your life?
- ❏ Are you working consciously towards fulfilling that purpose?
- ❏ How clear are you on your goal and the right direction for you at this time?
- ❏ How will you recognise resistance to any changes that might be necessary?

- ❏ When did you first become aware of a desire to take time-out?
- ❏ What prompted you originally to go on the camino?
- ❏ Did the prompt come from something that you felt needed changing?
- ❏ Make a list of what appears to be blocking any change from happening.

- ❏ What help might you need on a practical, emotional and spiritual level?
- ❏ How will you recognise the right help or correct answer?
- ❏ What are the joys and challenges in working towards your unique potential?
- ❏ What are your next steps towards fulfilling that potential?

How aware are you of the following? Score yourself on a level of 1 – 10 and compare these scores again on your return from the camino.

- ❏ Awareness of your inner spiritual world.
- ❏ Clarity on what inspires you and the capacity to live your passion.
- ❏ Confidence to follow your intuitive sense of the right direction.
- ❏ Ability to recognise your resistance and patterns of defence.
- ❏ Ease with asking for and receiving support from others.

Overview:

The Route: The Camino de Santiago from Lisbon to Porto has now been fully waymarked, thanks largely to the efforts of Alex Rato, Djalma de Sousa e Correia and the various pilgrim associations including the Asociación Galega de Amigos do Camiño de Santiago – AGACS. The first 3 stages, as far as Santarém, coincide with the caminho da Fátima (caminho de Tejo). In Santarém the 2 routes separate with the historic Camino de Santiago veering off to the northeast towards the Templar town of Tomar. As this 2011 edition goes to print the facilities along the section are still not sufficiently well developed to be able to endorse this route to pilgrims familiar with the Camino Francés and with expectations of a similar infrastructure. The Camino Português has all the qualities to re-emerge as one of the great caminos to Santiago and facilities are slowly being developed aided by the build-up for the 2010 Holy Year. The latest section (Lisbon to Porto) is ready to be enjoyed by fit and seasoned pilgrims able to converse in Portuguese. Infrastructure from Porto to Santiago is well developed and ready to welcome pilgrims of all abilities.

Lisbon is a wonderful city with an interesting mix of old and new. One of the smallest capital cities in the European Union it is relatively easy to navigate and it is full of vitality and a new sense of pride in its long and fascinating history. Originally known as Olisipo it was a major administrative centre and trading post for the Romans before the Visigoths took over eventually succumbing to 4 centuries of Arab rule before Afonso Henriques ousted them in 1147. In the 15th century it became the main base for the 'Discoveries' and many of the greatest explorers in history such as Columbus, Cabral, Magellan and Vasco da Gama set sail from here and established Lisbon as one of the great trading capitals of the world. Inevitably, an economy based on colonial spoils (rather than production) began to wane and the financial plight of Portugal took a lurch for the worse at precisely 9:40 a.m on November 1st 1755 when one of the most destructive earthquakes ever recorded hit the city. The Great Lisbon Earthquake and ensuing tsunami destroyed 90% of its finest buildings and killed a quarter of its population. The Marquis of Pombal emerged as the hero of the day and set about reconstruction in the form of the wide boulevards and squares that we see today. The tower of Belém and the adjoining Manueline-style Jerónimos monastery are 2 of the outstanding historic buildings that remain.

The airport is very close to the city centre (20 minutes – 15 minutes to the youth hostel at Moscavide, see page 38 for option) and buses leave every 15 minutes or so. The terminal has a tourist office, which provides a useful map of the city and a list of hotels (with booking service) and is open from 6 a.m. till midnight ✆ 218 450 657. If you arrive at **Santa Apolónia train station** (from Paris, Madrid etc) it is a short walk or taxi ride to the 'lower' area (along the river Tagus *rio Tejo*) known simply as the '*Baixa*' and forming the heart of the modernized city. On the main square adjoining the river is *Praça do Comércio* with Lisbon city's **Welcome Centre** and tourist information open daily from 9 a.m. to 8 p.m. ✆ 210 321 700. Spread out along the grid of streets between here and Praça Dom Pedro IV is the main shopping district **Rossio** with its numerous cafés and restaurants spilling out onto the pavements. This is also where you will find many of the city's smaller hotels and *pensões* (rooms are often located on the top floors). The austere building at the far end is the national theatre *Teatro Nacional de Dona Maria* and formerly the site of the Court of the Inquisition in front of which the hanging of heretics and ritual burning of many of Portugal's wise women took place. Just around the corner is the striking neo-Manueline (1886) façade of the old Rossio station and at the bottom end of Avenida da Liberdade are the helpful offices of the **Portuguese Tourist Board** ✆ 213 463 314. And overlooking all this history and activity (to the south) is the ***Bairro Alto***, which you can access via various antiquated elevators *Elevador San Justa, da Bica* and *da Glória*. This area includes the chic ***Chiado*** district with its elegant shops and cafés including the famous *A Brasileira*, haunt of many of Lisbon's literary figures (past and present) and the *Basilica dos Mártires* (issues credenciales).

To the north of the city we find the atmospheric **Alfama** quarter that rises to Castelo de São Jorge passing Lisbon's cathedral *Sé Velha* and the church of Santiago *Igreja de S. Tiago* on the way. The church is an ideal starting point for pilgrims to Santiago and occupies a delightfully elevated position just above the cathedral at the start (lower end) of the rua Santiago that leads to the castle and adjoining the Miradouro S. Luzia (tram # 28 that rattles its way past the main historic sites). The popular café and public viewing terrace has unrivalled views across the rio Tejo estuary. The church is (usually) open late afternoons from 16:00 to 19:00 with mass at 18:30. Inside there is a fine statue of Santiago Peregrino. The cathedral is an austere castellated structure that was restored after the earthquake, although the Alfama quarter was the least worst affected of the central city. The original foundations of the cathedral were laid in 1147 just after the town was captured from the Moors and, in a final flourish of triumph, built on the site of the former mosque. Ongoing archeological excavations in the cloister area have unearthed structures dating from 4th century B.C.E. The cathedral is open from 09:00 to 19:00 (17:00 Sunday, Monday and public holidays). Our first waymark appears on the east (lower) side of the entrance.

The Alfama also claims one of the best-known fado houses in Lisbon *Parreirinha d'Alfama* adjacent to Largo do Chafariz de Dentro. This mournful music quivers to the Portuguese guitar and the soloist *fadista* sings of the pining for things that are no more, or will never be – this is the core of fado with a secondary theme being the pathos of the emigrant and nostalgia for life in general *saudade*. Avoid the tackier tourist venues that are generally overrated and overcharge. Nearby is an interesting museum detailing the history of fado where you can familiarize yourself with this form of song at *Casa do Fado e da Guitarra Portuguesa*.

Iglesia de S. Tiago

Santiago Peregrino

Accommodation:
Turismo: Lisbon's Welcome Centre (daily c. 09:00 – 20:00) ✆ 210 321 700 Praça do Comércio, the main square down by the harbour. The offices of the Portuguese Tourist Board ✆ 213 463 314 are located on Av. da Liberdade.

❑ **YHA Pousada de Juventude**: Lisbon has no official pilgrim hostel but there are several youth hostels the most convenient to the camino is in Parque das Nações (see stage 1 for details). The main city hostel •**Pousada de Juventude de Lisboa** rua Andrade Corvo, 46 ✆ 213 532 696 is located in the Saldanha district (top end of Av. Liberdade, East of Parque Eduardo VII) and •**Pousada de Juventude de Catalazete** ✆ 214 430 638 on the Estrada Marginal in Oeiras some way from the centre but overlooking the beach beyond Belém.

❑ **Hoteles / Pensões:** *Alfama district* (nearest to our starting point at the cathedral) includes: •**Pensão São João de Praça** ✆ 218 862 591) town house with balconies onto the street and the adjoining •**Sé Guest House** ✆ 218 864 400 on rua São João de Praça, 97. The far side of the castle on Costa do Castelo, 74 is •**Pensão Ninho das Águias** ✆ 218 854 070. *Rossio and Baixa districts* (lower city centre) have a profusion of hotels, pensions and 'rooms'. Up market and up above Rossio in Chiado is the good value •**Hotel Borges** ✆ 213 461 951 on rua Garrett 108 (opposite the *Basilica dos Mártires* and adjoining the famous café *A Brasileira).*

❑ **Historic Buildings and Monuments:** Much of the historic fabric of the city was damaged during the 1755 earthquake. Amongst those that were saved or restored are 2 outstanding examples of Manueline architecture: ❶ *Mosteiro dos Jerónimos* XVIthc (work commenced in 1502) magnificent monastery and cloisters that capture this illustrious period in Portuguese history. In the entrance we find a statue to Henry the Navigator and the interior houses the tombs of Vasco da Gama and the 'Discoveries' poet Luís de Camões. Adjacent is the XVIthc *Torre de Belém* built as part of Lisbon's port defences. Also In this area is the modern Monument to the Discoveries *Monumento dos Descobrimentos* built to celebrate the 500th anniversary of the Henry the Navigator (trams E15 / E18). Of particular interest to pilgrims is ❷ *Basilica dos Mártires* Basilica of the Martyrs which has the only chapel dedicated to St. James. A pilgrim passport *credencial* is available from the sacristy. ❸ **Cathedral** *Sé*. Built in 1150 on Roman foundations to replace the former mosque. 400m above the cathedral is ❹ *Igreja S. Tiago* Church of St. James. ❺ *Castelo São Jorge* ruins of St. George's castle overlooking the city.

Rio Tejo from Rua Santiago

Castelo S. Jorge

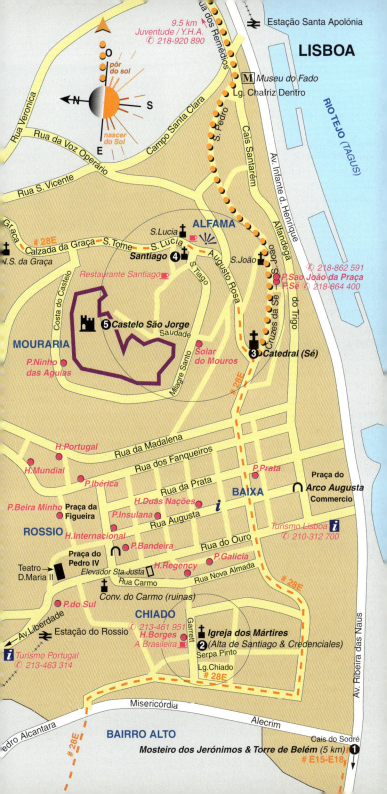

❏ **Injustice anywhere, is a threat to justice everywhere.** *Martin Luther King*

01 *615.6 km (382.5 miles) – Santiago*

LISBOA – ALVERCA do RIBATEJO
(Verdelha de Baixo)

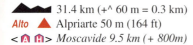

▬▬▬	--- -- 16.1 ---	52%
▬▬▬	--- --- 4.1 ---	13%
▬▬▬	--- --- 10.9 ---	35%
Total km	**31.1** km (19.3 ml)	

▲ 31.4 km (+^ 60 m = 0.3 km)
Alto ▲ Alpriarte 50 m (164 ft)
< 🅰 🅷 > *Moscavide 9.5 km (+ 800m)*

❏ **The Practical Path:** Traversing a city usually presents a challenge. However, navigating your way out of Lisbon is relatively easy as we head down to the mighty river Tagus *Rio Tejo* at the Expo'98 Maritime Park *Parque das Nações*. Then we follow the river to its confluence with the modest rio Trancão which we follow as it heads inland – leaving it to take a tranquil path up a green valley to the high point of today's stage at a mere 35m. It's then a gentle descent before entering the busy environs of Povoa de Santa Iria. Here we cross the rail line into an industrial estate to re-emerge just before reaching Alverca do Ribatejo where a short detour brings us to Verdelha de Baixo with a range of accommodation. Amazingly for a city route we find that half is on pathways with the waymarked route now avoiding most of the dangerous N-10.

❏ **The Mystical Path:** The wealth of Portugal was carved out of its colonial past and its sea ports were a gateway for the lucrative slave trade from Africa to the Americas. Our affluent Western lifestyle has created enormous injustices in wealth distribution. Chesterton wrote, "There are two ways to get enough; one is to continue to accumulate more and more. The other is to desire less."

❏ **Personal Reflections:** I nearly upset her begging bowl as I climbed over her outstretched legs sprawled across the steps. I was irritated at her pleading and avoided meeting her eyes... inside the church was like a refuge but also a reminder of my privilege and responsibilities. I sat by the chapel dedicated to St. James and vowed to give a tithe of my 'en route' expenses to those in need... she was no longer outside but other opportunities will present themselves.

0.0 km **Lisboa Cathedral** *Sé* The first waymark appears discreetly to the right of the cathedral steps, then down into rua São João da Praça, Largo de São Rafael, rua de São Pedro into Largo de Chafariz (Museu do Fado 0.5 km). *Option 1*: *Estação de Santa Ápolónia here we have an option to take the metro line to Estação do Oriente at the marine park or Sacavém) saving 7.0 + km of hard city pavements and opening the possibility to make it to Vila Franca de Xira for the end of this first stage.* **Option 2**: *page 38 for a 2nd option for stage 1.*

Museu Nacional do Azulejo

View over the Rio Tejo

For those intent on walking the entire route from the cathedral we continue via ruas Paraíso, Mirante (crossing rua Diogo Couto), Santa Apolónia, Calçada da Cruz da Pedra into rua Madre Deus to:

3.1 km **Museu Nacional do Azulejo** here we find the splendid museum of Portuguese tiles with courtyard cafe and baroque church all housed within a former Manueline convent *Convento da Madre Deus*. We now pass into ruas de Xabregas, Grilo and Beato passing the Convento and Alameda do Beato and into the Praça D L da Silva (public w.c. and striking façades of A P da Fonseca & Poço do Bispo). Cross the busy ring road (Av. Infante Dom Henrique) into the narrow rua Vale Formoso de Baixo (with its antigo teatro) to:

3.8 km **Túnel** take the underpass and up into Av. Fernando Pessoa and finally down to the Expo site and maritime park. The simplest way is to make your way directly to the harbour front and along the pedestrian walkways and the ***marina do Parque das Nações*** with its Oceanário (one of the largest oceanariums in the world), Pavilháo Atlántico, cable car *Teleférico* and up to the Lisbon's emblematic steel tower:

2.6 km **Torre Vasco da Gama** a multitude of bars and restaurants spill out onto the pavements with various modern hotels all developed as part of the Expo '98 site. The Vasco da Gama shopping centre has an information desk *Posto de Informação*.

Detour to Youth Hostel: 800m off route in nearby Moscavide is the modern youth hostel •**Pousada de Juventude** ✆ 218 920 890 on rua de Moscavide with 98 beds in rooms of 2 or 4 from €13 (pilgrim discount). Take the tree-lined Av. da Boa Esperança turning right at the roundabout (300m) into the tree-lined Alameda dos Oceanos and cross over (left) into rua de Moscavide (500m).

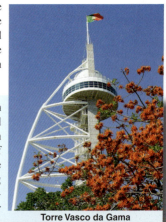
Torre Vasco da Gama

STAGE 01: 37

Ponte Vasco Gama — Statue of Catherine of Braganza *(Consort to Charles II)*

We now join the pedestrian walkways through the linear park along the banks of the rio Tejo. Amongst the various sculptures is a handsome bronze statue of Catarina de Bragança who left Lisboa in 1662 to marry Charles II. Her dowry included Bombay and tea! (she and her court introduced tea and 'tea time' to England). Continue under the magnificent 17 km-long Ponte Vasco da Gama bridge following the Tejo until it meets a small tributary **Foz del rio Trancão**. This is a good place to rest and view the route north up along the Tejo. There are bench seats and shade and the first concrete bollard marking the Caminho de Fátima (blue arrows to Fátima, yellow to Santiago (see photo right). We now follow the modest Trancão inland passing under the ring road (IC-2) and rail line at Sacavém. Shortly afterwards we pass restaurant *O Siphão* to meet up with the old N-10 (several •*café/bars* in the vicinity).

3.8 km N-10 **Ponte Sacavém** turn right over the bridge and immediately left along a path on the far side under the A-1 along a raised bank above the river passing ruins (right) before leaving the rio Trancão over a small stream.

3.6 km **Ponte** cross the stream and take the wide farm track up along a green valley where time seems to have stopped (except for the aircraft landing at Lisbon airport) and various Quintas lie abandoned in ruins. This leads to the high point of today at a mere 35m. An enterprising family are slowly bringing life back to the Quinta del Brasileiro *(opposite which is as a small bridge leading to* **Granja** *a short (200m) detour* ● ● ● ● ● *to this quaint village with variety of cafés and restaurants)*. From the bridge we join an asphalt road past factories (right) and continue s/o at the roundabout to the small village of:

5.5 km **Alpriarte** •*fonte* with welcoming •*bar-restaurante* (50m) and shop. Rejoin a farm track through cornfields and market gardens onto an asphalt road (don't continue on into Vialonga) but cross back *under* the flyover past the Olival Parque roundabout and down to the 2nd roundabout on the N-10:

3.6 km **N-10 Póvoa de Santa Iria** busy dormitory town of Lisbon with various •*café/bars* in the vicinity. We now turn right> *back* along the N-10 for 200m to cross the railway line turning <left into the industrial area of Póvoa and onto a path at the far end that winds its way through rough vegetation up to the first road bridge back <left over the railway line.

3.8 km **Ponte** bridge before entering the suburbs of Alverca do Ribatejo.

Detour 0.8 km *off* **route:** ● ● ● ● ● Note that, apart from the possibility of a floor with the voluntary firefighters *Bombeiros Voluntaríos*, there is no listed accommodation in Alverca itself. To stay the night in the area you need to leave the waymarked route at this point and make your way straight towards the **N-10** and turn <left at the petrol station **Jumbo [400m]** and continue past the major **AKÍ** store to the 2nd roundabout and cross over **[!]** to the start of Estrada de Alfarrobeira in.

1.3 km **Verdelha de Baixo** *(Total distance from Lisboa cathedral – 31.1 km).* Here at a major intersection of roads we find a variety of rooms and restaurants serving the workers from the adjacent industrial parks (busy during week days). They provide an inexpensive opportunity to find a bed for the night. Best bet is to try the first one on the corner: •**Restaurante A Faia** *Dormidas* ⓒ 219 574 103 and then work your way up the side road •**Alojamentos Particulares** Estrada de Alfarrobeira,10 ⓒ 219 580 475 with 50 beds from €15. Other possibilities. •**Restaurante A Lanterna** *Dormidas* ⓒ 219 576 488. Several other private houses along Estrada de Alfarrobeira may offer rooms. Note there is no accommodation in Alverca do Ribatejo (excepting the possibility of the •**Bombeiros Voluntários** ⓒ 219 581 551.

A Faia – Quartos

Alojamentos Particulares

Option 2 for stage 1: If you don't wish to take the above detour for accommodation into Verdelha de Baixo you can go directly to the youth hostel in *Moscavide* (either from the airport or the city centre) and then join the waymarked route along the rio Tejo to *Vila Franca de Xira* (see page 43 for list of hotels) a total distance of 31.2 km (instead of 31.1 km as described above).

REFLECTIONS:

Santiago Peregrino – rose window Lisbon cathedral.

❏ **It is more blessed to give than to receive** – *Acts 20:35*

02 *583.5 km (362.6 miles) – Santiago*

ALVERCA (Verdelha) – AZAMBUJA

▬▬▬ --- ---	1.0 --- ---	3%
▬▬▬ --- ---	16.8 --- ---	55%
▬▬▬ --- ---	13.0 --- ---	42%
Total km	**30.8 km** (19.1 ml)	

◤ 31.1 km (+^ 50 m = 0.3 km)
Alto ▲ Vila Nova da Rainha 30 m (98 ft)
<🅐 🅗> *Vila Franca de Xira 11.4 km*

❏ **Practical Path:** A level day's walk much of it parallel to the busy N-10 that we have to join at several stages so the majority of our journey is on asphalt and much of it through built-up industrial areas interspersed with some quieter country lanes around the fertile river valley *Vala do Carregado*. Note the first 3 days out of Lisbon (as far as Santarém) coincides with the route to Fátima known as the *Caminho do Tejo* (blue arrows to Fátima / yellow to Santiago).

❏ **The Mystical Path:** Giving and receiving are 2 sides of the same coin but it is giving to others with love and respect that provides true satisfaction. Accumulating for oneself alone is Self defeating. "It will be given you to see your brother's worth when all you seek for him is peace. And what you want for him *you* will receive." ACIM

❏ **Personal Reflections:** My roommate was French with penetrating eyes and dark beard. He told me he was anxious to get back to Toulouse but his bank had failed to transfer funds – he was short €20 for his fare. I judged him dishonest and chose not to help. It was only after we parted I realised my tithing commitment was exactly €20 and its distribution was proving oddly difficult – my mistrust and prejudice were deeper than I realised. Christ appears in many guises.

0.0 km **Verdelha de Baixo** If you stayed in Verdelha de Baixo return to the waymarked camino by the bridge over the railway.

1.3 km **Ponte** pass under the bridge and continue to the rail station and air museum *museo do Ar (photo)* turn left over the railway •*Cafés* and right into rua infante D. Pedro to skirt the town of **Alverca do Ribatejo** past the playing fields onto pathway and up through a large industrial area back to the N-10.

3.5 km **N-10** [!] This is a busy junction and

we have to cross over the N-10. Having made it to the far side we then continue alongside it for 2 kilometres passing under 2 grain chutes before re-crossing the N-10 [!] and taking the stairs down from the bridge to the rail station at Alhandra •*Café*. Waymarking here can be confusing but make your way north into the town centre (the rail line on your left and the estuary on your right prevents getting too lost!).

2.8 km **Alhandra** main square *Praça 7 de Março* •*Café/bars*. As in Alverca there is no official accommodation in this sizable town but there is a very basic *residencial* and a *bombeiros voluntários* also a variety of bars and shops.

The official waymarking now heads out past the municipal swimming pool back over the rail line on a metal footbridge and up to the busy N-10 again (see alternative below) which we follow all the way, passing the Naval School *Escola da Armada* veering off right at the impressive bullring *Plaza de Toros (see photo)*. We then follow the road to the level crossing over the railway line.

3.8 km **Vilafranca de Xira** *Option* [?]

Alternative (*same distance*) ● ● ● ● ● riverside pedestrian path *passeio ribeirinho pedonal* under construction sandwiched between the Tejo and railway. To access this alternative make your way from the central square in Alhandra to the river with its modern marina, sailing club and boat yards. Follow the path alongside the river and rail line as it narrows at the naval college and past the modern rail station. Keep to the river front and this will bring you to the level crossing to rejoin the waymarked route at the option point.

Vila Franca de Xira attractive town with wide range of *cafés e restaurantes* and accommodation including: •**Pensáo Ribatejana** ✆ 263 272 991 on rua da Praia adjoining the railway station, basic *residencial* with 8 rooms from €20 single or the more up-market •**Hotel Flora** ✆ 263 271 272 rua Noel Perdigáo,12 with 20 rooms from €37. •**Bombeiros Voluntários** ✆ 263 280 650 and on the outskirts •**Camping** ✆ 263 276 031 (summer only) and further out along the EN-1 •**Hotel Lezíra Parque** ✆ 263 276 670 from €75 single.

This busy town had links with the English crusaders (they came this way en route to the Holy Land) who named it Cornogoa (after Cornwall). It stands at the edge of Portugal's main wetland reserve *Reserva Natural do Estuario do Tejo* home to vast numbers of migrating (and domestic) wildfowl. Today it is better known for the breeding of fighting bulls and its popular 'running the bulls' that takes place during its well known fiestas – 'Red Waistcoat' *Festa do Colete Encarnado* that takes place during the first 2 weeks in July and again in first 2 weeks in October *Feira de Outubro* when accommodation is all but impossible to find.

The waymarked route continues along an attractive riverside park (between the railway and rio Tejo) out under the N-10 (which goes over the Tejo at this point) as the road veers left over the rail and down to a confusing roundabout on the old N-1. Here we take a leap of faith over to the far side (sign-posted Alenquer / Carregado) and out under a slip road and the A-1 (see photo right) up to the Lidl supermarket.

3.0 km **Lidl** turn right> down under the A-1 through an old industrial zone to the modern rail station in Castanheira do Ribatejo. Continue along the rail line to the old station at Carregado / Alenquer with several •*cafés.*

4.4 km **Carregado** we now turn inland along a drainage channel and turn right> by •*café/bar* over bridge past the power station *termoeléctica*. The route now continues under the A-1 again up to the N-3 and over into the village of.

4.6 km **Vila Nova da Rainha** •*cafés e restaurantes* the waymarked route continues through the village and rejoins the N-3 for a 6 km slog into Azambuja relieved only by a Repsol •*café* (left) and excellent fish •*restaurante* (right).

2.7 km Restaurante Mercearia do Peixe adjoining the filling station. Continue over roundabout past Galp •*café* (left) to the outskirts of Azambuja:

3.7 km Azambuja hotel•**Gaibéu** •*café* Aldi *supermercado* and *plaza de Toros* (left) hotel Gaibéu (right). Continue s/o over roundabout past the Páteo Valverde *Turismo* to the main square and *concello*.

1.0 km **Azambuja Centro** a pleasant town (population 7,000) with good facilities and popular fiesta during the last week in May *Feira do Maio* with its own 'running of the bulls.' The area is also known for its robust red wines coaxed from the Periquita grapes. The town has a good range of •*cafés bars & restaurantes* including the •*Páteo Valverde* (left) on entering with **tourist office** off the patio to the rear and museum with portraits of famous bullfighters of the town including one of the most famous female matadors, Ana Maria.

Accommodation including: •**Gaibéu** ✆ 263 401 641 modern hotel with 30 rooms adjoining the Galp petrol station at the entrance. •**Pensão Jacinto** ✆ 263 402 504 rua dos Campinos (tr. Da Misericordia). •**Pensão A Lareira** ✆ 263 475 115 rua Francisco Almeida. •**Casa de Hóspedes Jorge da Música** ✆ 263 401 555. •**Flor da Primavera** ✆ 967 067 381 rua Conselheiro Federico Arouca,19 (closed in 2010 check). •**Bombeiros Voluntários** ✆ 263 400 190) on rua José Ramos Vide.

REFLECTIONS:

❏ **Do one thing in this life – eradicate prejudice.** *Peter Ustinov.*

03 *553.7 km (344.1 miles) – Santiago*

AZAMBUJA – SANTARÉM

```
▬▬▬▬▬  --- ---  18.7  --- ---  58%
─────  --- ---  13.6  --- ---  42%
─────  --- ---   0.0  --- ---   0%
```
Total km   **32.3 km** (20.1 ml)

▲▲ 33.0 km (+^ 140 m = 0.7 km)
Alto ▲ Santarém 135 m (443 ft)
< Ⓐ Ⓗ > None

```
                                              Alto 135m ▲
100m - - - - - - - - - - - - - - - - - - - - - SANTARÉM
AZAMBUJA            Valada
  Río Tejo
0 km    5 km    10 km    15 km    20 km    25 km    30 km
```

❏ **The Practical Path:** Today we traverse the flood plains *lezíria* – half the route is via delightful farm tracks through this agricultural area with its crop fields, fruit and vegetable production (tomatoes) and vineyards. This is the market garden of Portugal covered with the rich alluvial soil of the Tejo which has now narrowed to a more intimate river as distinct from its estuary-form but all the more hazardous for that as it can (and does) rise and flood this totally flat terrain – a rise of 8 meters has been recorded! The only climb today is up to Santarém at 110m. Facilities are limited so carry some food and water. The only shade is occasional stands of poplar so take precautions against the sun.

❏ **The Mystical Path:** Everyone, without exception, is a child of the One God and to look on another with the vision of Christ is to recognise one's true Self in reflection. *The eye with which I see God, is the same eye with which God sees me.* Meister Eckhart.

❏ **Personal Reflections:** I looked out dreamily across the rio Tejo, contemplating the journey ahead and suddenly realised my camera was being lifted from my pocket. I lashed out in anger and recognised the young gypsy from an earlier confrontation. The strength of my reaction alarmed me. I write these notes in the calm of the evening and re-dedicate this journey to eliminating prejudice from my heart and to making every step a prayer for peace and understanding... *"He who angers you, conquers you."* Elizabeth Kenny.

0.0 km **Azambuja.** From the central square follow the waymarks that lead down rua Conselheiro Federico Arouca directly to the railway station up the metal staircase and over the N-3 and rail line to follow a quiet tree-lined road on the far side to a bridge.

1.8 km **Ponte.** Immediately over the bridge turn down sharp <left (waymark below road) and make your way along a delightful riverside path crossing over a side canal to skirt the quinta ahead and pick up wide farm tracks that wind their way to an asphalt road at:

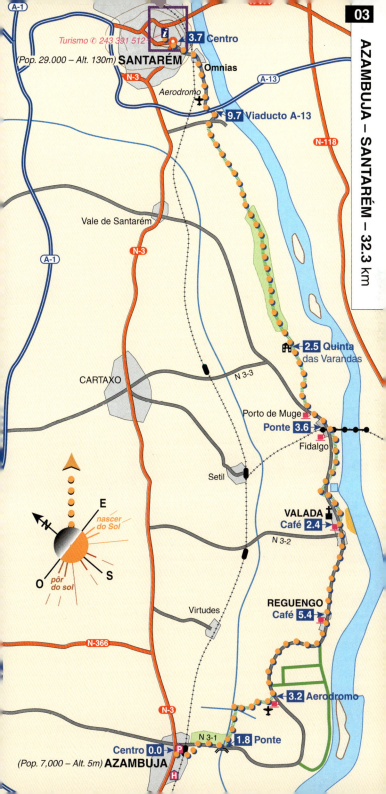

3.2 km **Aerodromo** •*café* serving the pilots but also welcomes the public. We now turn <left along the road to make out way back to the river. *[Note: after 400m old waymarks point right off the road but then evaporate in a maze of farm tracks through crop fields which requires you to make your way east as best you can to rejoin the road]* or simply stay on the asphalt road that bends first right and then left with the Tejo lying 'hidden' behind the high flood barrier that follows the river at this point passing a welcome sign as we enter:

5.4 km **Reguengo** welcome riverside village with •*café*:

2.4 km **Valada** •*café* a flood bank separates this attractive riverside village from the a sandy beach. A stone marks the flood level in 1979 when it rose to the top of the bank. The parish church *Iglesia de la O* dates from 16th c. We continue past a water treatment plant through Casal Fidalgo and leave the river bank at:

3.6 km **Ponte Porto de Muge** •*café* we now enter delightful 'sand' tracks that meander for 9 km through this rich agricultural area *Lezíria* with a variety of crops, especially tomato. One of the few signs of habitation is:

2.5 km **Quinta das Varandas** after which the first views of Santarém open up on the horizon ahead. We finally join an asphalt road to:

9.7 km **Viaducto A-13** pass under the motorway by a local aero club and under the railway in **Ómnias** for the final steep ascent up into:

3.7 km **Santarém Centro** Main roundabout *Largo Cândido dos Reis* with Hospital de Jesus Cristo church and the adjoining Santa Casa da Misericórdia. Santarém, a charming historic city, straddles a fortified hilltop well out of reach of the floodwaters of the Tejo. Its commanding position affords wonderful views of the river basin in particular from the viewpoint *miradouro* also called Gates of the Sun *Portas do Sol* where extensive gardens form a viewing platform on what was formerly the Moorish citadel. The town provided a major stronghold for the Romans and Julius Caesar chose it as the administrative centre *conventus* for the region. When the Moors arrived it became in turn a stronghold for Islam and was considered to be unassailable until the first king of Portugal *Dom Afonso Henriques* recaptured it in 1149 and returned the town to the Portuguese who have occupied happily it ever since. *Note: for detour to Fátima see page 10.*

REFLECTIONS:

Rio Tejo from Santarém

❏ **Historic Buildings and Monuments:** At the entrance to the town ❶ *Igreja do Hospital de Jesus Cristo XVthc* (adjoining the Santa Casa da Misericórdia). ❷ *Praça Sá da Bandeira* this exquisite square includes a flight of steps up to *Igreja N.Sra. da Conceiçáo e Seminário XVIIthc* which dovetails as the cathedral and on the opposite side is *Igreja N.Sra da Piedade*. Next on the circuit is the Manueline gem ❸ *Igreja de Marvila* with its wonderful display of ceramic tiles *azulejos* dating from *XVIIthc* although the original site was donated by D. Afonso Henriques to the Knights Templars in the XIIthc. ❹ *Igreja da Graça XVthc* with its fine rose window and which houses the tombs of Pedro Alvares Cabral (after whom the square is named) the 'discoverer' of Brazil whose simple stone slab is outdone by the ornate sarcophagus of Pedro de Menezes the first governor of Ceuta (Morocco). ❺ *Portas do Sol* 'Gate of the Sun' is a wonderful viewpoint *miradouro* occupying the site of the original Roman forum and the Moorish citadel. ❻ *Porta de Santiago* medieval pilgrims gateway.

❏ **Accommodation:** *Turismo* ✆ 243 391 512 rua Capelo e Ivens, 63 Close to the southern entrance: •Corinthia Santarém Hotel**** ✆ 243 309 500 on Av. Afonson Henriques. •Residencial Vitória ✆ 243 309 130 on rua Visconde de Santarém, 19. More centrally located are: •Pensão Muralha ✆ 243 322 399 rua Pedro Canavarro. •Residencial Abidis ✆ 243 322 017 rua Guilherme de Azevedo,4 and at no 24 •Casa de Hóspedes Central ✆ 243 322 399. •Pensão José Rodrigues ✆ 243 322 028 Trav. Do Frois,14 basic accommodation close to the tourist office. Near the Porta do Sol gardens at the northern exit is the quinta style TH •Casa da Alcáçova ✆ 243 304 030 and at the far (western) end of town opposite the Câmara Municipal •Residencial Beirante ✆ 243 322 547 on rua Alexandre Herculano. Other possibilities include: •**Santa Casa da Misericórdia** on Largo Cândido dos Reis with dormitory accommodation for groups of pilgrims to Fátima (may admit individuals pilgrims to Santiago). Further out beyond Casa Misericórdia in the south/ western suburbs at Av. Madre Andaluz •**Pousada da Juventud** Youth hostel ✆ 243 333 486 (Closed for renovations in 2010) also •**Bombeiros Voluntários** ✆ 243 323 122.

Praça Sá da Bandeira

Igreja da Graça

❏ **The possibility of the impossible is the subject of my novels.** *José Saramago*

04 *521.4 km (324.0 miles) – Santiago*
SANTARÉM – GOLEGÃ

▬▬▬	--- --- 16.6	--- ---	52%
▬▬▬	--- --- 14.6	--- ---	48%
▬▬▬	--- --- 0.0	--- ---	0%
Total km	**31.2 km** (19.4 ml)		

🏔 31.3 km (+^20m=0.1 km)
Alto 🔺 Santarém 135 m (443 ft)
< 🅰 🅷 > *Azinhaga (quinta) 24.3 km.*

Practical Path: Another pleasant days walking split between quiet country lanes and farm tracks running parallel to the river Tejo. The historic camino now leaves behind the concrete bollards and blue arrows that pointed to Fátima and we have the more humble yellow arrows to accompany us as we head into the flat terrain with our high point (once we have descended from Santarém) at Vale de Figueira at a mere 45m. We now abandon the A-1 motorway (for the time being) but facilities along this stretch are limited so stock up with water and some food before leaving Santarém. There is also little shade so take protection from the sun. Note that accommodation in Golegã is limited. **Intermediate accommodation:** *Azinhaga – 24.3 km with local shops, cafés and restaurants.*

❏ **Mystical Path:** Let me live in my house by the side of the road, where the race of men go by; they are good, they are bad; they are weak, they are strong, wise, foolish – so am I; then why should I sit in the scorner's seat, Or hurl the cynic's ban? Let me live in my house by the side of the road, and be a friend to man. *Sam Walter Foss*

❏ **Personal Reflections:** I was cold and wet and the batteries in my GPS suddenly went flat. I wearily retraced my steps and met her locking up the office by the side of the road. She knew of a place to sleep and, perchance, it was her birthday so she would be delighted to celebrate and share a meal with me. As I luxuriated in a hot bath it was not only the batteries that were being recharged – my heart was being filled with gratitude for unexpected friendship and trust offered to a total stranger by a lady at the side of the road in Azinhaga.

0.0 km Centro – head out on rua 1st de Dezembro <left into Tr. das Capuchas into Av. de 5th Outubro to **Porta do Sol [1.0]** out through St. James Gate *Puerta de São Tiago* and head down steeply [!] on woodland paths (left) to cross the EN-114 [!] and Igreja Santa Cruz down to the rail line at **Ribeira de Santarém [1.1]** •*café/bars* passing the fonte de Palhais and medieval bridge to turn right> over the rio Alcorce onto quiet country road to farmhouse and path [1.1]:

3.2 km Camino turn <left by house onto delightful path that now veers right> through crop fields running parallel to the road which we cross at:

3.4 km Cruce **X** and continue on path to rejoin road up to isolated quinta:

2.1 km **Quinta Cruz da Légua** where we continue along the flat flood plains of the Tejo passing quinta Boavista into a quiet village typical of the *lezíria*:

3.0 km **Vale da Figueira** *Centro* with central •*café-bar* by the church. Continue up through the town and turn down right> at next •*café-mini mercado* **[0.2 km]** onto an earth track turning <left into a cork tree plantation. **[!]** *The waymarking here is spasmodic but the route takes an easterly direction until just before entering Azinhaga where it turns north again. Use the sun compass to help in general orientation.* Veer right> at next T-junction **[1.2 km]** and continue to **bridge [1.7 km].**

3.1 km **Ponte** over the rio Alviela (tributary of the Tejo) and keep s/o along track before turning <left **[1.0 km]** to pass working farm and quinta **[0.5 km]**.

1.5 km **Quinta** the route now alternates between country lanes and farm tracks through crop fields, mostly corn *maizales* veering right> **[0.9 km]** then <left **[1.3 km]** onto road (into Reguengo do Alviela) and immediately right> onto path by line of trees turning right> **[1.4 km]** towards woodland **[!]**.

3.6 km **Bosque** small woodland copse where waymarking may be indistinct in this area but we make our way along the edge of a field to the small wood directly ahead and out onto a track the far side keeping s/o **[1.6 km]** around old sand and gravel pits passing a water treatment plant **[1.3 km]** emerging onto asphalt road into the town centre **[1.0 km]**.

3.9 km **Azinhaga Centro** turn right> in Largo da Praça by Foundation offices (corner right) dedicated to the works of Nobel Laureate José Saramago who was born in the village in 1922 and died in 2010. He became the first Portuguese writer to win the Nobel Prize for literature in 1998 and his works have been published in over 30 languages. He wrote: *"As citizens, we all have an obligation to intervene and become involved – it's the citizen who changes things."* Azinhaga is an attractive town with a resident population of 2,000 supporting a variety of •*café-bars* and connections to the original medieval pilgrim route. In rua da Misericordia we pass an ancient pilgrim hospital adjacent the 14thc Capilla del Espíritu Santo and at no 28 (covered in creeper) we find the delightful quinta •**Casa da Azinhaga** © 249 957 146 a restored 18thc manor house that retains its 'olde worlde' charm coupled with the luxury of a swimming pool, 7 rooms from €70.

Casa da Azinhaga

Continue straight on at the roundabout *Rotunda do Campino* past the ruins of 15thc Capela San João Ventosa (right) and turn <left onto path turning right> at the gates of Quinta da Broa to the bridge over the rio Almonda:

STAGE 04: 55

1.9 km Ponte we now stay on the road all the way into Golegã passing:

3.8 km Cruce X (detour left for Reserva Natural) continue s/o passing lake (right) and at the end of the tree-lined park turn right up into the main square:

1.7 km Golegã *Centro* The central square has popular cafés and tourist office (summer only) and the 14thc parish church *Igreja Matriz N.Sra. da Conceiçao* with beautiful Manueline door (see photo below). The other area of activity is around the large main square *Largo do Marquês de Pombal* (equestrian arena). Golegã is a lively town (population 6,000) whose roots go back to the 12thc when a Galician woman (from "Galego" *Golegã*) set up an inn for travellers and pilgrims on the Royal Way *Estrada Real* from Lisboa to Porto. Golegã is now better known as the 'horse capital of Portugal' famous for its national (and international) horse fair *Feira Nacional do Cavalo* held during the first 2 weeks in November (St. Martin's Day) when accommodation for miles around is booked out a year in advance! Apart from the equestrian events there is also the obligatory 'running of the bulls' and bullfighting *a la Portugues*. Towards the top of rua José Relvas (on the direct route into town) is *Casa-Museu de Fotografia Carlos Relvas* with the ornate house in which his early photographic material is displayed.

❏ **Accommodation:** *Posto de Turismo* ✆ (351) 249 977 361 centrally located on the camino in Largo Imaculada Conceição Nearby / rua Afonso Henriques. The limited (and generally expensive) accommodation includes: •**Hotel Lusitano** 4 star luxury ✆ 249 976 933 with 24 rooms from €130. **A.N.T.E.** •**Lusitanus** ✆ 249 976 933 with 6 exclusive rooms (part of the main equestrian centre). Best bet •**Restaurante O Té** ✆ 249 976 404 rua José Relvas, 119 who have rooms from €15 and will direct to other accommodation if full. •**Apartamentos Calvo Branco** bungalow accommodation (see photo below – consider sharing) part of the convenient •**Parque Campismo** ✆ 249 976 222 and under the same management, located in Largo Parque Campismo (off rua D. Joao IV as you enter the town) where we also find the •**Bombeiros Voluntários** ✆ 249 979 070. Some private houses and restaurants may also offer rooms: •*Restaurante Lusitanus* ✆ 249 977 572 on Largo do Marquês de Pombal.

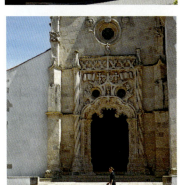

❏ **Practise random acts of loving kindness and senseless acts of beauty.**

05 *490.2 km (305 miles) – Santiago*

GOLEGÃ – TOMAR

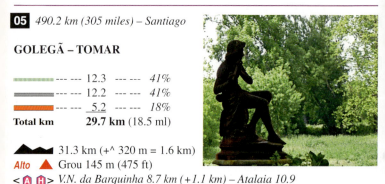

▰▰▰▰▰	--- ---	12.3	--- ---	*41%*
▬▬▬▬	--- ---	12.2	--- ---	*41%*
▬▬▬▬	--- ---	5.2	--- ---	*18%*
Total km		**29.7 km** (18.5 ml)		

⛰ 31.3 km (+^ 320 m = 1.6 km)
Alto ▲ Grou 145 m (475 ft)
<🅐 🅗> *V.N. da Barquinha 8.7 km (+1.1 km) – Atalaia 10.9*

Practical Path: We set out today towards to one of Portugal's most notable manor houses – *Quinta da Cardiga*. The first half is along quiet country lanes relieved, occasionally, by farm tracks as we head back towards the Tejo where it takes a pronounced bend away from our path at Vila Nova da Barquinha where we leave it for the last time. This is the point where we also leave the flat alluvial plains and head into more interesting countryside with gentle rolling hills covered in woodland offering us some shade for the first time. We also encounter villages at regular intervals with the possibility of refreshments and we end this stage in the historic Templar town of Tomar where the welcome felt by the medieval pilgrim is extended to those of us who follow in their footsteps. **Intermediate accommodation:** *Vila Nova da Barquinha (off route) and Atalaia.*

❏ **Mystical Path:** Love simply *is* and needs no defence. It is the desire for love that makes it manifest and dissolves the barriers erected in a vain attempt to keep it hidden. Camões says it thus:

> *The lover becomes the thing he loves*
> *By virtue of much imagining;*
> *Since what I long for is already in me,*
> *The act of longing should be enough.*

❏ **Personal Reflections:** I arrived in the heat of the afternoon and rested by the gate – I didn't have long to wait and was treated like an old friend with love and kindness. I merely mentioned an interest in visiting the castle at Almourol and was driven there without a moments hesitation along with a visit to Constância beautifully located at the confluence of the Tejo and Zezere. It was here, in the 16thc, that Portuguese poet Luís Vaz de Camões was forced into exile and wrote some of his masterful verse, oft compared to that of Shakespeare.

0.0 km **Golegã** *Centro* despite its compact size it is easy to lose your way amongst the maze of streets – use the sun for orientation (if you stayed here last night then head towards the rising sun (ahead right) on the north/eastern side of

town) into rua D. Afonso Henriques and s/o over the bypass road onto track **[0.9 km]** to intersection with asphalt road **[1.9 km]:**

2.8 km **Cruce** turn <left and s/o at sign *S. Caetano* and veer right> at next sign *Malã* onto poorly waymarked track **[!] [0.3 km]** (an option here is to continue by road into S.Caetano). The original waymarks may have been ploughed up but head towards the large quinta and buildings across the field (or around its edge) to an asphalt access road to quinta do Matinho **[1.1 km]** and s/o to the tree-lined avenue and historic buildings **[2.1 km]** at:

3.5 km **Quinta Cardiga** take a rest in the shade and soak up the peaceful atmosphere with its images of old and new world wealth and privilege. A leisurely stroll down the tree-lined avenue is to take a trip down memory lane with old retainers trying hopelessly to maintain a semblance of order out of the fading opulence. Strategically located on the banks of the Tejo it started

Quinta da Cardiga

life as a castle given by D. Afonso Henriques into the care of the Templars which, along with Almourol (see later) formed part of the defensive system against both Spanish and Arab invasion. From castle it became royal palace, home to religious orders, hospital for pilgrims, home to nobility passing into... history?

Continue over the stone bridge *Ribeira da Ponte da Pedra* over a stream that enters the Tejo immediately to our right (the gardens of the quinta front the river). The route now wends its way past Pedregoso passing sign for V. N. Barquina and across the main road (EN-3) and railway line.

2.4 km **V. N. da Barquinha** *Options:* **[?]** We now have several options.
Detour ● ● ● ● ● *[1]* Vila Nova da Barquinha ½ km detour to the attractive and historic town centre beautifully preserved with all facilities including a riverside park and accommodation •**Pensão Soltejo** ✆ 249 710 231 and •**Bombeiros Voluntários**. *Detour [2]* If time and energy allow then a further excursion of 4 km along the banks of the Tejo to ***Almourol castle*** is worth considering but would require spending the night in Atalaia, Barquina, Tancos or Entroncamento. In the summer a boat trip also runs from the town of Tancos which can be accessed either by riverside walk, rail or taxi. This magnificent stronghold of the Templar knights stands on a tiny rocky island just off the northern bank of the river. *Detour [3]* If accommodation

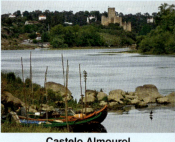
Castelo Almourol

at V. N. da Barquinha is full then additional facilities are available in the large commercial town of Entroncamento – a 2 km detour on the far side of the IC-3 / N-365 (see map). From the railway line in V. N. Barquinha make your way up through the residential suburbs of V. N. Barquina that merge into Atalaia via ruas de São Matias and Patriarca D. José to:

2.2 km Atalaia •Casa do Patriarca
© 249 710 581 fine manor house with 6 rooms and shaded gardens (right) directly on the camino with restaurant nearby. Continue up to the top of the rise to the well preserved 16th c Parish church (National monument) with its beautiful Manueline porch **[0.2 km]**. We now head down towards the N-110 and turn right> onto track **[0.5 km]** immediately *after* the sign for leaving Atalaia, opposite industrial building *(not the first track with dog kennels)*.

[!] *Extra vigilance is needed through the next section (as far as Grou) as recent clear-felling of timber in the area may have removed many of the waymarks so look carefully for signs on pylons and rocks that maybe slightly off route. If new waymarks are clear then follow them otherwise follow the original route as follows:* Keep to the main track through woodland up to a central clearing and intersection of forest tracks **[1.1 km]** (pylon to the right). Veer <left and then immediately right> *(the main track continues up left to a radio mast and eventually meets the A-23 before reconnecting to the original waymarked route described next).* There are several indistinct paths that now head over to our left parallel to pylons towards a small derelict building *ruinas* on the horizon beside a bridge *ponte* **[0.6 km]** over the A-23 motorway which is hidden in a cutting in the landscape at this point (see photo below).

2.4 km Ponte A-23 cross the bridge and turn <left back above the A-23 before turning up right> **[0.3 km]** onto a steep path through the trees up to a clearing where overhead cables cross and several paths branch off **[0.9 km]**. Take the central path s/o to intersection and turn <left **[0.3 km]** and immediately right> down into the valley ahead (see photo right) and at the bottom turn <left (quinta straight ahead through trees) and right> over river-bed **[1.2 km]** and up steeply where the forest track yields finally to an asphalt road into Grou **[1.4 km]**

4.1 km Grou extensive views towards Tomar •*Café Palmeira Alto* (often closed and •*fonte* maybe dry). Continue along asphalt road passing modern church (up to our right) down to the valley floor with •*fonte* **[1.3 km]** and up again into the sprawling village of Asseiceira with several cafes to the centre **[0.4 km]**.

1.7 km Asseiceira •*Café O Flecha* mini-mercado. Proceed down to the main road **[1.0 km]** turn right> along N-110 **[!]** into Guerreira **[1.3 km]**.

2.3 km **Guerreira** *Detour* •*Café Flor da Guerreira* at this point there is a short (½ km) detour into Santa Cita with accommodation •**Residencia S. Cita** © 964 682 805. The camino now continues along the main road over river *Ribeira da Bezelga* to roundabout under the IC-3 flyover (the new bypass around Tomar) following the signs to Zona Industrial / Leiria to bridge over the railway.

1.5 km **Ponte** immediately the far side of the rail bridge turn down right> onto path alongside railway keeping s/o at level crossing and up onto asphalt road **[2.0 km]** (Casal Marmelo) and s/o (bridge on right) to top of rise passing •*Cafe O Zé* and mini mercado (•*fonte* opposite) turning right> at T-Junction over the railway down to the main road *Tomarpeças* **[1.7 km]**.

3.7 km **N-110** Turn <left along the main road into São Lourenço •*cafe-restaurante* **[1.2 km]**. The tiny chapel opposite was built in the maneuline style in the mid 16thc. *The chapel commemorates the spot where, in 1385, the troops of D. Joao I joined forces with those of D. Nuno Álvares Pereira prior to the epic battle of Aljubarrota which resulted in the defeat of the Spanish and established the independence of Portugal under Dom Joao I (king John 1st). This decisive victory led to the construction of the monastery of Santa Maria da Vitória na Batalha (battle) now a UNESCO World Heritage Site where the king along with his English born wife, Philippa of Lancaster lie buried. The blue and while tiles azulejos depict this famous meeting.*  Behind the chapel is a memorial column *O Padrao de D. Joao II*. The route now follows the narrow main road **[!]** parallel to the river Nabão into Tomar with rail station under the bridge (left) up the commercial rua António Joaquim de Araújo past the restaurant and pension Trovador and access to the bus station (left) to roundabout with stone arch and taxi rank **[1.4 km]**. The waymarked route now enters the historic old town *cidade antigo* between cafe O Infante and the refurbished Hospital de N. S. da Graça into the main square Praça da República with statue of the founder of Tomar and Grand Master of the Knights Templar Dom Pais who overlooks the beautiful Manueline church of S. João Baptista (see photos below). The camino continues down the pedestrian street rua Serpa Pinto (Corredoura) to the medieval bridge over the rio Nabão and tourist office **[0.5 km]**.

3.1 km **Tomar** *Centro* Centre of the town and tourist office (right).

STAGE 05:

REFLECTIONS:

Convento do Cristo *(above)* Quinta da Cardiga *(below)*

Tomar is *the* quintessential medieval pilgrim town and the most perfect example of Templar layout and architecture to survive to this day. The main sites of historic interest are shown on the town plan opposite (described overleaf) numbered ❶ – ❻. The Templar castle (picture previous page), Convent of Christ and the incomparable *Charola* occupy a commanding location overlooking the town and have been declared a World Heritage Site. Successive Grand Masters including King Henry 'The Navigator' helped to plan the Great Discoveries from here. Gualdim Pais, founder of Tomar is buried in the Templar Mother church on the far side of the river. This historic town has a population of 20,000 and excellent facilities with a good range of accommodation in all price brackets. The helpful regional tourist office is prominently located opposite the old bridge *Ponte Velha* at the start of the main pedestrian street – rua Serpa Pinto (locally referred to as Corredoura) and is a good place to start a tour of the town. Consider spending a rest day here to explore its Templar past and to soak up the peaceful atmosphere that pervades the old town.

❏ **Accommodation:** *Turismo* rua Serpa Pinto (Ponte Velha) ✆ 249 329 000. •**Pensão União** ✆ 249 323 161 rua Serpa Pinto, 94 with 28 rooms and popular with pilgrims. Close by on the same side •**Pensão Luz** ✆ 249 312 317 rua Serpa Pinto, 144 with 24 rooms. •**Pensão Cavaleiros de Cristo** ✆ 249 321 203 rua Alexandre Herculano,7 (street behind) with 17 modern rooms in central but quieter location. •**Residencial Sinagoga** ✆ 249 323 083 rua Gil Avo,31 (street behind Herculano) with 23 comfortable rooms with air conditioning. •**Pensão Luanda** ✆ 249 323 200 Av. Marques de Tomar, 15 (the main road leading out of town from the old bridge) with 13 rooms and above the restaurant of the same name facing the river. Directly opposite (far side of Av. Marques de Tomar and the rio Nabão) is the delightfully old fashioned •**Estalgem de Santa Iria** ✆ 249 313 326 situated on a lovely island site *Parque do Mouchão*. At the top end of the market off Av. Marques de Tomar further out of town is the luxury 4 star •**Hotel dos Templarios** ✆ 249 310 100 and at the other end of the scale and town is the possibility of a bed in the •**Bombeiros Municipais** in rua de Santa Iria and the •**Casa de Dormidas Convento** ✆ 249 311 903 on Av. Cãndido Madureira,18 and further out still (5 blocks away) on rua 10 de Agostso de 1385 we find •**Residencial Trovador** ✆ 249 322 567.

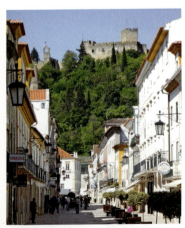

Town Centre & Templar castle *above*

Convento de Cristo *Chapter window*

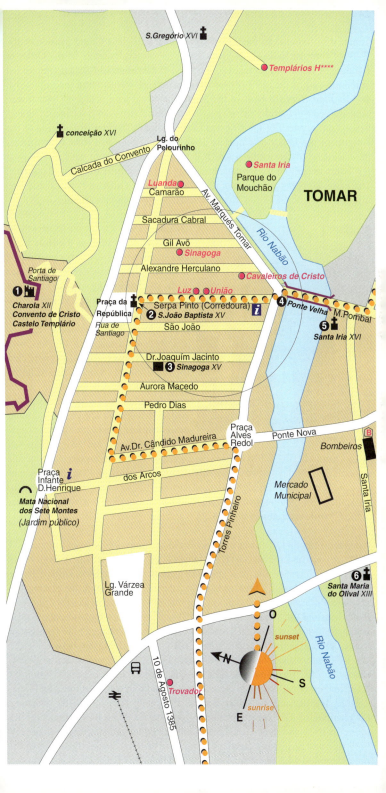

Tomar was founded in the 12thc by Gualdim Pais, first Grand Master of the Knights Templar, who established Tomar as the headquarters of the Order in Portugal. A statue of Pais takes centre stage in the beautiful *Praça do República* at the top end of the main pedestrian street where we also find the impressive ❷ *São João Baptista* built in the Manueline style with octagonal bell tower, opposite is the graceful 17thc town hall and rising above it all is the incomparable beauty and mystery of the Convent of the Knights Templar (transferred to the Knights of the Order of Christ in 1344) ❶ ***Convento de Cristo*** which forms the backdrop of the whole town. It is a pleasant 15-minute walk but allow a few hours to explore its dramatic buildings and beautifully maintained gardens. The entire complex forms the cradle of the Templar Order in Portugal and was inscribed by UNESCO as a World Heritage site *Patrimônio Mundial* in 1983.

Convento do Cristo – Charola

Gualdim Pais was a crusader knight who spent many years in the Holy Land and returned to supervise the building of the fortress and the *Convento de Cristo* with its fascinating chapel *Charola* based on the octagonal shape of the Temple Mount in Jerusalem (alluding to the wisdom within Solomon's Temple). This became a hallmark of the Order whose roots were directly connected to the Temple where the original knights were based and from which grew its phenomenal power base and esoteric traditions. The chapel's double octagonal form gives the impression of a round building – indeed it was known as the Rotunda. Its richly embellished interior is full of mystery and occult symbols and the layout was reputedly designed to allow the knights to attend mass on horseback. The high altar and surrounding alcoves were subsequently decorated with monumental paintings and murals (a major restoration program of the Charola area commenced in 2008 and is ongoing).

When the Templar Order was outlawed by king Philip of France and suppressed by the papacy in 1312 the surviving knights fled to Portugal where Dom Dinis gave them sanctuary and in a stroke of genius re-branded the knights under the title the Order of Christ redesigning the famous insignia by placing the red cross on a white band symbolizing that the old order was now 'purified' which satisfied the Vatican and the vast Templar property including the Tomar headquarters now passed to the new order under the patronage of the Portuguese throne. Prince Henry 'the Navigator' became Grand Master between 1417 and 1460 and established his court here. Dom Manuel succeeded as Grand Master in 1492 (becoming King a few years later) and Columbus, Vasco da Gama and other 'discoverers' were almost certainly received in these buildings as Dom Manuel and the Order became intricately involved in the financing and planning of the expeditions to the 'New World'. João III succeeded to the throne in 1521 and under his stewardship the Order became more religiously orientated and its hitherto political power base began to wane. It now became a more identified with monastic discipline and rule. The Great Cloister adjoining the chapter house was commenced at this time and marks the arrival of the Renaissance classical style in Portugal. The interconnecting courtyards (7 in all) and extensive halls and dormitories which welcomed pilgrims en route to Santiago give some impression of the grand scale of the whole complex and the beauty and diversity of its architectural forms which represent some of the finest examples of Romanesque, Mozarabic, Manueline and Portuguese Renaissance periods. Of particular note is the exquisite Chapter Window (see photo previous page) with its intricate sculptured maritime elements and topped by the cross of the Order of Christ.

The complex was allegedly connected by secret tunnels to the town below and to the Templar mother church St. Mary in the Olive Grove ❻ *Santa Maria do Olival.* A drinking well to the right of the church was reputedly disguised as an aerating shaft as the tunnel itself was kept sealed. The church was the resting place of over 20 Templar knights and several Grand Masters including that of the town's founding father Gualdim Pais. In one of the many atrocities perpetrated against the Order the bodies were disinterred but fear of a political backlash convinced the Establishment to re-inter the body of Pais. In a further act of cultural and historical sacrilege a new bypass was recently constructed through this ancient historical site – the modern power base may have shifted to the motoring lobby but the custodianship of the church still resides in the loving care of António who provides a rich source of information. The simple layout of the church contains many hidden symbols of the Order.

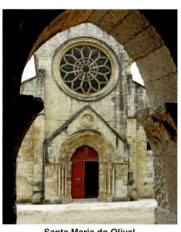
Santa Maria do Olival

Tomar has other sites to enthral the visitor and these include the 16th c chapel to the patron saint of Tomar ❺ *Capela de Santa Iria* which adjoins the lovely stone bridge over the river Nabão ❹ *Ponte Velha*. Near Praça República is the well-preserved ❸ *Sinagoga e Museo Luso-Hebraico Abraham Zacuto* in rua Joaquim Jacinto, 73. 15th c synagogue named after the astronomer who made the navigational equipment for Vasco da Gama's discovery of the Americas. The town also hosts the famous Festival of the Trays ***Festa dos Tabuleiros*** with obscure origins dating back to the 16th c and generally considered to be related to the cult of the Holy Spirit. It is held in July every 4 years with the next one in 2011 (the last one in 2007 attracted over 600,000 visitors). The procession of the trays consists of around four hundred young women each carrying on her head a tray with loaves of bread and crowned with a white dove – the symbol of the Holy Spirit. The headdress weighs in the region of 15 kg so young men assist in the procession by escorting each maiden.

❏ **Non nobis, Domine, sed nomini tuo da gloriam!** *Psalm 113*

06 *460.5 km (286.1 miles) – Santiago*

TOMAR – ALVAIÁZERE

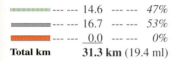

▬▬▬	--- ---	14.6	--- ---	47%
▬▬▬	--- ---	16.7	--- ---	53%
▬▬▬	--- ---	0.0	--- ---	0%
Total km		**31.3 km** (19.4 ml)		

4.1 km (+^ 560 m = 2.8 km)
Alto ▲ Alvaiázere 310 m (1,017 ft)
<A H> None

Physical Path: A day of varied terrain as we climb out of the flat plains of the Ribatejo into the central province of Beira Litoral over several hills *serras* to the high point today which is Alvaiázere itself at 310m. The surface underfoot likewise changes from town pavements into dirt farm tracks, roman roads, woodland paths and quiet country lanes. Few of the tiny hamlets we pass through have facilities so stock up on water and some food before leaving Tomar. **Intermediate accommodation:** None. Note there is currently only one *residencial* in Alvaiázere – consider booking ahead.

❏ **Mystical Path:** *Not unto us, o Lord, but unto your name grant glory!* The words of this psalm were chosen by the Templar Knights as their Motto and could serve us well today. Self-glorification is a condition of our ego-orientated world and has made us blind to the Source of our true identity.

❏ **Personal Reflections:** He was a mine of information but responded only to what was asked – humbleness exemplified. He indicated the general direction of the secret symbol but invited me to feel its power rather than observe its form. The Holy Grail is an inward understanding not a physical object. We have been looking in the wrong direction and found only emptiness in our blindness.

0.0 km **Tomar** *Centro* We leave town via the old bridge *Ponte Velha* over the rio Nabão veering left into rua Voluntarios da República and straight over the roundabout into rua de Coimbra, veering left into rua Antonio Duarte Faustino by the bullring *Praça de Touros* steeply up into rua de Vincennes and military complex (right) to the high point of this stage (110m) in new town *Cidade Nova* •*Café* **[1.8 km]** before finally dropping down into rua Ponte Peniche onto a wide track through olive orchards to the medieval stone bridge **[1.2 km]**.

3.0 km **Ponte de Peniche** The delightful earth track continues into a pine and

eucalyptus forest. The new motorway IC-9 has cut through the original path at this point so avoid old arrows that direct you up right but continue s/o and then down under the IC-9 **[0.3 km]** to pick up the path again down to the rio Nabão and turn right> along the river bank past a weir before turning up right> **[0.8 km]** onto a steep path that cuts its way through the rock under power cable to take a track along to the asphalt road **[2.2 km]** and turn down right> and then up into the village of Casais **[1.2 km]**.

4.5 km Casais *Iglesia* (at the top end of the village) with café behind (often closed). The route now continues down steeply into the hamlet of **Soianda [1.5 km]** with •*Café Balrôa & mini-mercado*. Continue s/o over **stream [1.5 km]** and through the village of **Calvinos [0.6 km]** turning <left (towards Chão das Eiras) in Cabeleireira **[0.6 km]**.

3.6 km Casais •*Café Cabeleireira & mini-mercado* (the last opportunity to buy refreshments before reaching Alvaiãzere). Continue along to the main road and turn <left along a short stretch of the N-110 to the bridge in Ceras.

3.1 km **Ponte Ceras** Cross the N-110 but ***not*** the road bridge and take the side road *rua lagar do Boucha* to cross the original bridge over the Ribeira do Chão das Eiras. The road now turns right uphill before we leave the asphalt and turn sharply up left onto a delightful forest path leading into and through the straggling hamlet of:

2.0 km **Portela de Vila Verde** with fine views over the countryside. No facilities excepting a water tap •*fonte* (right) at the far end of the hamlet. **[!]** While the route is generally well waymarked it now crisscrosses a maze of small country lanes through tiny hamlets so stay focused. The path maintains the high ridge past Vila Verde to turn off <left onto a forest path.

3.2 km **Camino** through mixed woodland (eucalyptus and pine) where waymarks are less obvious but generally maintain the contour line and s/o at cross of woodland tracks **[1.5 km]** past water tower **[0.1 km]** (white building off the path left, which marks the high point of this stage at 305m). Continue down passing specimen cork tree and continue s/o on over crossroads **[1.4 km]**.

3.0 km **Cruce** *Tojal* sign Alvaiãzere Sul. We now have a long stretch of asphalt passing sign for Relvas and again Relvas TR **[1.8 km]** (•*Quinta Catarina* © 236 636 314 *a 1½ km detour*). Continue s/o to Casa Torre at Cortica **[1.5 km]**:

3.3 km **Cruce** *Cortica* turn right at crossroads and left (800m) onto a series of crisscrossing cobbled lanes (well waymarked) through the straggling hamlets of Outerinho and Feteiras •*Bar*

up into the southern suburbs of Alvaiãzere where, on rua Augusto Martins we find the restaurante and pensão:

5.6 km **Alvaiãzere** •**Residencial O Braz** ⓒ 236 655 405. The limited facilities (several pleasant cafés and shops) are situated around the attractive central square and church located a further ½ kilometre. •**Bombeiros Voluntários** ⓒ 236 650 510. Alvaiázere from the Arabic *Al-Baiaz* 'land of the Falconer' has a population of 8,000.

REFLECTIONS:

❏ **Theirs is an endless road, a hopeless maze, who seek for goods before they seek for God.** *Bernard of Clairvaux*

07 *429.2 km (266.7 miles) – Santiago*

ALVAIÁZERE – RABAÇAL

▬▬▬ --- ---	14.3 --- ---	44%
▬▬▬ --- ---	18.2 --- ---	56%
▬▬▬ --- ---	0.0 --- ---	0%
Total km	**32.5 km** (20.2 ml)	

🗻 35.1 km (+^ 520 m = 2.6 km)
Alto ▲ Vendas 470 m (1,542 ft)
< 🅐 🅗 > *Ansião 14.5 km*

Physical Path: Another delightful day of undulating terrain through afforested valleys interspersed with olive groves and small crop fields that brings us into Ansião, conveniently located around ½ way – a good place to take a midday break or possible stopover for the night. Note an alternative route to and from Fátima connects at Ansião so be careful not to follow any blue arrows!

❏ **Mystical Path:** There are many paths back to our divine origins but many that lead us in the opposite direction. We do well to remember that... *money will buy a bed but not sleep, books but not brains, food but not appetite, finery but not beauty, medicine but not health, luxury but not culture, amusement but not happiness, a crucifix but not a Saviour, a temple of religion but not heaven.*

❏ **Personal Reflections:** She gave me a smile of such penetrating love that I was momentarily stilled, like one of her flock of peacefully grazing sheep and goats...

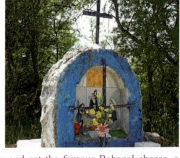

And now I sit in this welcoming hostelry and eat the famous Rabaçal cheese, a mixture of local sheep and goat milk with the unique flavour of the pasture of this peaceful landscape... and the love of the shepherdess. I feel blessed and satiated.

0.0 km **Alvaiãzere** From the *residencial* we proceed straight into the town centre •*café* down towards the main street turning right> to main crossroads and municipal gardens **[1.1 km]** where we veer up right and then <left **[0.5 km]** (sign-posted Laranjeiras) and follow the road up **[1.7 km]** into

3.3 km **Laranjeiras** •*Café Olá* we continue up steeply up through the Serra dos Ariques attentive for the waymarks as we twist and turn into **Vendas** •*fonte* **[1.2 km]** s/o to high point of this stage at 470m after which we turn right onto track **[1.9 km]** along to the pretty chapel **[1.0 km]** in:

4.1 km **Venda do Negra** *ermita*. The route to Ansião now passes through a series of straggling hamlets (no facilities) along alternating surfaces of asphalt, earthen tracks, cobblestone lane-ways and woodland paths. We pass first through **Gramatinha** and **Casais Maduros** and continue upwards (passing water tower left) into Casal do Soeiro where turn off <left onto path:

3.6 km **Casal do Soeiro** *camino* here we branch off <left onto a woodland track (various gravel walking trails) down to the asphalt road (several wayside shrines) s/o over roundabout into the bustling market town of Ansião arriving at the main square with parish church (right). Proceed down the main street to the centre with tourist office, adjacent parish council office *Junta de Freguesia* opposite the •Adega Típica.

3.5 km **Ansião** *Centro*. The town is one of the larger municipalities we pass through with a population of 13,000 and source *nascente* of the river Nabão. *Note: Ansião offers a main detour to Fátima indicated with blue arrows.* It is has a good range of facilities and a choice of accommodation which includes: •**Residencial Adega Típica** ✆ 236 677 364 where Carlos (speaks English) and his brother João run this popular establishment (traditional

Portuguese cooking) in rua Combatentes da Grande Guerra (see photo above with municipal offices and jurisdictional pillar *picota*). •**Nova Estrela** ✆ 236 677 415 Av. Dr. Victor Faveiro which also has a welcoming restaurant. •**Pensão Larsol** *Avelar* ✆ 236 621 287 rua Nova, Avelar. At the other end of the bridge (on the way out) •**Solar da Rainha** ✆ 236 676 204 Alto dos Pinheiros just beyond the IC-8 overpass, 14 rooms and restaurant. •**Bombeiros Voluntários** ✆ 236 677 122. The tourist office in the centre is due to re-open in 2011. Free internet access is available in the modern municipal library.

Leave Ansião over the 17[th]c bridge *Ponte da Cal* under the IC-8 up past Solar da Rainha, around a new sports ground through Além da Ponte and **Netos** to:

STAGE 07: 73

3.7 km Netos *Camino* turn <left onto a forest track that undulates sharply through pine and eucalyptus woodland where sap is still collected in funnel shaped containers (see photo right). The woodland is interspersed with olive groves and we suddenly emerge at a major crossroads with petrol station in Freixo:

2.0 km Freixo *Cruce* •*café* (*Detour* ● ● ● ● ● *2½ km to A Santiago da Guarda with its medieval Tower and fortified Palace and nearby accommodation at* •*Casa Vázea* ✆ *236 679 057*). To continue to Rabacal proceed in the direction of A Santiago but then turn right> (100m) off the main road and right> again onto a short stretch of path to Casais da Granja. The route now alternates between asphalt and narrow lanes with dry stone walls and paths (overgrown in places – push through or seek alternatives). Just before entering Junqueira (small hamlet ahead) the route leaves the asphalt road to take a track up through scrub and woodland to:

3.7 km Alvorge •*café/bar* and grocery shop in this attractive hilltop village (*accommodation possibility 3 km off route in Vale Florido* •*Quinta do Sobral* ✆ *236 551 117*). Continue over the crossroads veering right steeply downhill on new asphalt access road and turn off left onto rough path **[0.4 km]** through scrubland down to the valley floor with lavadero. Cross main road **[0.7 km]** onto open path that meanders above but parallel to the road before turning down sharply onto asphalt road **[1.7 km]** which we follow back down towards the main road, ignoring 1st path but taking the 2nd path off right> **[0.4 km]** the path is overgrown and can be wet underfoot, cross stream and turn right> on main road in the small hamlet of **Ribeira de Alcalamouque [1.5 km]**

4.7 km Ribeira de Alcalamouque no facilities. Continue through the town and turn off right> onto cobblestone lane that alternates between track and path past abandoned quinta (left) onto asphalt road, turn <left to cross river and up into Rabaçal turning right> at T-junction to:

3.9 km Rabaçal •**Casa de Turismo do Rabaçal** Dª Alice ✆ 918 752 990 / 917 620 982 with 29 beds and located on the main street rua da Igreja. Pilgrim discount available €15. Adjacent is the cultural centre and museum *museso romano* ✆ 239 561 856 which also arranges tours of the Roman Villa with its perfectly preserved mosaic floors at the far end of town as we exit. Rabaçal has several pleasant restaurants and bars offering the popular local cheese.

(*Detour* ● ● ● ● ● *5 km to Penela, one of the oldest municipalities in Portugal founded by D. Afonso Henriques in 1142 as part of the defensive system in the reconquest. Its beautifully preserved castle sits atop the hill* pena *and is a listed monument. Penela has several pensões in the town including:* •*Bigodes* ✆ *239 569 129. Penela Turismo* ✆ *239 561 132.*)

Residencial (left) **Museo** (right)

❏ **Live out of your imagination, not your history.** *Steven Covey*

08 *396.7 km (246.5 miles) – Santiago*

RABAÇAL – COIMBRA

		10.3	--- ---	*35%*
		15.6	--- ---	*53%*
		3.6	--- ---	*12%*
Total km		**29.5 km**	(18.3 ml)	

▃▄▅ 31.6 km (+^ 420 m = 2.1 km)
Alto ▲ Alto Santo Clara 215 m (705 ft)
< Ⓐ Ⓗ > Condeixa a Nova 12.8 km (+1 km)

Practical Path: The terrain is gentler now as we leave the hills *serras* behind, our highest point of the day is Alto de Santa Clara at 190m overlooking Coimbra and the Mondego river valley. We follow part of the original Roman road that linked Olisipo (Lisboa) with Bracara Augusta (Braga) and pass the famous Roman ruins of Conimbriga. This first part of the day is through quiet countryside alongside the rio dos Mouros with a mixture of pine and eucalyptus woodland interspersed with vineyards and olive groves. However, the latter half of this stage ends less romantically as we navigate through the maze of roads and motorways that weave around the outskirts of Coimbra.

❏ **Mystical Path:** "Healing does not mean going back to the way things were before, but rather allowing what is now to move us closer to God" *Ram Dass*. Come back to the present – arrive into now – embrace the joy of this moment – inhabit your Self – laugh out loud – dance with the angels – come alive.

❏ **Personal Reflections:** I let my mind wander and my feet followed aimlessly, oblivious to the glorious Landscape Temple surrounding me; I might as well have been walking in my own back garden for all the benefit I was receiving or giving. As I retraced my steps I began to examine my choice – to stay dwelling on the past or focused on the glorious present – the switch is simple awareness.

0.0 km **Rabaçal** From the *residencial* continue due north down the main street out of town past the Roman villa (off route left) along the Via Romana and veer right> onto path **[1.3 km]** over riverbed **[1.2 km]** up into Zambujal **[0.7 km]**.

3.2 km **Zambujal** central square with parish church and •*café*. Continue through the village and down over the river and over the road **[0.9 km]** and straight into Fonte Coberta **[1.4 km]**.

2.3 km **Fonte Coberta** Chapel and image of Santiago (photo above). Proceed

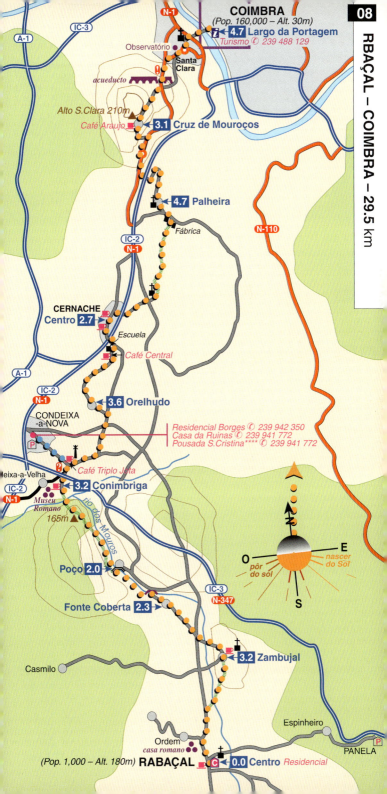

out of this historic pilgrim hamlet onto path and veer <left onto a delightful track just before the 17thc ponte Filipina (see photo above). The track now runs parallel to the rio dos Mouros into:

2.0 km **Poço** another tiny hamlet. We continue on a remote track alongside the river climbing gently up into woodland before dropping down more steeply to cross a tributary of the rio dos Mouros up to the historic Roman site at:

3.2 km **Conimbriga** (Condeixa-A-Velha) The largest and best preserved Roman settlement in Portugal and classified a National Monument. The Romans arrived here in 139 BCE under the command of general Decimus Junius Brutus who established a base on what was a Celtic settlement (*Briga* is Gaelic for 'fortified place'). Excavations have unearthed Iron Age remains going back to the 9thc BCE. The extensive ruins  occupy an attractive wooded site and include a museum with •*café* and good views down the valley. We exit the ancient site via a tunnel under the modern motorway IC-3 and make our way towards the antennae adjoing •*Café-Bar Triplo Jota* where we have an option.

Detour ● ● ● ● ● *Condeixa-A-Nova 1 km off route. This regional centre for hand-painted tiles has a range of facilities and accommodation. On the way into town we pass the up-market •**Pousada de Santa Cristina** ⓒ 239 941 286 and in the centre of town 2 basic hostels: •**Residencial Borges** ⓒ 239 942 350 rua Dona Elsa Sotto Mayor with 12 rooms and the adjacent •**Casa de Hóspedes Ruinas** ⓒ 239 941 772 with 11 rooms. The lively town also supports several bars and restaurants.*

Just before Bar Triplo Jota the waymarked route continues s/o along a series of intersecting secondary roads. Stay focussed so as not to miss any of the frequent turnings into and through:

3.6 km **Orelhudo.** Continue up passing •*café* **[1.5 km]** and turn <left after school over the IC-2 into Cernache past Correio to the town centre **[1.2 km]**.

STAGE 08: 77

2.7 km Cernache *Centro* •*cafés / restaurantes*. Continue through the town turning right> at roundabout under the IC-2 and s/o at crossroads up to church and the start of forest track **[1.6 km]** which continues for a delightful **[2.5 km]** eventually dropping down to modern factories to turn <left onto main road. We now cross over up into **[0.6 km]**:

4.7 km Palheira *Iglesia* the route now undulates sharply up to alto (190m) before dropping down steeply again (previously via concrete pedestrian bridge over the IC-2) but now waymarked to cross under the motorway into Antanhol ascending once more turning right> at major new roundabout and then sharp <left steeply up to the high point of this stage Alto de Santa Clara (215m) and:

3.1 km Cruz dos Mouroços *Alto de Santa Clara* •*café* From the church square *Plaza de la Iglesia* we get the first view over the Mondego river valley as we descend steeply down to the maze of roads and flyovers that bypass Coimbra 'old town'. Ongoing roadworks may obliterate some waymarks but the first obvious guide is the Roman **aqueduct [1.1 km]** now sliced in half to allow one of the new roads to plough through the middle, as do we (but watch out for new or temporary waymarks that may offer a detour in this area). Continue down to the valley floor and turn up right> at **junction [1.8 km]** into rua Central da Mesura and up into rua do Observatório passing the observatory (left) before cresting the rise into a modern suburb •*cafés / restaurantes* s/o over roundabout with panoramic views over Coimbra. We now begin the sharp descent down into Santa Clara, a satellite town of Coimbra with a population of 10,000. We pass a military barracks incongruously built adjacent to **Convento Santa Clara [1.8 km]** The lower 'old' *Convento de Santa Clara-a-Velha* was the original resting place of the convents founder Santa Isabel, wife of King Dom Dinis and subsequently the patron saint of Coimbra. It also housed the murdered

remains of the tragic Dona Inês de Castro (see below) but the waters of the Mondego River were constantly flooding the convent and so a new one *Convento de Santa Clara-a-Nova* was built during 17thc further up the hill. The convent is an austere building; the two redeeming features include a fine cloister and Isabel's tomb (that of Inês was re-interred in Alcobaça).

The life and gruesome death of *Dona Inês de Castro* is the subject of many an epic story line and poetry and formed the subject (and title) of Victor Hugo's first play. Beautiful daughter of a Galician nobleman she caught the eye of Dom Pedro who vowed to marry her. Pedro's father King Afonso IV fearing Spanish influence on account of the Galician connection forbade the marriage. However they married in secret but Afonso hearing of the union had her murdered in the grounds of the mournful park close by (to the right of our route) known as 'The Garden of Tears' *Quinta das Lágrimas*. When Dom Pedro succeeded to the throne in 1357 he exhumed her body from the convent here and had her corpse crowned and seated on a throne in Santa Cruz (see Coimbra) where courtiers were forced to pay homage and obliged to kiss her decaying hand.

The life of pilgrim Queen Elizabeth *Santa Isabel* 'The Peacemaker' is a more uplifting story. Daughter of King Pedro III of Aragon she was married off to the king *Dom Dinis* at the age of 12 and suffered greatly under his austere rule and bouts of jealousy. She used to infuriate her husband by giving constantly to the needy. One of the early miracles associated with her (that would lead eventually to her beatification) was when she hid gold coins to bring to the poor disguised in a basket and was stopped and searched by her husband but the gold had turned to roses thus escaping (or perhaps inflaming) his wrath. When Dom Dinis died in 1325 she distributed her remaining wealth to the poor and became a Poor Clare in the convent here (which was sumptuously embellished by her).

We now make our way down and over the mighty river Mondego whose source is the Serra da Estrela and crossing the Ponte de Santa Clara into the welcoming square *Largo da Portagem* that marks the entrance to the city:

4.7 km Coimbra *Largo da Portagem* with popular cafés and helpful tourist office *Turismo* (right). Coimbra was capital of Portugal from 1145 until 1255 but is better known for its famous university founded in 1290. The prestigious university crowns the hill and its students bring a lively atmosphere to this ancient and historic city formerly the Roman town of Aeminium with a population of a mere 100,000. Indeed one of its main charms is its compact size, which makes it easy to visit the main sites, some directly linked to the medieval camino de Santiago. Spend a day in this enchanting city if you can for, like Tomar, there is much to do and see. The main historic and tourist sites are all grouped around the city centre and lie either directly on or within a few hundred metres of the waymarked camino.

❏ **Accommodation:** *Turismo* Largo da Portagem ✆ 239 488 129

Hoteles and Pensões: on or immediately adjoining the waymarked camino (within 100 meters) includes: Largo da Portagem •**Pensão Larbelo** ✆ 239 829 092. Adjacent *left* •**Pensão Atlantico** ✆ 239 826 496 •**Hotel Astória***** ✆ 239 853 020 •**Pensão Internacional** ✆ 239 825 503. Adjacent *right* •**Pensão Avenida** ✆ 239 822 156. •**Pensão Parque** ✆ 239 829 202. •**Pensão Jardim** ✆ 239 825 204. Between Igreja Santiago and the rail station •**Pensão Moderna** ✆ 239 825 413, rua Adelino Veiga 49. •**Pensão**  **Dómus** ✆ 239 828 584 rua Adelino Veiga 62. There are several other hotels and Pensões in the busy streets in the area of the railway station itself. *Note* there are 3 railway stations in Coimbra, the central station 'A' Estação Nova is the one referred to here. On the far side of the university in rua Henrique Seco is a modern youth hostel •**Pousada Juventud** ✆ 239 822 955 a 20 minute walk or take bus Nº 46 from the central station 'A'. •**Bombeiros Voluntários** Av. Fernão Magalhães, there are a number of other hotels in this area. Take your pick of the excellent and inexpensive restaurants catering to all tastes and pockets down virtually every street which includes the ever popular but tiny Zé Manel on rua Forno (behind the Astoria).

❏ **Historic Buildings and Monuments:** *(see city plan)* ❶ *Conventos Santa Clara* on the West side of the river (on the way in). From Largo da Portagem the waymarked route goes down rua dos Gatos into Adro de Cima and Adelino Veiga passing the 18th c Igreja de São Bartolomeu and the ancient Hospital Real into Praça do Comercio lined with bars and restaurants and open air market to ❷ **Igreja de Santiago** 12th c church evoking the medieval pilgrimage. The flight of steps (right) brings us (off route) up to the main pedestrian shopping street rua Visconde da Luz. Turn left to the heart of the city in *Praça 8 de Maio* and ❹ **Igreja de Santa Cruz** (photo far right). The monastery was founded in 1131 making it one of the oldest buildings still extant and housing the tombs of King Afonso Henriques and Sancho I. The Manueline 'Cloister

Igreja de Santiago *(with waymark left)*

of Silence' was added in 1517 and the triumphal arch in the 18th c. Adjoining it (right) and built on the original monastery buildings is the popular neo-Manueline café Santa Cruz with its vaulted stone interior. Also on the square is the Câmara Municipal behind which is the Jardim da Manga.

This minimal 'tour' would not be complete without a visit to the historic cathedral. Return via the pedestrian shopping street, past Santiago church and turn left up steps under ❺ **Arco de Almedina** the original main gate in the medieval defensive wall that ran for 2 kilometres around the base of the hill. This is still the main entrance to the Old City or *High Quarter*. Continue up steeply into largo da Sé Velha where we find ❻ **Sé Velha** the old (original) cathedral before that function was transferred to the soulless Sé Nova situated further on up. One of the most important Romanesque monuments in Portugal built in 1162 on a former ecclesiastical site dating from the 9th c. Amongst the many ancient tombs is that of a former archbishop of Santiago de Compostela, D. Egas Fafes with a scallop shell emblem set in azulejos tiles. A side door provides access to a lovely Gothic cloister – the oldest extant cloisters in Portugal and well worth the minimal entry fee with proceeds going to community services.

Sé Velha – Cloisters

Sounding a different note but adjacent to the cathedral is fado restaurant •*O Trovador* with its atmospheric interior of ceramic tiles and wood panelling. Coimbra fado shares the same sombre melodies heard in the fado houses of Lisboa and Porto but supposedly with more scholarly lyrics! Just above the cathedral is the renowned **Museu Machado de Castro** on Largo Dr. José Rodrigues and just above it we come to Largo da Sé Nova with the New Cathedral, which was founded by the Jesuits. If you intend to visit the university buildings this is the time as you are now effectively at the crown of the hill where the various faculties are located. The end of the academic year is marked with rowdy celebrations *Queima das Fitas* the 'burning of the ribbons' held in April. From here you can find your way down (or get deliciously lost) amongst the maze of narrow winding streets. Providing you head north (sun to your left if its afternoon) you will arrive back in the main shopping street.

COIMBRA

REFLECTIONS:

❏ **Bacchus hath drowned more men than Neptune.** *Thomas Fuller*

09 *367.2 km (228.2 miles) – Santiago*

COIMBRA – MEALHADA

▬▬▬▬▬▬ --- ---	7.1 --- ---	32%
▬▬▬▬▬▬ --- ---	12.2 --- ---	54%
▬▬▬▬▬▬ --- ---	3.1 --- ---	14%
Total km	**22.4 km** (13.9 ml)	

▰▰▰ 23.3 km (+^ 180 m = 0.9 km)
Alto ▲ Santa Luzia 145 m (475 ft)
< 🅐 🄷 > None

Practical Path: The terrain is now markedly different from the previous stage being virtually flat as we pass along various river valleys crisscrossed with flood and irrigation channels *acequia* (reminiscent of the Ribatejo plains). Our high point is around Santa Luzia at 145m. While we have short stretches of the roman road *calzada romana* much of today is spent on asphalt and there are several dangerous stretches of main roads where extra vigilance is required. This is also one of our shortest stages so there is no necessity to leave Coimbra early. **Intermediate accommodation:** *None – but several villages en route with small shops, cafés, bars and restaurants.*

❏ **Mystical Path:** Between inebriety and sobriety lies a state of equilibrium; embracing a super-sensible reality while honouring the god of harvest and grapes. Robbie Burns reflected thus: "I love drinking now and then. It defecates the standing pool of thought. A man perpetually in the paroxysm and fears of inebriety is like a half-drowned wretch condemned to labor unceasingly in water; but a now-and-then tribute to Bacchus is like the cold bath – bracing and invigorating."

❏ **Personal Reflections:** It was like a battlefield, the bodies of the vanquished strewn all over the square. Some students were still comatose, others lay moaning in the cold light of dawn trying to awaken from the festivities. I picked my way out of the city and recalled my own youthful period of excess. Perhaps I am now more interested in quality rather than quantity, waking rather than sleeping. Despite the chaotic scenes around me, the light of this new day filled me with a sense of hopefulness, we will arise from our stupor.

0.0 km Coimbra *Largo da Portagem* This stage is measured from *Largo de Portagem*. You can [1] proceed directly down Av. Emídio Navarro alongside the river to rejoin the waymarks at the central rail station [100 m] or [2] follow the waymarked route to the *Igreja de Santiago* and thence back to the central station **[0.5 km]** 'A' *Estação Nova* and out along the rio Mondego past the bus station and under **[!]** the maze of high level roads giving access to Ponte do Açude **[1.0 km]** (N-1 and IC-2) under the railway to the roundabout **[0.9 km]**:

2.4 km Rotatória continue s/o roundabout and veer right> **[0.3 km]** (before Repsol petrol station) onto an old asphalt road with the environs of Coimbra now firmly behind. Continue alongside overgrown canal parallel to rail line and turn right> over bridge **[2.9 km]** up to main road crossing **[0.2 km]**.

3.4 km Cruce *Adémia da Baixo* •*café* s/o and turn <left at sign for Cioga do Monte **[1.4 km]** passing •*fonte* up to **Cioga [0.9 km]** •*café-mercado* and on up steeply to cross A-1 motorway and down gently to village square **[1.2 km]**:

3.5 km Trouxemil *Plaza* •*cafés, bares e restaurantes* turn up <left into **Adões [0.7 km]** •*café e mercado* through **Sargento Mor [1.1 km]** •*café e mercado* and up gently to join the busy N-1 •*café* to traffic lights **[1.8 km]**:

3.6 km Santa Lúzia *Luminoso* •*cafés* continue s/o along the N-1 to branch off right> through the centre of **Carqueijo [2.0 km]** •*café* and cross back over the N-1 at lorry park **[0.7 km]**.

2.7 km Camino •*restaurante* take the path into the eucalyptus forest offering welcome respite from the traffic and continue over railway at *A Mala* into:

2.4 km Lendiosa chapel but no facilities. Veer right past •*fonte* and onto path by river through woodland and up to roundabout at the entrance to Mealhada.

3.1 km Rotatória with the god Bacchus astride a wine barrel. Cross and turn <left over rail veering right> at Instituto da Vinho, past Correios to the centre.

1.3 km Mealheada *Centro* central park with •*cafés* and shops.

Mealhada is a busy town just off the A-1 and straddling the N-1 and rail line with a population of 5,000. The name derives appropriately from Meada 'meeting of the ways' and it was also a major crossroads town in Roman times being milepost *miliário* XII on the Coimbra *Aeminium* – Porto *Cale* highway. A famous wine growing area where the municipal pamphlet takes a quote from Victor Hugo "God created water but man made wine." and urges us to "… render homage on our knees our hands in prayer, this is Bairrada wine, the divine liquid awaiting us." Praise indeed! And so that the culinary highlights of the district are not left out it leaves us with another popular saying, "God created the suckling pig, the devil the hedgehog!" Mealhada is famous for its spit roasted month-old piglet dish *Leitões*. However, our focus is, perhaps, more on accommodation possibilities and the pilgrimage ahead.

❏ **Accommodation:** •**Pensão Castela** ✆ 231 202 275 basic but centrally located adjacent to the church. Further out but directly on our route (and the N-1) is the popular pilgrim pension •**Residencial Oasis** ✆ 231 202 081 / 914 626 362 with 15 rooms and a bit further on (just off route) is •**Hotel Quinta dos Três Pinheiros***** ✆ 231 202 391 part of the Best Western chain but don't let that put you off – this is good value, set  well back from the N-1 and with a pleasant restaurant. Further out (the other side of town) is an up-market inn •**Estalagem Azevedo dos Leitões** ✆ 231 209 880 on the N-234 just before the A-1 flyover. •**Bombeiros Voluntários** ✆ 231 202 122 on rua Bernardino Selgueiras.

REFLECTIONS:

❏ **"If we are not fully... in the present moment, we miss everything."**
Peace Is Every Step: The Path of Mindfulness in Everyday Life *Thich Nhat Hanh*

10 *344.8 km (214.3 miles) – Santiago*

MEALHEADA – ÁGUEDA

▓▓▓▓▓ --- ---	3.1 --- ---	*12%*
▬▬▬▬▬ --- ---	20.9 --- ---	*82%*
▬▬▬▬▬ --- ---	1.4 --- ---	*6%*
Total km	**25.4 km** (15.8 ml)	

▲▲▲ 26.2 km (+^ 160 m = 0.8 km)
Alto ▲ Anadia 85 m (279 ft)
<🅰 🅷> *Anadia 7.7 km.*

Practical Path: Another fairly level stage as the gently undulating terrain follows the path of the Cértima river valley (a tributary of the Vouga which we will pass tomorrow). It's also another relatively short stage but with much asphalt to contend with as we skirt several industrial areas. Vineyards and a stretch of woodland relieve the monotony of the road network and we have the town of Águeda, built around the banks of the river, to explore on our arrival.

❏ **Mystical Path:** Between alertness and stupor lies a liminal space of mindlessness. Day-dreaming can be a restful if the dreams are peaceful but it is not a place from which to navigate the paths of life with authority and power. To come fully alive we need to come fully present and act from mindfullness. Awareness is the key.

❏ **Personal Reflections:** I had feasted on the local speciality and fallen under the spell of Bacchus and was feeling somewhat the worse for wear. So much for my judgement and condemnation of the youthful citizenry of Coimbra. Here I am the following day lost because my mind is foggy from an excess of wine the previous night and I missed a key waymark. Mindfullness is the way of the pilgrim.

0.0 km Mealheada *Centro* from the town centre we make our way back to the N-1 passing *Residencial Oasis* and turn right> **[1.4 km]** by modern restaurant Espelho d'Agua in the *direction* of Sernadelo veer off right> by house with modern concrete slatted windows **[0.2 km]** onto path through woodland **[0.6 km]** take left hand fork **[0.2 km]** s/o into **Alpalhão [1.0 km].**

3.4 km Alpalhão *Igreja* turn right> past church and into and through **Aguim [1.5 km]** (no facilities) and turn right> onto another woodland track **[1.0 km]** and s/o main road and roundabout *towards* Anadia past modern sports grounds *zona desporto* and continue up to next roundabout at top of the hill above **Anadia [1.8 km].**

4.3 km Rotatória *Anadia* here we have an option to detour into the town:

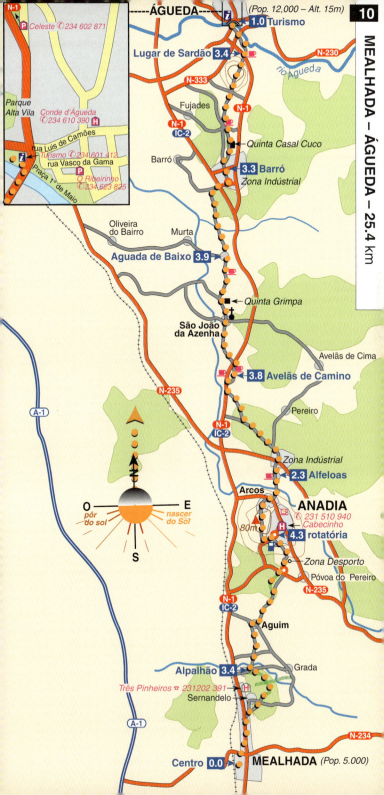

Detour ● ● ● ● ● *Anadia* 1 km off route. The wayamrked route bypasses this lively market town with a good range of facilities and accommodation including modern •*Hotel Cabecinho**** Ⓒ 231 510 940 just down from the roundabout at the top of town and close to •Centro Social São José de Cluny.

Turn <left at the roundabout past the petrol station •*café* and shops and turn up right> past the cemetery s/o up to our high point of this stage (75m) to drop steeply down passing •*fonte* into **Arcos** *Igrexa* **[1.4 km]** •*café* turn <left and s/o over river into **Adfeloas [0.9 km]**.

2.3 km **Adfeloas** •*café* s/o over the busy N-235 past various factories back down to the main road (traffic lights) into Avelas de Caminho.

3.8 km **Avelãs de Caminho** variety of •*cafés-restaurantes* adjacent to the main road including the popular •*Queiróz*. The suffix *caminho* denotes associations with the medieval camino. At the far end of the town we veer off <left by chapel into **São João da Azenha** past Bodega offices and **capela St. João [1.9 km]** continue along the quiet country lane passing **Quinta da Grimpa [0.4 km]** connected with the Bodega in São João and the famous Bairrada grape. The quinta's fine Manueline features were restored from another site. We now head into the Município passing •*Café Rossio* **[1.0 km]** and up into the village of **Aguada de Baixo [0.6 km]**.

3.9 km **Aguada de Baixo** *Centro* •*café-pastelaría* continue s/o over river bridge **[0.6 km]** and turn right under the IC-2 / N-1 **[2.2 km]** and into the industrial area of **Barró [0.5 km]**:

3.3 km **Barró** *Zona Industrial* as we leave the industrial area we veer right> off, but parallel to the main road on the original Royal Way *Estrada Real* passing Quinta Casa dos Cucos turning up <left by •*café* to drop down steeply to cross the busy [!] N-1 at:

3.4 km **Lugar de Sardão** •*café* s/o through this ancient quarter with murals onto open ground (flood area) and through a tunnel under the by-pass and up over the old bridge *Ponte Velha* across the rio Águeda to:

1.0 km **Águeda** *Turismo* Largo Dr. Elísio Sucena with helpful tourist office in this attractive tree-lined square at the bottom end of the town by the river. Águeda is an attractive town with a municipal population of 14,000. The main activity is centred on the lower town and the river area and main shopping street rua Luis de Camões with interconnecting mosaic-lined pedestrian streets off it. *The camino continues left along the river in the direction of A Parades*

❏ **Accommodation:** *Turismo* ℂ 234 601 412 Largo Dr. Elísio Sucena (by the bridge). Accommodation in the lower town: •**Pensão O Ribeirinho** ℂ 234 623 825 rua Vasco da Gama, 88 welcomes pilgrims with 7 rooms above the restaurant (see photo right). •**Hotel Conde d'Águeda** ℂ 236 610 390 modern hotel on Praça de Águeda. •**Bombeiros Voluntários** ℂ 234 623 122 Av. 25 de Abril. *(The 'hotel' on Praça de Maio is not recommended).*

In the upper town past the Hospital Conde de Sucena (near the rail station) is •**Residencial Celeste** ℂ 234 602 871 on the N-1 (1 km). Along the N-1 into town in Vale do Grou is •**Motel Primavera** ℂ 234 666 237.

REFLECTIONS:

❏ **We are all prostitutes… no matter how moral one takes oneself to be.**
— *R. D. Laing*

11 *319.4 km (198.5 miles) – Santiago*

ÁGUEDA – ALBERGARIA
A-VELHA

▬▬▬ --- ---	3.1 --- ---	19%
--- ---	13.2 --- ---	81%
--- ---	0.0 --- ---	0.0%
Total km	**16.3 km** (10.1 ml)	

▲ 17.9 km (+^ 320m = 1.6 km)
Alto ▲ Serém de Cima 125 m (410 ft)
<🄰 🄷> None

Practical Path: Another easy day's walking and the shortest stage with reasonably flat terrain, the high point being Albergaria itself at 130m. Again the majority is on asphalt roads relieved by a magical path through pine and eucalyptus woods along the original Via Romana XVI over a beautiful stone bridge across the rio Marnel – the ancient ambience and tranquillity marred only by the main road. While there is not much to do in Albergaria A Velha it is a pleasant town that provides an opportunity to just hang out and soak up its peaceful atmosphere. Accommodation is limited so consider booking ahead.

❏ **Mystical Path:** The rape and pillage we see all around us, of our earth, our children and each other is calling for urgent change. The masculine principle is out of balance and requires the restoration of the Sacred Feminine as a crucial phase in the evolution of our human consciousness. It is time for healing as we begin to embody the qualities of Love, Wisdom and Compassion – the Divine Mother, Sophia, Tara... Known by different names but One and the same Source.

❏ **Personal Reflections:** The goddess of love appears to have joined the god of harvest along this ancient stretch of calzada romana; Venus tempting the modern traveller with her charms. The fishnet tights looked out of place on the Roman bridge but blended easily in the modern motel. I, too, sell myself every time I try and manipulate the universe around me to meet my own needs. The Coimbra students have taught me not to be too hasty in judging others.

0.0 km Águeda *Turismo* we continue out along the river via *rua 5 de Outubro* in the direction of *A Parades* and veer off right> **[0.5 km]** up steeply and cross over railway **[0.5 km]** down steeply and up right again *rua do Portinho* to industrial estate **[1.6 km]** and s/o over the N-1 **[!]** **[1.3 km].**

3.9 km **Cruce** welcoming •*café-pastelería* on the far side. We now follow a secondary road (parallel with the N-1) directly into **Mourisca do Vouga [1.3 km]** with large mansions built in more prosperous times, many now semi-derelict. The town offers various •*cafés, restaurantes e mini-mercados* we

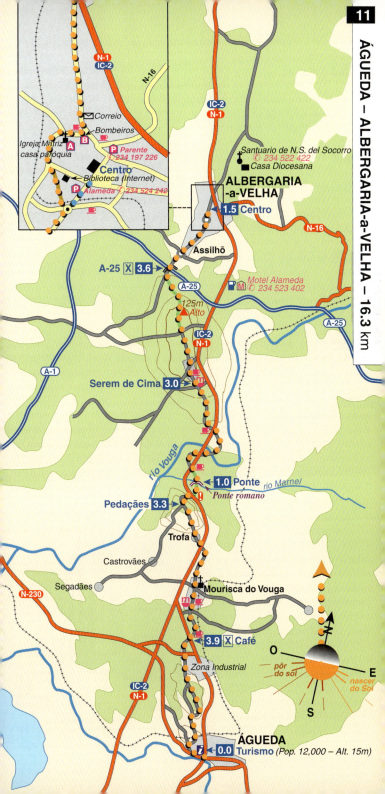

continue back over the **N-1 [0.8 km]** by traffic lights into **Pedacães [1.2 km]**.

3.3 km **Pedacães** veer right> into *rua de Espanha* and head down steeply, passing the Concelho Lamas do Vouga (school) to a dangerous bend on the **N-1 [!] [0.7 km]** cross over with care onto a stretch of Roman road *rua da Ponte Romana* passing over the recently restored medieval bridge (with Roman foundations) **Ponte de Marnel [0.3 km].**

1.0 km **Ponte de Marnel** dating from the 2nd century, part of the original Via XVI. On the far side is •*Café Espírito Santo*. Cross back over the **N-1 [!] [0.4]** into Lamas do Vouga and under flyover and up to the original bridge over the river Vouga at **Pontilhão [0.8]** (Roman remains in the area and site of an archeological dig) and s/o to cross back over the **N-1 [!] [0.8]** •*café* and up steeply to **Serém de Cima [1.0]:**

3.0 km **Serém de Cima** •*Café S.António* •*Mercado Casa Leonel* continue up past •*Café-Pastelaría O Pelurinho* **[0.4 km]** cross road and at T-Junction continue s/o ahead into eucalyptus forest **[0.9 km]** the welcome respite from the asphalt road brings us to our high point of this stage (125m). The woodland track leads us to a bridge over the motorway **[2.3 km]:**

3.6 km **Ponte A-25** cross over, s/o at roundabout and up into Largo da Misericórdia on the outskirts of Albergaria. Continue down the wide access street to roundabout with modern fountain at the entrance to town (Options).

1.5 km **Albergaria-a-Velha** *Centro [Note:* to access central accommodation and main square continue 200m s/o over the roundabout to *Plaza principal e Casa da Alameda].* However, the poorly waymarked route bypasses the town centre by taking a narrow path just to the left of the roundabout over the rail line and up into town where we turn right by the parish church *Igreja Matrix* with pilgrim accommodation on the floor *suelo* available in the adjacent parish hall. The nearby fire-station *Bombeiros* directly on the waymarked route (see town plan) is sometimes used to supplement the basic facilities.

❏ **Accommodation:** •Casa da Alameda ⓒ 234 524 242 old world charm in this centrally located hotel on *Alameda 5 de Outubro* with 14 rooms and popular adjoining restaurant (behind the bar with ironmongery shop!) full of character and excellent local fare. Run by the amiable Carlos Vidal whose family also owns •**Motel Alameda** ⓒ 234 523 402 two kilometres back on the N-1 (km 280) and can arrange transfer if the accommodation here is full or closed. Further into town (200m) in rua Doutor Brito Guimarães we find •**Pensão Parente** ⓒ 234 197 226. The •**Bombeiros Voluntários** is in rua Dr. José Henriques located 100m past the Igreja Matrix *(Pensão Parente is located a further 100m left past the Bombeiros).*

Casa da Alameda

Igreja Matrix

Concelho

There is an appealing harmony to Albergaria-a-Velha, founded in the 12th century on the royal command of Dna. Teresa in 1120 to welcome pilgrims (albergue), a command that the towns folk seem happy to fulfil 9 centuries later. Here is a place where old and new blend seamlessly – the façade of the historic Capelo Santo António sitting easily with the art-deco of the Cine Teatro. Whether writing your inner reflections in the shade of the alameda or availing of the free internet in the municipal library, enjoy the welcoming atmosphere.

REFLECTIONS:

❏ **Life is like riding a bicycle. To keep your balance you must keep moving.**

12 *303.1 km (188.3 miles) – Santiago de Compostela*

ALBERGARIA-A-VELHA – SÃO JOÃO DE MADEIRA

▬▬▬ --- ---	5.2 --- ---	18%
--- ---	20.6 --- ---	70%
--- ---	3.4 --- ---	12%
Total km	**29.2 km** (18.1 ml)	

31.5 km (+^ 460 m = 2.3 km)
Alto ▲ São João da Madeira 240 m
< Ⓐ Ⓗ > N. Sra. do Socorro 3.4 (+0.5 km) – Oliveira de Azeméis 19.8 km

Practical Path: We start today with a stretch along a lovely forest road through eucalyptus and pine but the route becomes progressively more urbanized as we approach São João da Madeira and have to cross the main road and railway many times. The terrain is now more irregular as we pass through several river valleys separated by gentle hills. Facilities along this stretch are good with several opportunities to eat and sleep along the way.

❏ **Mystical Path:** When we are out of balance we begin to wobble and fall further from our centre. We become irritable, tired, confused with the apparently limitless choices around us and distracted from our true purpose. As we move forward with awareness we regain our balance and find a new sense of peace and poise amid the mayhem. We become free to choose the right direction.

❏ **Personal Reflections:** The bundle on her head was almost as big as her body and yet she carried it with such poise. This theme of balance continues to flirt with me along the way. Between the sacred and the profane, between love and fear lies a place of acceptance and equilibrium. If I judge another as inferior or superior I make a distinction that drives the wedge of separation ever deeper into my human drama and psyche. I will keep moving forward and restore my equanimity.

0.0 km **Albergaria-a-Velha** We leave town via the fire-station *Bombeiros* and post office *Correio* (see town plan) and cross over the N-1 to forest track **[1.6 km]** turning <left at junction of tracks **[1.3 km]** to crossroads **[0.5 km]**

3.4 km **Cruce *N. Sra. do Socorro*** with statue of Our Lady *[•Casa Diocesana © 234 522 422 ½ km off route up the road to the right. This modern retreat house is located atop a small wooded hill adjoining the Igreja N. Sra. Do Socorro and viewpoint. Accommodation may be available to pilgrims (generally going to Fátima) it is advisable to phone in advance to check availability].* The waymarked route continues s/o along a quiet asphalt road before turning off

12

ALBERGARIA – SÃO JOÃO – 29.2 km

Inset map 1 (São João da Madeira - Centro)
- St. Antonio
- 11 Outubro
- Oliveira Junior
- Av. Dr. Renato
- Dr. Macie
- Solar São João 256 202 540
- Centro Praça Luís Ribeiro
- São João A.S. 256 836 100
- Liberdade
- Praça 25 de Abril
- V. João Madeira
- João de Deus
- Araujo
- Igreja
- Largo Souto
- Antonio M. Pinho

Inset map 2 (Oliveira de Azeméis - Centro)
- 25 de Abril
- A. Pinto de
- Largo S. Miguel
- Bento Cerqueira
- Praça José da Costa
- La Salette 256 674 890
- Largo da República
- Centro
- Av. Dr. A dos Reis
- Dighton 256 682 191
- Dr. M Arriaga
- Almeida
- Taxi Anacleto 256 682 541
- A-1

Route

- **SÃO JOÃO da MADEIRA** (Pop. 21,000 Alt. 240m) — 3.0 Centro
- Quinta
- N-227
- Faria de Cima — 3.1 X Caminho de ferro
- Vila de Cucujães
- São Roque
- Mangas
- Ponte 3.3 — rio Ul
- Santiago da Riba–Ul
- Figueiredo
- IC-2 / N-1 — 230m
- **OLIVEIRA de AZEMÉIS** (Pop. 12,000 - Alt. 220m) — 3.7 Centro
- Ul — 105m — Ponte medieval
- Travanca Ponte 3.6
- N-224
- Caniços
- fonte Bemposta — 210m — passarela
- Pinheiro da Bemposta — 5.4 X café
- Alviães
- Cristelo
- Escusa
- Casaldima
- Branca XVII S.da Alegria
- **ALBERGARIA-a-NOVA** — 3.7 Centro
- Carvalhal
- Santuario de N.S. del Socorro
- Casa Diocesana 234 522 422
- IC-2 / N-1
- 3.4 X estátua
- A-1
- **ALBERGARIA A-VELHA** — Centro 0.0
- N-16
- A-25

Compass
- O pôr do sol
- E nascer do Sol
- S

<left **[0.8 km]** onto woodland path emerging onto asphalt road to cross over railway onto N-1 **[2.0 km]** before veering off left to bypass town centre to re-emerge on the far side of Albergaria-A-Nova back on the **N-1 [0.9 km].**

3.7 km **Albergaria-A-Nova** •*café e mini-mercado*. *Note: from here to São João da Madeira we crisscross the N-1, the railway and a series of secondary roads that makes it impossible (and unnecessary) to detail all the twists and turns. It is sufficient to know that waymarking is adequate and with attention to signs no undue problems in navigating should arise).* Continue along the N-1 and turn off <left **[0.5 km]** to join railway line over crossroads bypassing **Branca [1.8 km]** (no facilities) with *Igreja Matrix* consecrated in 1695 (left). The terrain now becomes more undulating as we crisscross our way up to **Pinheiro da Bemposta [3.1 km]**.

5.4 km **Pinheiro da Bemposta** •*Café-Pastelaría Sorveto* •*fonte*. We continue up and over the N-1 via footbridge *passarela* and up again steeply passing Primary school *Escola Primária da Areosa* to high point (alto 217m) with view over the valley (left) and ancient fonte (right). Continue down and over **[!]** the N-1 (traffic lights) at **Caniços [1.9 km]** *•cafés* through an industrial estate and urbanised area and over motorway **[1.7 km]** into:

3.6 km **Travanca** continue down over stream and turn up sharp right to pass *under* the N-1 **[0.9 km]** onto path alongside railway **[!]** *(it may look abandoned but there are several daily services)*. We now have a delightful one kilometre stretch of original pilgrim pathway as we descend down into the river valley along the *rua do Senhor da Ponte no Caminho de Santiago* over the rio Anceira via the Roman bridge **[0.6 km]** over railway back onto the asphalt road turning left into rua Cruceiro up rua da Portela through the suburbs into the (part) pedestrianised street *rua António Alegria* to the central square **[2.2 km]**.

3.7 km **Oliveira de Azeméis** *Centro* Largo da República with the historic town hall *Câmara Municipal*. This town presents a confident air with a growing population in excess of 12,000. It has all the facilities associated with a modern town but also an historical centre. The waymarked route brings us past the parish church of saint Michael *Igreja Matrix de São Miguel* mentioned in documents

Igreja de São Miguel

Câmara Municipal

as far back as 922 and an adjoining Roman milestone *Miliário* as evidence of the towns earlier foundations as part of the Via Romana XVI. We also find links with the camino de Santiago and the first 'official' camino bollard from the Xunta de Galicia. The town also has an important Marian shrine *La Salette*. The feast day of N. Sra. de La Salette takes place on 2nd Sunday in August and attracts huge crowds when beds are virtually impossible to find. The fine houses built at the end of the 19th century are known as *casas de brasileiro* built by former emigrants returning with their new found wealth. The story of their lives is captured by Portuguese writer Ferreira de Castro whose own house has been turned into a museum *casa-museu* in the village of Ossela 5 km to the East.

❏ *Turismo* (Summer only) ✆ 256 674 463 Praca José da Costa (see map). **Accommodation:** •**Pensão Restaurante Anacleto** ✆ 256 682 541 on rua António José Almeida (beside the taxi rank). •**Residencial La Salette** ✆ 256 674 890 on rua Bento Carqueja. At the 'top' end is the 4 star •**Hotel Dighton** ✆ 256 682 191 on rua Dr. Albino dos Reis (opposite the *Câmara*) ask for a pilgrim discount which might bring an individual room down to €45 depending on season. •**Bombeiros Voluntários** ✆ 256 682 745 in rua Dr. José Henriques. Wide choice of **restaurants**, several directly en route including the trendy •*Art Club* opposite Residencial La Salette in the centre.

We continue our way up along rua Bento Cerqueira past the Correios crossing rua 25 de Abril and then heading steeply down over the river turning <left at roundabout [**1.0** km] and up through the northern suburbs and industrial area, crisscrossing the railway with several short stretches of cobblestone as we make our way out through the historic area **Santiago de Riba-Ul** passing •*Café Santiago* [**1.2** km] and down to the bridge over the river Ul [**1.1** km].

3.3 km **Ponte do Salgueiro** ancient stone bridge with miniature roadside shrines carved into the granite columns. We now make our way up past •*Café O Emigrante* [**0.4** km] through Vila da Cucujães (Galp) [**1.1** km] •*café* with the former Benedictine monastery *Mosteiro de Cucujães* prominent on the hill. We now have a short section of path leading to bridge and railway [**1.6** km].

3.1 km **Ponte do Caniço** cross over rail for the last time and over the bypass and the major roundabout at the start of the modern suburbs of São João da Madeira. Here we continue s/o (*The Park of the Lady of the Miracles* Parque da Senhora dos Milagres *right*) as we head up Avenida Dr. Renato Araújo signposted *Centro* veering right at the 2nd roundabout into rua Padre António Maria Pinho past the parish church of St. John the Baptist *Igreja Matriz (the original roman military thoroughfare Via XVI passed to the rear)*. We now turn left into rua Visconde de São João da Madeira up into the central square.

3.0 km **São João da Madeira** *Centro* **Praça Luis Ribeiro** with range of *cafés, bares, restaurantes* and •*Hotel São João e* •*Pensão Solar São João*.

São João da Madeira is an historic town of Roman origin but you wouldn't know that from the modernity that surrounds us. An industrial town built on the back of its worldwide reputation for the manufacture of hats and shoes with *Museo da Chapelaria* on the camino in rua Oliveira Júnior, 501. The area around the central square (a rotunda) is pedestrianised and has the 2 best hotel options and several café-bars including •*Café Concha Doce* with its prominent pilgrim shell, the only evidence that we are actually directly on 'the way'.

❏ **Accommodation:** on the central Praça Luís Ribeiro •**Residencial Solar São João** (popular with pilgrims, photo right) ✆ 256 202 540 at Nº165 and •**A.S. Hotel São João** ✆ 256 836 100 at Nº7 a 2 star budget hotel with 36 rooms. 4 star luxury at the ultra-modern •**W.R. Hotel São João da Madeira** ✆ 256 106 700 on rua Adelino Amaro da Costa (off Av. da Liberdade towards the Parque Milagres). •**Bombeiros Voluntários** ✆ 256 837 120 off the central Largo Conde Dias Garica or its modern counterpart off rua Oliveira Figueiredo in the eastern suburbs. *Turismo* ✆ 256 200 285 'fluctuates' between a kiosk on Praça Luís Ribeiro and Av. Liberdade.

Amongst the more notable buildings are: ● Chapel and Park of Our lady of the Miracles *Capela e Parque de Na Sra dos Milagros* built in the 1930's in the Neo-Romanesque style located near the roundabout on the way into town close to the railway station. ● The Parish church of St John the Baptist *Igreja Matriz de S. Joao Baptista* reconstructed in 1884 with an altarpiece dating from the previous century, Off rua Visconde de São João da Madeira (also on the way in). ● Chapel of St. Anthony *Capela de Santo António* built in 1937 in the Neo-Romanesque style and located immediately behind the central square in Largo de S. Antonio. ● House of Culture *Casa da Cultura* one of the finest examples of a *Casa de Brasileiros* housing the town's Art Centre, exhibition rooms and auditorium, located off Alão de Morais beyond the Bombeiros.

STAGE 12:

REFLECTIONS:

❏ **Greater is He that is in you than he who is in the world.** *1 John 4:4*

13 *273.9 km (170.2 miles) – Santiago*

SÃO JOÃO DA MADEIRA – PORTO

▬▬▬ --- ---	2.8 --- ---	8%
▬▬▬ --- ---	20.6 --- ---	60%
▬▬▬ --- ---	<u>10.9</u> --- ---	32%
Total km	**34.3 km** (21.3 ml)	

▲ 36.8 km (+^ 505 m = 2.5 km)
Alto ▲ Malaposta 315 m (1,033 ft)
<🅰 🅷> *Grijó 19.0 km (+ 1.5 km)*

Practical Path: As we approach Porto the road network becomes ever more congested so prepare for the long slog into the centre along hard city pavements This is a *very* long stage, much of it on main roads with fast moving traffic across undulating terrain, so you will need to leave São João at first light. The medieval monastery at Grijó offers some respite around halfway. Accommodation is also possible here (1½ km *off* route – see map) and the noise and danger of the roads is relieved by a short but delightful stretch of medieval road through woodland beyond Grijó. Consider taking a rest day in Porto to recover from your exertions and to explore this fascinating city littered with historic monuments.

❏ **Mystical Path:** Physical sight shows us the superficial world of the ego fashioned by humanity with its incessant demands. Below the surface lies our true Identity. This higher Self is recognised by seeing it in others. The confusion between outer and inner between the ego and the divine forms the crux of our problem – one problem, one solution. It is time to awaken our spiritual vision.

❏ **Personal Reflections:** How many more crossroads will I meet today – each one requiring a choice of direction... but I need to remind myself that I journey on two different levels. If I heed only the signs to Santiago I head towards an empty casket. The signs to the Source are not so obvious… but I miss them at my peril. I need to stay alert amongst the labyrinth of highways and byways if I am to reach my true Destination.

0.0 km São João da Madeira *Centro* from the Praça Luís Ribeiro we head out along rua Oliveira Júnior (to the left side of the Banco Espiritu Santo) passing *Museo da Chapelaria* (left) [**0.5 km**] veering <left opposite Repsol garage past disused industrial buildings s/o over crossroads by *supermercado* and crossroads in **Arrifana** [**1.1 km**] *Igreja Matrix* with fine façade of blue and white tiles *azulejos*. Continue up steps into rua S. António and turn <left as

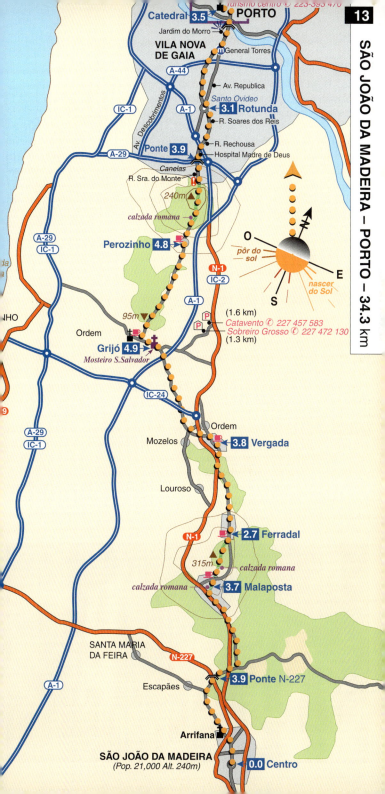

the road follows the undulating terrain to a bridge over the N-227 [**2.3 km**].

3.9 km Ponte *N-227* We cross the bridge over the N-1 *Restaurante Concorde (•Hotel Feira Pedra Vela Ⓒ 256 910 350 – off route along the N-1)* pass Galp petrol station *café* through Sanfins and turn off right> to the Roman road in Malaposta. This marks the high point of this stage at 315m.

3.7 km Malaposta *Calzada Romana* •*Café Solar*. A well preserved stretch of the original Via XVI which is rudely cut off 90m later by the main road but it continues the far side in rather less pristine condition but with an additional 400m through shaded woodland. [The Calzada Romana becomes, variously *Rua da Estrada Romana* or the Royal Way *Estrada Real*]. We emerge in the straggling village of:

2.7 km Ferradal •*Café Ferradalense e mini-mercado*. The route now winds itself through the urbanised neighbourhoods of Souto, Redondo, Carvalhosa, Monte Grande, **Lourosa** •*café* along the N-1 •*cafés* veering off into:

3.8 km Vergada •*café-restaurantes e mini-mercados*. We now turn <left into rua Joaquim do Porto through **Mozelos** crossing the N-1 [**!**] down steeply *[good viewpoint of the complicated web of roads ahead and the distant sea. However, waymarking is good so keep focused on the friendly yellow arrows but with one eye on the fast moving traffic.]* Continue down through **Vila de Nogueira da Regedoura** and down under the IC-24 and down again under the A-1 into the surprisingly lush and relatively tranquil Grijó valley turning <left along the high stone walls of Grijó monastery *Café Mosteirinho*:

4.9 km Grijó 13[th]c **Mosterio S. Salvador de Grijó** here the medieval Italian pilgrim Confalonieri stayed during his pilgrimage from Rome to Santiago. The original buildings were consecrated in 1235 and were an important stop for both physical and spiritual nourishment to pilgrims in the following centuries. A sense of peace continues to pervade the parkland and offers the modern pilgrim a brief respite from the traffic. Adjoining the monastery are the offices of the parish council *Freguesia de Vila Grijó* and public toilets. The waymarked route continues straight on down the Avenida do Mosteiro into Grijó town.

Detour 1.3 km: ● ● ● ● ● Porto is still 4 hours away along busy main roads and, while not ideal, there is the possibility of accommodation in this area. If you need to stop you can retrace your steps back around the walls of the monastery to the *crossroads (300m)* and instead of veering back right under the A-1 you continue straight on under a different section of the *A-1 (200m)* via rua do Sr. do Padrao and follow it all the way to the end as it twists around to a *staggered crossroads (400m)*. Here we turn left and immediately left again up into rua de Americo Oliveira. The accommodation is situated up towards the top end – it's a steep *climb (400m)* to: •**Pensão Sobreiro Grosso** Ⓒ 227 472 130 rua Américo de Oliveira, 807 with 28 rooms and restaurant under same management in separate building on lower road. Continue up past the restaurant for *another (300m)* to •**Pensão Residencial Catavento** Ⓒ 227 457 583 on Largo das Vendas, 88 in a prominent (noisy) location directly on the main road N-1.

Note: Despite the proximity to Porto there are still a few stretches of the original medieval pilgrim route ahead over the Serra dos Negrelos to relieve the noise and monotony of the roads. Waymarks now have to compete with other signs and you also need to stay alert to the fast moving traffic. Note the position of the sun and as you head due north keep it in the same general position which should be behind you over the left shoulder in the early afternoon to guide you into and through Vila Nova de Gaia which offers a range of intermediate accommodation. If you are not familiar with Porto it is probably best to go direct to the cathedral (along the *top* of the bridge – see alternative route later). This is the logical 'end point' of the Lisbon section where you can give thanks for your safe arrival, pick up a pilgrim passport *credencial* and / or stamp your existing one. Adjacent to the cathedral is a tourist office with map of the town and list of hotels. Just below the cathedral is a range of budget hotels and other accommodation (see under Porto).

From the Mosterio S. Salvador de Grijó head on down the Avenida do Mosteiro turning up right around the walls of the monastery in the general direction of Vila Nova de Gaia. At this junction is the Capela de S. António (directly ahead) and •*cafés*. This marks the low point of this stretch (95m) and we now climb steadily along a maze of roads (well waymarked) passing various roadside cafes all the way up to:

4.8 km **Perosinho** welcoming •*café-restaurante* just beyond the crossroads is the council office and parish church and suddenly we find ourselves amongst the pines and eucalyptus of the delightful Serra de Negrelos on the ancient Roman road *calzada romana*. This brings us to the high point (240m).

We now head into the residential suburbs at Senhora do Monte down rua da Serpa steeply to the N-1[!] Antalis HQ where we turn <left along a dangerous stretch of the rua da Senhora do Monte [!] with no pavement (photo right) into Rechousa and Vila de Pedroso and bridge over the motorway.

3.9 km **Ponte A-29** •*cafés* (there are

now roadside cafés all the way into Porto). Continue s/o over the motorway still on the N-1 passing Hospital Madre de Deus and Galp filling station and head down *under* the A-1 motorway [**1.6** km] and up tree-lined rua da Palmeira into the commercial rua Soares dos Reis and to major roundabout [**1.5** km].

3.1 km **Rotunda de Santo Ovídeo** *[Note: The N-1 now becomes the Avenida de República which we follow parallel to (and join later) all the way to* **Ponte de Dom Luis I** *– the main bridge over the rio Douro linking Vila Nova de Gaia with Porto and the cathedral.]* We head across this busy high level crossroads still on rua Soares dos Reis and wend our way over the city bypass A-44 *Cintura Interna* [**1.2** km] also referred to as Avenue of the Discoverers *Avenida dos Descobrimentos* into the Mafamude district past public gardens past *Casa de Juvenude (right) this is* not *a hostal* continue s/o into rua S. Francisco Sá Carneiro and s/o at roundabout (following signs to *Centro Historico*) over a wide grass platform (over the railway) to the metro station Estação de General Torres [**1.1** km] back onto the Av. República to the delightful gardens overlooking the mighty rio Douro **Jardim O Moro** [**0.5** km] **OPTION** [**?**]:

Note [1]: Jardim O Moro is a good place to pause for breath – this has been a long stage and we are near the end point. [2] Take a moment to get your bearings – the viewpoint here gives a panoramic view of Vila Nova de Gaia spilling down *this* side to the Southern banks of the river with its Port wine lodges. On the *far* side is the city of Porto with the cathedral up to our right and the harbour area Ribeira down to the left and the main shopping area and hotels spread out behind it. [3] If you don't have reserved accommodation then decide now where to head for. [4] at this point the waymarked route goes sharply down via Calçada da Serra to cross over the lower tier of the iconic metal bridge and then proceeds either back up (steeply) to the cathedral or into and through the city centre. If you have no fixed plans it may be better not to loose this high contour but continue over the upper level of the bridge directly ahead [**0.1** km] and continue up to the next crossroads [**0.5** km] and turn <left straight down to the natural end point of this stage – the cathedral [**0.1** km].

3.5 km **Porto Catedral** *Sé* the waymarked route from Porto starts from this point. Adjoining the cathedral entrance (by the statue of Vimara Peres atop his steed) is a *Turismo* and the offices of *Porto Tours* in the tower just below. See city map and details of accommodation in the next section.

STAGE 13: 105

REFLECTIONS:

Cais da Ribeira with river barges **Barcos Rabelos** and **Catedral** *Sé (top left)*

Historical Sketch: Porto is beautifully situated on the banks of the 'River of Gold' *Rio Douro*. It is a city full of life and vigour, completely authentic and justifiably proud of its long history. It was here in the 12th century that Portugal took its name as an independent nation. By the 14th century it had well-established trade links and we begin to see the emergence of a wealthy merchant class and the building of substantial civic structures. Henry the Navigator was born here in 1394 and we can still visit his house below the square bearing his name. By the 15th century the city was playing a leading role in the maritime discoveries of the New World. The historical centre was declared a World Heritage site in 1996 and in 2001 Porto was chosen as the European City of Culture. In 2004 it proudly hosted the European football championships – Porto and football are synonymous! Today the city has a population of around ½ million with 1½ million in the greater catchment area. All this grew out of a modest Celtic settlement atop what is now Cathedral Hillock *Colina da Sé*, a rocky promontory from which the old quarter tumbles down to the river at the *Cais da Ribeira*.

Arriving in Porto. If you are starting your pilgrimage in Porto and arrive by air there is a tourist information counter in the arrivals hall ✆ 229 432 400 (08:00 – 23:00) with map of the city and hotel information. A regular shuttle bus operates to the city centre and takes around an hour for the 14 km trip. Or take the efficient metro from the station in the airport itself. If you arrive by train that there are 2 rail stations. The main station *Estação de São Bento* is in the centre. The modern *Estação de Campanhã* is a few kilometres east and the old *Estação de Trindade* has now been revamped as the ultra modern hub of the efficient metro.

❏ **Tourist offices** *Turismo*: The main city tourist office opens 09:00 – 17.30 (19:00 July–Sept). *[1] Turismo Centro* ✆ 223 323 303 rua Clube dos Fenianos, 25 (effectively a continuation of Avenida dos Aliados adjacent to the *câmara* at the top end of Praça da Liberdade) *[2] Turismo Ribeira* ✆ 222 060 412 down near the river on rua do Infante D. Henrique,63. *[3] Turismo Sé* ✆ 223 325 174 Terreiro da Sé by the entrance to the cathedral in the former city hall. *[4] Turismo Portugal* (for information outside Porto) ✆ 927 411 817 Praca D. Joao I, 43.

❏ **Accommodation:** Oporto has a wide selection of *hoteles, pensões*, rooms *quartos,* and beds *camas* in all price brackets. The city centre is full of good value options – the tourist offices provide an extensive list that includes the following (marked on the city map) all of which are concentrated in the old historic city, within ½ kilometre of the camino itself.

Accommodation: At the top end of the scale is the five star •**Hotel Infante de Sagres** ✆ 222 008 101 on Praça Dona Filipa de Lencastre, 62 with single from €150. Around the corner is •**Hotel Internacional** ✆ 222 005 032 on rua do Almada, 131 (part of the camino to Braga) where for ½ that price you will find a comfortable modern room. Just above it on rua da Fábrica, 27 is the refurbished •**Pensão Grande Hotel Paris** ✆ 222 073 140 popular with pilgrims with single from €45 and where the breakfast room spills out onto a delightful olde-world garden. A few doors further up is •**Residencial Grande Oceano** ✆ 222 038 770 at rua da Fábrica, 45 where €35 buys you a basic single for the night and up at the top of the street we can reduce the bill further in •**Pensão Duas Nações** ✆ 222 081 616 in Praça Guilherme Gomes Fernandes, 59 where we find a spotlessly clean room for around €30 and all these options within a minutes walk of each other! Other nearby accommodation popular with pilgrims (some with pilgrim discount) are centred around the noisier Avenida dos Aliados and include: •**Pensão Paulista** ✆ 222 054 692 at Nº 214 •**Pensão Chique** ✆ 222 009 011 at Nº 206 •**Pensão Universal** ✆ 222 006 758 at Nº 38 •**Residencial Dos Aliados** ✆ 222 004 853 overlooking Avenida dos Aliados (above Cafe Guranay but with entrance around the back off rua Elíso de Melo, 27. On the far side of the avenue, around rua Santa Catarina are several *pensões* with rooms from around €30. Here we also find the fabulously old-fashioned •**Grande Hotel do Porto** ✆ 222 076 690 at Nº 197 (near the café Majestic) with single rooms from €90. •**Hotel da Bolsa** ✆ 222 026 768 on rua Ferreira Borges (just above the Bolsa Exchange) is good value for such a prominent location. Talk of a pilgrim hostel has still produced no concrete plan but in the meantime there is the Youth Hostel •**Pousada da Juventude** ✆ 226 177 257 on rua Paulo da Gama which is situated 4 km west of the city centre close to the mouth of the Douro.

Eating Out: A basic tourist menu around the popular Ribeira will cost around €20. *Taverna do Bebobos*, Cais da Riberia 21, is one of the more popular and expensive. *Adega S. Nicolau* on rua S. Nicolau is reasonable value and has a few outside tables with fine views of the river and bridge. Amongst the best value is the atmospheric *O Muro* on Muro dos Bacalhoeiros 88; this is a pedestrian walkway above street level with views over the river. If you want to experience the haunting Portuguese music *fado* two popular fado houses are in this area *Casa da Mariquinhas* on rua São Sebastião and *Mal Cozinhado* on rua Outeirinho – both will try and sell you an expensive and mediocre dinner but it is possible to prop-up the bar instead and drink overpriced wine while you listen to the melancholy voices accompanied by the Portuguese guitar.

Praça da Liberdade & *Rua dos Aliados leading to* **Paços do Concelho** *(centre)*

For economy you can still find a basic menu in the old town away from the main tourist areas for around €10. Artist Sónia Honório offers a cosy culinary experience at the atmospheric *Taipas I Feijao* on rua das Taipas,17 while around the corner in rua de S. Miguel 19 is a rare vegetarian (vegan) option at the multi-cultural *O Oriente no Porto*. Back towards the centre on the corner of rua da Fábrica and Conde Vizela is a more traditional option *Churrasqueira Central Dos Clérigos*. The trendy *Café Guarany* is centrally located on Av. dos Aliados. At the other end of the scale (and the other side of the Avenida dos Aliados) is *A Brasileira* on rua do Bonjardim (opposite the old city theatre). Here you might start with an aperitif in the spacious Art Deco cafe adjoining, dine in the restaurant and then make your way up to the *Majestic Café* on rua de Santa Catarina for liqueur and coffee. The majestic is one of the best known Belle Epoque cafés in Portugal with beautiful interiors and the possibility of live piano music in the background, but don't expect change out of €50 for the evening's entertainment.

❏ **Historic Buildings and Monuments: City Excursion:** Allow time to visit the historic city centre and absorb some of its magnificent sights. From the west door of the Cathedral (the start of stage 14 to Santiago) in the old medieval quarter known as the *Bairro da Sé* to the beginning of the pedestrian street rua Cedofeita in the quarter known as *Cordoaria* is less than 2 km (see city map). You can walk this stage in under an hour. However, if you intend to visit the interior of any of the buildings along the way then you need to allow more time. Indeed to soak up the atmosphere of the Cathedral and its cloisters would require at least an hour in itself. Several further options are available from the Cathedral. You can take the tourist tram for a 90-minute tour of Vila Nova do Gaia. If you shudder at the notion, don't! For around €10 you can rattle instead through the cobblestreets and

Henry the Navigator & Cathedral Towers

over the famous bridge Ponte de D. Luís I. Your money buys you a visit to one of the oldest port wine lodges in Portugal, including a tasting session where you get to sample a ruby and perhaps a less familiar white port. The tour then returns to the Cathedral via the lower section of the bridge, past the old customs hall *Alfândega Nova* and up past the main rail station *Estação de São Bento*. If a port wine lodge is not of interest, then just behind the cathedral at 32 rua Dom Hugo (around the back of the Archbishop's Palace) is the beautiful former house and museum (mostly Islamic art and artefacts) of the Portuguese poet *Guerra Junqueiro*. The office of the tour company *Porto Tours* is situated in the medieval tower 50m below the Cathedral. Here you can book for any of the extensive city and river Douro tours operated by the company. These include bus tours of the city and environs and a one-day cruise up the Douro, returning by train. There are also tours to the prehistoric rock art valley at Vila Nova de Foz Côa, off the river Douro. The following Porto 'excursion' follows the waymarked route from the cathedral to the start of the pedestrian street rua de Cedofeita (1.6 km) – and then loops back to the river – mopping up the remaining 'must see' sights on the way!

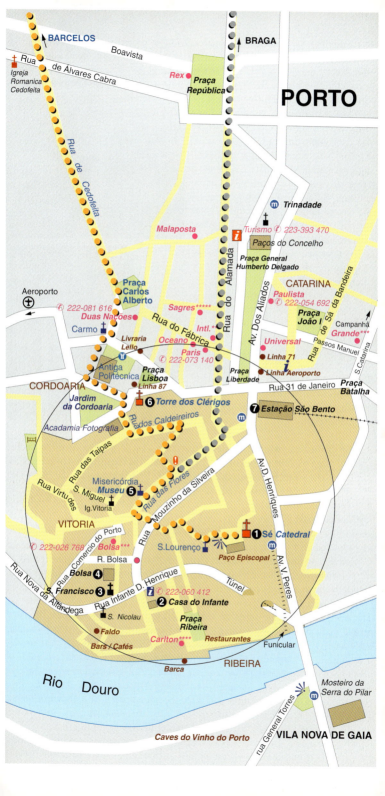

❶ **Cathedral** *Sé* prominently positioned on an elevated site overlooking the city and river Douro. Like most medieval cathedrals it has been altered and embellished many times since its inauguration in the 12th century, most notably in the Baroque period. However it never lost its austere Romanesque form of fortress-church. Enter through the West door below its fine rose window and just inside is the information desk where you can obtain the official *credencial* (€1) or have your existing 'passport' stamped. An additional €2 secures a ticket to visit the 14th century Gothic cloisters with its interesting chapels and also provides access to the Chapter House *Casa do Cabido* and the cathedral treasure on the first floor. Many visitors never discover the wonderful notary chamber room on the second floor (immediately above). Richly adorned with hand painted tiles *azulejos* and a stunningly beautiful painted ceiling, with St. Michael making up the central panel over-lighting proceedings below. But, most significantly, here you will find a delightful 16th century statue of Santiago Peregrino, pilgrim staff in hand – an opportunity, perhaps, to obtain a blessing on your own pilgrimage ahead (see photo right)

Pick up the first waymark opposite the cathedral west door and proceed down the cobbled ramp past the offices of Porto Tours located in the medieval tower (right) and down the steep steps into the Largo Dr. Pedro Vitorino with the imposing 16-18th century Mannerist façade of the Church of St. Laurence *Igreja de S. Lourenço* built into the steep rock-face (left) and down again to cross the busy rua Mouzinho da Silveira and up into Largo São Domingos turning right into rua das Flores passing ❺ 18th century Church of Mercy *Igreja da Misericórdia* with museum and on to the imposing edifice of the former Companies office *Casa da Companhia* on the corner of rua das Flores 69 and rua do Ferraz. *Note*: [!] This is the point where the alternative route, *caminho interior* via Braga separates from the main way *caminho central* – don't confuse them.

The main central route turns up sharp <left into rua do Ferraz past the tiny chapel dedicated to Saint Catherine of the Flowers *Capela de Santa Catarina das Flores*. *[Formerly the pilgrim association office* Associação Dos Amigos do Caminho de Santiago *and its president Djalma de Sousa e Correia who did so much to open and waymark the modern camino. The association has remained dormant awaiting a new champion since 2008.]* At the top of rua do Ferraz turn right> into rua dos Caldeireiros and up to the large open area at the top *Campo Mártires da Pátria* that merges into the *Jardim de João Chagas* and here on the left is the imposing façade of the former remand prison *Cadeia da Relação* which is now a beautifully refurnished arts and photographic exhibition centre. On our right is one of Porto's most emblematic buildings ❻ Clergymen's Tower

Torre dos Clérigos an impressive 18th century baroque tower and, at 75m high, the city's main landmark and worth the €2 entrance fee for the 225 steps and the grand 360 degree vista from the top. After you have stretched your quadriceps, the adjoining church *Igreja dos Clérigos,* built in a beautiful elliptical shape, is a delightful environment in which to flex your soul muscles. The architect, Nicolau Nasoni, is buried in the church in recognition of his dedication and skill in, 'creating such a beautiful and towering monument to God'. Pick up the waymarks again at the *Jardim de João Chagas* and cross diagonally over the park past the former Polytechnic Academy *Antiga Academia Politécnica* to the blue and white tiles *azulejos* of the 18th century *Igreja do Carmo*. It is separated from the neighbouring Carmelite convent church *Igreja das Carmelitas* by one of the narrowest building in the world – barely a metre wide! It acted as a physical barrier between the monks and the nuns who, by convention, could not live in adjoining buildings. The waymarked camino now continues straight ahead into rua de Cedofeita.

To continue this excursion of Porto's main sites head back towards the city centre, down past the handsome statue of the Lions and into rua das Carmelitas where at number 144 is the intriguing bookshop *Livraria Lello (see photo below)*. Described as 'the most beautiful bookstore in the world', it really is an architectural delight. Have a browse or a cup of coffee atop the sweeping staircase. Continue down to join the rua Clérigos just below the church and into Liberation Square *Praça da Liberdade* with its impressive statue of D. Pedro IV. At the top end is the imposing façade of the town hall *Paços Concelho Câmara*. No need to walk up the intervening Avenida dos Aliados unless you want to visit the main tourist office *Turismo* on the left side of the Câmara. It is now only a short hop *under* the Praça de Almeida Garrett to ❼ main rail station *Estação de São Bento (*named after the Benedictine monastery built here in the 16th century. Step inside its grand entrance hall with magnificent display of *azulejos* (over 20,000) depicting transport scenes and historical events including the battle of Valdevez in 1140 when the king of Portugal *Afonso I (Afonso Henriques)* defeated the Spanish under king Alfonso VII of Leon thus securing Portugal's independence from Spain. Other panels show the Conquest of Ceuta in 1415 and the arrival in Porto of D. João I and Philippa of Lancaster.

At this point we can return to the cathedral now visible up Av. Vimara Peres or head down the wide rua Mousinho da Silveira towards the river into Praça do Infante Henrique where we find an impressive statue to this most famous son of King D. João I – Henry the Navigator (1394 – 1460) who was a major force in the Portuguese discoveries of the New World. He looks down to the harbour and the house where he was born ❷ *Casa do Infante* (also referred to as House of the Navigator) and museum in the rua Infante Dom Henrique.

Perhaps it's time to cool off by the harbour and quench your thirst at any of the numerous bars, cafés, restaurants and fado houses that surround this historic and lively riverside area *Cais da Ribeira* or take a river trip on one of Porto's iconic river barges *Barcos Rabelos* now converted to transport tourists rather than Port wine. Around €9 will secure a memorable 1 hour boat ride under 6 of the city's bridges and down to the river mouth. If you have time or energy to spare head back up to Praça do Infante Henrique to visit the fabulous interior of ❸ *Igreja de São Francisco* now de-consecrated and turned into a museum but well worth the €2 entry fee to soak up some of its quiet and cool interior bedecked with gilded carvings (some of the most impressive in all of Portugal). A combined ticket provides access to a small museum opposite the church entrance (adjoining the ticket office) and the sombre catacombs below. A short walk back into Praça do Infante Henrique and we arrive at the city's splendid stock exchange building ❹ *Palácio da Bolsa*. You can see the vast inner courtyard at the entrance without having to take the €7 guided tour, although you will miss the magnificent Arab Hall (well worth the visit) and a chance to dine in the adjacent restaurant.

Starting Out – Options for Stage 14 (the first stage for the majority of pilgrims starting the Camino Português from Porto itself). Many will have allocated a fixed amount of time with the intention to walk the entire camino, without recourse to public or private transport, along the waymarked route from either Lisbon or Porto cathedral to Santiago. This is shown as option A below:

[A]. The route through Porto involves a long slog through the suburbs and one particularly dangerous section just beyond Araújo. Like any stage through a major city there will be challenges and these include the difficulty of seeing the waymarks with all the competing signs and street advertisements. The route *is* well waymarked but you have to stay very focussed and this attentiveness must also be directed towards the fast moving city traffic, which is noisy and hazardous. So you might consider the following alternatives.

[B] From Matosinhos along the Atlantic coast to Vila do Conde. This makes a wonderful alternative depending on favourable weather. While it is not waymarked you can't get seriously lost if you keep to the coast. 70% is alongside or on sandy beaches where you can walk barefoot and paddle your way up the coast – but avoid swimming (unless there is a lifeguard) as the currents here can be dangerous. An early start will allow time to enjoy the many beaches and sites along the way, including the archaeological remains of Castro S. Paio dating from the Iron Age and reputedly the earliest Portuguese example of a fort that used the sea as part of its defensive system. There are plenty of beach cafés and restaurants along the route for refreshments. This alternative is 22.1 kilometres from Praia Leça da Palmeira (Matosinhos) to the centre of Vila do Conde but note that [1] sand slows the pace considerably and [2] beaches have a pronounced camber towards the sea and it is essential to change your gait from time to time to avoid muscle strain. One way to avoid injury is to walk backwards (not *back!*) at regular short intervals and also use the board-walks where available. Note also that if is it windy (it often is along this exposed Atlantic coast) then you may have to abandon this option as the wind blows the sand across the face and eyes and it can become difficult (or impossible in high winds) to continue along the beach itself. The limited feedback to this route has been positive although one pilgrim mentioned that she missed the opportunity of meeting other pilgrims and the reassurance of the arrow waymarks. See page 122 for full details to this route.

[C] Metro to Maia and pick up the waymarked route at Igreja de Maia [+0.7 km]. A good option for those who want to avoid the city pavements and drab suburbs and the dangerous central reservation on the N-13 just beyond Araújo. For this alternative take the metro from *Trindade* in the direction of *Ismai* and alight at *Fórum Maia*. Walk *back* to crossroads *Centro*

Commercial [200m] turn right> cross motorway (w.c left) and continue up to rejoin waymarked route at Igreja de Maia [500m]. ***Note***: apart from avoiding the hazards of the city roads this option cuts 11.7 km from this stage out of Porto making it possible to reach the splendid new pilgrim hostel in ***São Pedro de Rates 25.9 km (incl. metro access – see stage 14a on map).*** The new (2010) hostel in ***Tamel S. Pedro Fins at Portela – 25.3 km (from Rates)*** makes a logical alternative to stage 15. Following this itinerary reduces stage 16 from 33.6 to 24.2 km making a more comfortable 3rd stage to the new (2009) pilgrim hostel in ***Ponte de Lima – 24.2 km from Portela.*** A variation on this theme is:

[D] Metro to Vilar do Pinheiro and pick up the waymarked route in Mosteiró [+1.1 km]. Popular alternative with logical changes in the next stages as detailed under 'C' above. Note that the metro line is this latter case is from *Trindade* in the direction of *Póvoa de Varzim*. Alight at Vilar do Pinheiro and turn right (east) out of the metro and s/o over the N-13 [600m] and turn left at T-

junction to join the waymarked route at cafe S. Gonçalo [0.5 km] pass Farmacia to welcoming cafe D.José in Mosteiro. ***Note: Total 19.4 km to Rates.***

Whichever route you decide to follow – heed the maxim 'early to bed and early to rise' so that you can make the most of this day out of Porto city. Make sure everything is packed and ready for the physical path ahead and make time to recall your intention for the inner journey. Our invocations are powerful conduits for the experiences that will follow. Whether we are conscious of it or not, *every* thought sows a seed for good or ill and draws to us peace or strife – the law of Cause and Effect is immutable! So may your every step become a prayer for peace. *Blessings along the outer and inner pathways that lie ahead...*

❏ **Look at every path closely and deliberately. Then ask yourself, and yourself alone, one question, 'Does this path have a heart?' If it does, the path is good; if it doesn't, it is of no use.** *The Teachings of Don Juan*

14 239.6 km (148.9 miles) – Santiago

PORTO – VILARINHO
(VILA DO CONDE – RATES)

```
                 0.0              0%
                15.6             60%
                10.3             40%
Total km        25.9 km (16.1 ml)
```

27.0 km (+^ 220 m = 1.1 km)
Alto ▲ Igreja Maia 125 m (410 ft)
<🅐 🅗> Maia 11.7 (+0.7) km – Padrão Moreira 14.6 km

The Practical Path: Despite the comprehensive waymarking, this first stage out of the city is likely to prove taxing (see alternative routes). Commercial advertising and street signs compete for your attention and if you get distracted it is easy to get lost – stay very focused. The main waymarked route also requires you to cross the central barrier of a busy stretch of dual carriageway just north of Araújo which is very dangerous [!] take special care (or take one of the alternatives). The city pavements and cobbled laneways are hard underfoot and today there is little respite from traffic. While the highest point of this stage is Maia at only 125m there is plenty of demanding undulations to test the muscles of those pilgrims starting out at Porto. All grist for the mill and remember – things can only get better, and they do!

The Mystical Path: Have you found the first waymark that points you in the direction of your true Destination? Does it look familiar or are you left in doubt as to the right course to take? One thing is certain, it will only be found by following the wisdom of the heart. Everything you see with the physical eye is likely to lead you away from the mystical. We have become intoxicated with the things of this world and fallen into a deep stupor. We search for relics housed in stone buildings that mask the true home of spirit. In our drunkenness we have forgotten the way Home... and yet feelings of alienation and loss stir us to awaken.

Personal Reflections: "… in the distraction of the city roads I forgot the waymarks to the inner path. I pause to clear my mind of the anger I directed towards a dangerous driver. Psychic rubbish is every bit as noxious as the physical rubbish that I now observe all around me… I start to pick up litter and, feeling momentarily self-righteous, remind myself of the many times that I have littered the landscape and suddenly become aware of a bright red rose just above my head – still part of the sense-perceptible world but reflecting, perhaps, a deeper reality; symbol of a higher truth. Yet in my initial anger I so nearly missed it…"

Leaving the cathedral *Sé* we pick up the first waymark opposite the main west door and zig-zag steeply down (as described fully on page 110) and cross the busy **rua Mouzinho da Silveira [0.3 km]** up into Largo São Domingos veering right> into rua das Flores passing the Igreja da Misericórdia and then up sharp <left into into the narrow **rua do Ferraz [0.3 km] [!]** *(Note the waymarked route to Braga 'caminho interior' continues straight on along rua das Flores into rua do Alamada. Be careful not to confuse these waymarks at this early stage).* Continue to the top and turn right> into rua da Vitória and then sharp <left into rua dos Caldeireiros and up to the expansive plaza at the top *Campo dos Martires da Patria* with Torre dos Clerigos (right) and the imposing former remand prison *Cadeia da Relação* (left) **[0.5 km]**. Cross over to the park past (right) the neoclassical building (part of the university's science faculty *faculdade de ciências)* into Praça de Gomes Teixeira. On the corner (left) is the Carmelite church *Igreja do Carmo* evident from its distinctive blue and white tiles *azulejos*. From here we pass into the Praça de Carlos Alberto and the start of the pedestrian shopping street **rua de Cedofeita [0.5 km]** which now runs in a straight line to the crossroads at rua de Álvares (Sacadura) Cabral **[0.6 km]**:

2.2 km **Cedofeita / Option.** Crossroads and optional short detour ¼ km *down left* into rua de Sacadura Cabral to Cedofeita church. (Praça da Republica is *up right* rua de Alvares Cabral ½ km for those accessing the route from there):

Detour ● ● ● ● ● **Igreja de Cedofeita:** a 250m detour will bring you to the *site* of one of the oldest Christian buildings in Europe (its red tiled roof visible down to our left.) The foundations of the Igreja de Cedofeita were laid in the middle of the 6th century, viz. 555 A.D. by the Suevian king Theodomir. What we see today is, in most part, a 12th century Romanesque building constructed over the original foundations

Igreja de Cedofeita

For the waymarked route continue s/o over the crossroads into rua do Barão de Forrester over the wide rua da Boavista passing under railway up to the chapel occupying an island site **largo da Ramada Alta [0.6 km]** veering <left then right> into rua de Nove de Julho. Cross the busy rua de Egas Moniz passing under block of apartments over rua da Constituiçao under more apartments and veer <left into rua de Oliveira and up to the crossroads and **Igreja de Carvalhido [0.9 km]** with notable exterior adorned with *azulejos*. Continue s/o into rua do Carvalhido merging into rua do Monte dos Burgos past the Hospital da Prelada (left) under the city bypass *Via de Cintura Interna* A-20 **[0.8 km]** *[entrance (left) to the former city campsite in the grounds of the Quinta da Prelada]*. Continue s/o up to the busy city ring road **[0.8 km]**.

2.9 km **Estrada da Circunvalação [!]** s/o into rua Nova do Seixo merging into rua do Recarei through seemingly 'endless' modern suburbs out under the new A-4 motorway **[3.0 km]** into rua de Gondivai up to the junction (right) of **rua dos Bombeiros [0.5]** and optional detour.

3.5 km **Rua dos Bombeiros.** Junction and Detour. •*Bombeiros Voluntarios*

Detour ● ● ● ● ● **Mosteiro Leça do Balio:** a 1 km detour to this historic 12th century Romanesque monastery. Queen D. Teresa granted the land in 1116 to the Military Order of St. John and it became the burial place of various Hospitaller knights. Some maintain that this is the location of the secret marriage between the future king of Portugal, Don Pedro I and Doña Ines de Castro who took their vows here in defiance of his father's wish that he marry Doña Constança. The tumultuous love affair ended with the gruesome murder of Doña Ines (see under Coimbra). *Directions:* at the junction of rua de Gondivai with rua dos Bombeiros turn right (signposted Mosteiro) and continue past the fire station *bombeiros Voluntarios de Leca do Balio* over rail line [300m] turn down over access roundabout under the N-13 flyover [300m] and the Monastery and cemetery are visible ahead amongst the woodland [400m]. Return the same way for a 2 km round trip.

Mosteiro Leça do Balio

For the waymarked route continue s/o along rua de Gondivai over **railway [0.7 km]** cruceiro in **Araújo [0.3 km]**:

1.0 km Araújo *Capela* (right) small chapel adjoining the popular Sacred Oak Cafe •*Café Carvalho Santo* and shaded park with seating. Good place to stop for a rest and to take our bearings (the modern Porto suburbs effectively end here). The café is named after a miraculous event 200 years ago when a hurricane tore through Araújo and demolished everything in sight, save the ancient oak tree that stood here.

Wood from the tree is used in the pulpit in the adjoining XVIII[th]c church of St. Peter *Igreja de São Pedro de Araújo*. A tiny statue of St. Peter is embedded in the oak which still occupies the centre of the square.

Option. From Araújo there is an option to continue straight on along the main road towards Padrão Moreira (with selection of hotels). While this alternative route follows the busy main road it avoids having to cross the central road barrier on the 'original' route, which is dangerous and requires a measure of agility. If your mobility is impaired you should consider this option although it, too, is busy with its own hazards. Be vigilant whichever route you choose and remember there is no guarantee of safe passage in this life and *that* realization may help us come to terms with the inherently impermanent nature of all physical form.

● ● ● ● ● For the *alternative* route
0.0 km Araújo s/o along rua de Custio, cross metro line down to the rio Leça and over the **Ponte de Moreira [2.1 km]** up and over the IC-24 and turn right> on the N-13 and s/o over roundabout **[1.0 km]** (Quinta do Mosteiro left) turn right> after cemetery past •*Café Mosteiro* **[0.7 km]** turn right> at T-junction up to rejoin main route at traffic lights at crossroads

[1.4 km] (sign for Zona Industrial Maia and a bank and •*café* on the corner)

5.2 km Cruce *Moreira* If you need accommodation at this point there is a selection ½ kilometre back down to the *Cruz das Guardeiras* on the N-13.

•**Estalagem Lidador** Ⓒ 229 436 220 single from €30. •**Residencial Puma** Ⓒ 229 482 128 single from €40. Other possibilities ½ kilometre further on towards the airport •**Pensão Aeroporto** on rua das Pedras Rubras Ⓒ 229 429 334 or 1½ kilometres further out along the N-13 towards Vilar do Pinheiro to •**Residencial Santa Marinha** Ⓒ 229 271 520 (Anna Maria da Silva) from €25 single with (modest) breakfast. Situated slightly back from busy N-13 up the steps on the first floor and popular with pilgrims (good restaurant on the ground floor).

From Araújo we leave behind the city environs and head onto quieter roads. The cobblestone roads *estradas de pedra arredondada (Spanish: adoquinado)* may be attractive but the granite setts are very hard underfoot. This granite surface makes up much of Portugal's rural road network and lack of maintenance compounds the problems as missing setts are a hazard to walkers. Use the alarming sound of car tyres on cobbles to keep you alert!

(*We now step onto the historic camino as the original route makes its way down to and over the river leça via the medieval bridge Ponte de Barreiros.*) Just past the covered cross in Araújo (scallop shells and other pilgrim motifs on the shaft) turn down right> onto the first of many cobbled lanes *Travessa D. Frei Manuel Vas Concellos* (Note: Portuguese names bear both the father's

and mother's family lines) which winds its way down to the stone bridge and the rio Leça **Caution** *Cuidado* **[!]** Take great care on the crossing the dual carriageway. Wait patiently until *both* sides of the dual carriageway are empty before crossing as you need to make it over to the other side in one movement – you don't want to be caught in the middle! If you are nervous about hopping over the central barrier, you can take a short detour: ½ kilometre up to your right to a traffic crossing and then head back down to rejoin the waymarked route (total 1 kilometre extra). However, this is also not a route planned for walking pilgrims and is likewise potentially hazardous.

STAGE 14: 119

Once over the main road we climb up into rua do Souto under the rail bridge and past the exclusive restaurant •*Quinta As Raparigas (left with Santiago statue in niche)* and up again past the manor house Quinta das Conegos (right) to the câmara Municipal de Maia, turning <left up past the council offices to:

2.1 km **Igreja da Maia** *Capela de Na. Sa. do Bom Despacho* with its lovely façade of *azulejos* and the high point of this first stage at 125 m.

Detour: [1] ● ● ● ● ● From here it is ½ km down (right) to the ultra modern centre of the new town at Maia which has several expensive hotels including •**Central Parque** ⓒ 229 475 563 with 40 rooms, single from €50. This is also where pilgrims who took the metro to Maia start their camino. [2] ● ● ● ● ● Just past the church we come to the •*Bar do Zoo* and a short 50m detour down to our (left) to the shaded and peaceful *Zoo do Maia* with •*Café*.

Continue down the cobble laneway to the crossroads by Quinta de Santa Cruz past •*café* and over another crossroads to emerge onto main road turning <left and then right> (signposted Zona industrial Maia 1) to pass the •*Fonte do Godim* **[0.7 km]** where you can fill up with the invigorating waters of this well where the 'water is of high chemical and bacteriological quality' *agua de alta qualidade química e bacteriológica*. Now it's up again under the motorway underpass in the direction of Gemunde. Veer <left by shaded park in Guarda with its tiny chapel dedicated to S. António. Follow sign for the industrial zone (Z.I. Maia 1) up to another high point passing 2 •*cafés* **[1.2 km]** to the next major crossroads and option point **[1.0 km]**:

2.9 km **Cruce** *Moreira* crossroads with bank *Espirito Santo* and adjoining •*café*. This is where pilgrims who took the alternative road route join from the left. See alternative route for accommodation options ½ km (left) to the main crossroads at *Cruz das Guardeiras* on the N-13. The historic camino continues straight on between modern industrial buildings, to **crossroads [2.5 km]** with another option for accommodation.

● ● ● ● ● *A short detour left into Vilar do Pinheiro to the N-13 [300m] and turn left again back along the main N-13 for another [300m] to* •**Residencial Santa Marinha** *described under the alternative road route from Araújo.*

Continue s/o at the crossroads (signposted Mosteiró) passing •*café* (left) in the hamlet of Venda. The path continues along narrow cobbled laneways into the village square in **Mosteiró [1.3 km]**:

3.8 km **Mosteiró** with a pleasant shaded square •*café*. The waymarked route keeps to the left past the café *[and is joined by pilgrims coming from the Metro option to Vilar do Pinheiro]* as it meanders up into **Vilar [1.0 km]** with the parish church up a long avenue (right) s/o over crossroads along the busy N-306 past •*bar* (left) •*café-snack bar* (right) **[2.2 km]** to crossroads in Gião **[0.5 km]**:

3.7 km Cruce *Gião* Option
Detour: •**Quinta das Alfaias** Ⓒ 252 662 146 set in lovely gardens located 1.7 km *off* route along a quiet asphalt road in the direction of Casal / Fajozes. Directions: Turn left at crossroads and veer right 0.5 km straight to quinta 1.2 km.

Continue s/o crossroads in Gião past *Quinta do Alferes* to next **crossroads [1.8 km]** (Vairão *Museu* right) and up to the traffic lights at the next major **crossroads [1.5 km]** in:

3.3 km Vilarinho small but busy town at junction of the N-306 and N-104 (*The latter links Vila do Conde on the coastal route with Trofa adjacent to the Braga route.*) The town has a welcome shaded central park off which are several bars and cafés includng the popular •*Café-pastelaría Nova Aurora* and the adjoining •*Restaurant Castelo* at the far end (right) of the square.

If you started at Porto cathedral or otherwise plan to stay at the new pilgrim hostel here then turn right> up through the shaded park to the welcoming and helpful chemist •*Farmácia Rei* Ⓒ 252 661 610 on the main road (09:00 – 19:00) who hold a key or on Sundays enquire at the Bomba Gasolina Repsol near the crossroads. The hostel is situated in a small sports pavilion *pavilhão desportivo* around the corner behind the chemist (follow sign to the school).

0.5 km Albergue. The accommodation has recently been extended to 16 beds and basic facilities with showers and w.c.'s and kitchenette. If the albergue in Vilarinho is full the options are [1] to proceed to the extensive new hostel in Rates (11.4 km – allow 4 hours) or detour to Vila do Conde (6 km – allow 2 hours or take a taxi (10 mins c. €10) or the infrequent bus to Vila do Conde. See  alternative route [D] for accommodation in this delightful seaside town.

Vila do Conde — Harbour with 17th century Capela do Socorro

REFLECTIONS:

Alternative Route [D] ● ● ● ● ● **Porto (Matasinhos) to Vila do Conde 22.1 km**. The best place to start this coastal alternative is to make your way to the lifting bridge *ponte móvel* in Matosinhos where crossing the bridge is a fine symbolic start to the journey. Once over the bridge turn immediately left and make your way to the sea at Praia Leça da Palmeira. The route now follows the coast all the way into Vila do Conde with accommodation. The connecting route from Vila do Conde to the main route in São Pedro de Rates is not well waymarked but relatively easy to follow and is described in detail. There are several options to get to Matosinhos **[1]** The quickest and easiest is to take the metro from Trindade in the direction of ***Senhor de Matosinhos*** and get off at the penultimate stop – ***Mercado*** (40 mins). *[Note that if you miss the Mercado stop you can simply walk back from the terminus. Note also that the central metro stations at São Bento or Aliados will require a change at Trindade].* **[2]** Take any bus route that ends in Mercado (by the *ponte móvel*) route numbers 1, 19, 86, 89, 92, 61. Line 1 (500) follows the coast from Praza Almeida Garrett or São Bento in the centre to Mercado via Foz do Douro. Route 76 from Cordoaria or 44 from Boavista and 507 from the centre go to Praia de Leça itself. Note that bus route and numbers in Porto can change (and often do!) so check at the tourist office or bus stop schedule *before* heading off.

0.0 km Matosinhos *Ponte Móvel* take the spiral staircase and cross the lifting bridge, a moving symbol (literally and metaphorically) as we leave the city behind and take our first tentative steps on this coastal route towards Santiago. Take the spiral staircase down at the far end and out towards the coast passing the impressive stone fort **castelo [1.1 km]** along the wide boulevard to pass the lighthouse **faro [1.8 km]** which acts as a pilgrim 'beacon' and on to the chapel **capela [0.3 km]** built on a rocky promontory over the sea:

3.2 km Capela •*café* we now head past the gates of the ugly gas-fired power station **[1.0 km]** emerging onto the first of many board-walks **[1.0 km]** along Praia Paraiso in Parafita and Praia Memoria to memorial obelisk **[1.7 km]**.

3.7 km Obelisco •*café* The tower apartment blocks of Póvoa de Varzim are now visible in the distant horizon (Vila do Conde is *this* side of Póvoa). *Note: Take the board-walks wherever possible (they're great to walk on) but be selective. e.g. it might be preferable to take to the sandy beach here for 100m to rejoin the board-walk further on rather than take the board-walk back to the road.* We now head onto Praia Cabrada over small rivulet to 'Sea House' museum:

3.6 km Casa do Mar Traditional stone fisherman's shed and adjoining replicas of Roman Salt Tanks *Tanques Romanos Salga*. Continue via wooden bridge over river **[1.3 km]** to small cove below S. Paio **[1.0 km]** where we make our way up onto a narrow path that skirts the beach and winds its way up towards the pillar on the headland onto a boardwalk with information panels (Portuguese and English) on the history of this Iron Age settlement built around the Capela de **S. Paio [0.5 km]**.

2.8 km **S. Paio** •*café* pre-historic castro and chapel occupying a prominent position on the headland. Archeological investigations continue to explore the myths and meaning of this ancient settlement. Continue onto Praia de Moreiró and into the famous fishing village of **Vila Chã [1.3 km]** •*cafés* to Fishermans Square *Largo dos Pescadores* •**Café Tony** © 917 487 512 may have holiday rooms to let (depending on season) also •**Parque de Campismo**. The waymarks split here and the choice is to go s/o right by asphalt road or turn left to take the shorter route across a sandy beach with pronounced camber – both routes bring us to **Praia Mindelo [2.2 km]**.

3.5 km **Mindelo** •*café* the coastal road now veers inland and we come to a long and more remote beach separated from the road by an extensive area of sensitive dune land vegetation. The shortest route is along the beach or over the sand dunes till ½ km before the harbour wall a major apartment development opens up over to our right at:

2.2 km **Árvore** we continue along the beach to the 2nd **[1.0 km]** of 4 ramps that come down through the dunes to access the beach (any ramp will take you to the access road but the 2nd is the most direct). Head s/o directly over the road (round stone tower right) and down a dust road (old harbour and swamp left) over bridge **[0.4 km]** and turn <left up into rua Francisco Goncales Mosteiró and we head towards the Convento Santa Clara building visible on the horizon above the town of Vila do Conde. Pass shipyard (left) and <left onto asphalt road (sign Junqueira) •*Café Vila Azur* **[0.6 km]** past chapel (ruins) and up to the main road and turn <left to cross bridge over the rio Ave to riverside park. Turn right to continue to S. Pedro de Rates or s/o to the centre of Vila do conde and tourist office **[1.1 km]**.

3.1 km **Vila do Conde** *Centro Turismo*

For those who have walked the coastal route from Porto you can now enjoy this delightful town with its medieval quarter around the harbour, dominated by the prominent white dome of the early 17th century *capela do Socorro*. This tiny circular chapel built 1603 in the Moorish style with *azulejos* displaying the adoration of the Magi. Nearby is a museum of boat building and replica of a Portuguese caravel *(Vila do Conde was a major centre of early boat building activity in Portugal's great exploration period)*. The narrow cobbled alleyways wind around the perfectly preserved medieval fishing quarter that leads into the central square on the far side of which is the fine 16th century parish church *Igreja Matriz*. If you want to swim in the sea head west past the municipal swimming pool to the sandy beach behind St. John the Baptist Fort (15 minutes from the town centre).

Overlooking the town is the impressive *Convento de Santa Clara* (we pass under it on our way to S. Pedro de Rates). The walk up to the top is rewarded with wonderful views of the entire town and coastal area. At the side of the convent are the remains of a remarkable Roman aqueduct that fed the entire complex with water from the nearby hills.

Turismo ✆ 252 248 473 the helpful tourist office occupies an ivy-clad building on rua 25 April (part of the central square) Taxis (adjoining) ✆ 252 631 933
❑ **Accommodation:** *Budget from €25 single* •**Hospedaria O Manco D'Areia** ✆ 252 631 748 Praça da Republica (€15 for pilgrims sharing) adjacent to the stylish •*Le Villageois* restaurant (no longer has rooms) •**Pensão Patarata** ✆ 252 631 894 overlooking the harbour on Cais das Lavandeiras with restaurant and bar on the ground floor. •**Residencial Princesa do Ave** ✆ 252 642 065 rua Dr. António Sousa Pereira •**Hospedaria Venceslau** ✆ 252 631 748 rua das Mós. *In the middle price bracket from €35:* •**Estalagem do Brazão** ✆ 252 642 016 Av. Dr. João Canavarro good value and welcoming to pilgrims. *At the luxury end from €60 single:* •**Hotel Santana** ✆ 252 641 717 rua de Santana (over the bridge on the far side of the river). •**Hotel Forte de São João Baptista** ✆ 252 240 600 Av. Brasil newly renovated luxury in this historic building on the sea. Best to avoid June and July when motor racing through the town and summer tourists make accommodation scarce, expensive and noisy. Merging into Vila do Conde to the North is the burgeoning modern seaside and dormitory town **Póvoa do Varzim**, not recommended for a visit but with many additional hotels if necessary.

COASTAL ROUTE – STAGE 14: 125

To return to the historic waymarked route at São Pedro de Rates [9.8 km]

`0.0 km` Vila do Conde *Ponte* Leave by the main bridge and follow the river Ave upstream past the Convento de Santa Clara and over the **metro line [0.4 km]** •*cafés* past vacant corn silos turn right> at **T-Junction [1.6 km]** under the **A-28** into **Touguinha** •*café-pastelaria* up and s/o over the roundabout **[1.3 km]** and down to join the N-309 in **Touguinhó** passing •*cafés* and shops to crossroads and bridge over the river Este (tributary of the Ave) **[1.4 km]**:

`4.7 km` Ponte *Rio Este* •*café [Note: an alternative route to Rates goes left up the hill at this point via Touguinhó and Rio Mau but this is along the busy 206 and is not recommended].* For the recommended route turn right> (signposted Junqueira) cross the bridge (cascades upstream *cascatas de Touguinho*) into rua Rio Este [!] blind corner (this continues a short but dangerous stretch of the N-309) past the impressive gates of Quinta da Espinheira (right) to turn <left off the N-309 just past bus-stop and up into rua Central **[0.9 km]** past Fonte da Garrida (left) veering <left past Centro Médico da Junqueira and steeply up past •*café* (right) continue s/o (ignoring any turnings off this central road) up to Junqueira parish church *Igreja Matrix* **[1.2 km]** which marks our high point of this stage (60m) and continue s/o down passing school (right) and •*café-panidoce* (left) to crossroads **[0.5 km]**:

`2.6 km` Cruce *Junqueira* •*café* continue s/o down to monastery church ahead *Igreja de São Simão da Junqueira* with statue of Santiago Peregrino in the right-hand niche. Cross over the A-7 motorway **[1.5 km]** and optional detour:

Megalithic Mound *Megalítico do Fulom* (Mamoa do Fulão) located in the pine forest immediately (right). The wooden railing around this prehistoric site is visible from the road. The burial chambers date back to 3,000 B.C.E and was excavated some years ago. The west-facing opening is discernible in the second of the two mounds. It is a little visited site, which adds to the mysterious atmosphere that surrounds this peaceful glade, disturbed only by the proximity of the new motorway. If you have particular interest in these mamoas you can telephone for further information © 252 631 087.

To continue – follow the road down to rejoin the waymarked route from Vilarinho at the bridge over the **Rio Este [0.7 km]** and up into **Arcos [0.3km]**. From here on the route follows the traditional route to S. Pedro de Rates.

`2.5 km` Arcos *Quinta S. Miguel*

❏ **The Path around our home is also the ground of awakening.**
Thich Nhat Hanh

15 *213.7 km (132.8 miles) – Santiago*

VILARINHO – BARCELOS

▬▬▬▬ --- ---	7.2 --- ---	26%
▬▬▬▬ --- ---	15.1 --- ---	56%
▬▬▬▬ --- ---	5.0 --- ---	18%
Total km	**27.3 km** (17.0 ml)	

▲▬ 28.3 km (+^ 210 m = 1.0 km)
Alto ▲ Goios 150 m (492 ft)
<🅰 🅷> Arcos 7.5 km / Rates 11.4 km / Pedra Furada 18.5 km

```
                                            295m ● Monte Franqueira
                                    150m ▲ Alto (Goios)
VILARINHO         Arcos Rates  Pedra Furada                      BARCELOS
  Río Ave          Río Este                                       Río Cávado
0 km      5 km          10 km       15 km       20 km       25 km
```

The Practical Path: A varied day where we encounter our first delightful woodland paths around Arcos. 50% of this stage is along quiet country lanes, mostly screened by eucalyptus and pine woods, offering shelter from wind and shade from the sun. While this requires walking on asphalt this is somewhat kinder underfoot than the traditional granite cobblestones. There are also some stretches along the N-306 with very poor sight-lines that require extra vigilance for the in-frequent but fast traffic along it. **Intermediate Accommodation:** *Arcos 7.5 km – São Pedro de Rates 11.4 km – Pedra Furada 18.4 km.*

❏ **The Mystical Path:** We have mastered how to travel to the moon but we don't know how to find inner peace. *Charity begins at home* is an old saying containing much wisdom. The breakdown of relationships is endemic in our affluent western world – we don't need to switch on the television to witness war. We are at war with ourselves, with our families, with and between our local communities and within our own country. If we want to create peace in our world we don't need to step outside our neighbourhood – we just need to develop an open door and an open-heart right here and now.

❏ **Personal Reflections:** "…I was covered in dirt and sweat and suffering from heat exhaustion and dehydration and nearly missed the café entrance. The cool interior and the smile on the patron's face embraced me in welcome. Before I had spoken a word he guided me to a table and poured a fresh orange juice – it was unasked for and tasted like nectar. But the greatest gift was the spontaneous display of generosity. Before I left this haven of hospitality António had pressed the key of his apartment into my hand, *'treat my home as if it were your own,'* he said simply… I write these notes in his apartment overlooking the broad sweep of the river Cávado. He is at work in his restaurant till late but I look forward to having breakfast with him. I want to understand what makes one man open his home to a total stranger while another bars it to his own family…"

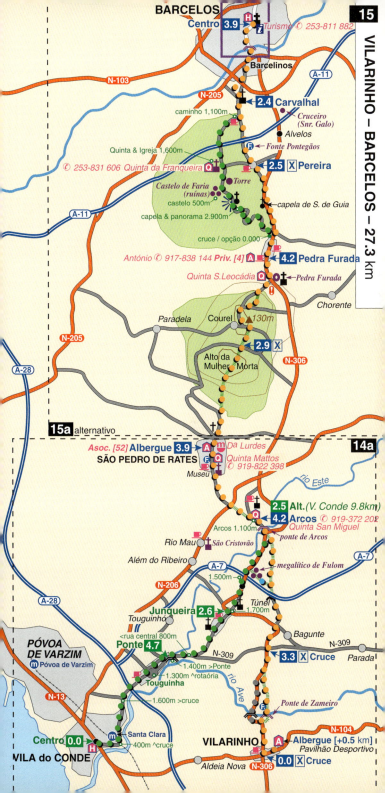

From Vilarinho continue straight through the crossroads in the direction of Fontaínhas (turn right at the crossroads if coming from the albergue + 0.5 km). Stay on the main road N-306 and turn off **right>** **[1.2 km]** and follow the track down to the beautiful medieval bridge over the rio Ave **Ponte Dom Zameiro** **[0.5 km]** with old mill buildings down river. The bridge has been damaged on several occasions in recent years. *(Note: If the bridge is impassable – don't panic! Continue along the river bank and veer up to rejoin the main road and proceed over the modern bridge ½ km down river (see photo right) and continue on the road till you join the waymarks again).* Proceed over the river Ave to pass •*fonte* (left) and continue up to the **crossroads [0.3 km]**

small hamlet straddling the crossroads and overlooking the river Ave with bar and chapel *Capela de N.S. da Ajuda*. Continue up into woodland and back onto **main road [0.6 km]** *(alterative bridge route joins here in the area of Castro de Santagões)* turn right> and continuing to **crossroads [0.7 km].**

3.3 km **Cruce** with roadside shrine Outeiro Maior (right) Junqueira (left) continue s/o passing the **Casa do Alto [0.5 km]** (high point of the day at 125 m) before veering right> onto the cobbled rua de São Mamede **[0.7 km]** through Boa Vista passing the ruins of the old pilgrim and coaching inn *Estalagem das Pulgas* and under the new A-7 **motorway [1.6 km]** (linking Póvoa de Varzim with Familicão). Here the pretty village of Arcos now opens to view straight ahead. *Optional detour (adds ½ kilometre to the waymarked route): a forest track to the left runs alongside the motorway to the megalithic burial mound* **Megalítico do Fulom** *described under alternative route from Vila do Conde.*

We now make our way down the rough path to the **rio Este [1.0 km]**. A sandy river bank makes a good place for a picnic, or a swim? Proceed over the Ponte de Arcos and up the cobbled lane with the walls of the Quinta São Miguel (right). If you are staying the night here continue on past the waymarked route for 50 metres and the entrance to the Quinta is opposite the **church [0.4 km]** in:

4.2 km **Arcos** adjoining the church is the welcoming •**Quinta São Miguel** ℂ 919 372 202 with 5 rooms, single from €45 with breakfast in this delightfully restored 18th century manor house with swimming pool. The owner António Rodrigues speaks English and is very supportive of pilgrims. Dinner is also available. There is a pleasant •*café-bar* around the side of (behind) the church.

Leaving Arcos The waymarked route veers off by the handsome *cruceiro* at the side of the quinta and around the edge of the village up onto an earth **track [0.4 km]** into eucalyptus woods and over busy main road **N-206 [!] [1.1 km]**

by timber yard *(an alternative route from Vila do Conde, via Rio Mau joins from the left)*. Continue onto cobble **lane [1.2 km]** over abandoned **railway [0.4 km]** to the parish **church** in **São Pedro de Rates [0.3 km]**. The town is a delightful blend of old and new with the parish church dedicated to St. Peter, a local saint much revered in the area and reputedly ordained by St. James himself on his evangelisation of the peninsula. It was originally built as a monastery church by the Order of Cluny (a powerful influence on the camino) in the 11th century over the remains of earlier pagan temples of Roman and pre-Roman origins. The church belfry is a separate structure to the rear. An adjoining ultra modern museum (with public toilets) displays some artifacts found during excavation, most dating from 12th century but with some exhibits from the Roman period. Just beyond the church an extensive square opens up *Praça dos Forais* with the diminutive Chapel to Our Lady of the Square the *Capela do Sra. da Praça*

with the historic Town Cross *Pelourinho* adjoining. At the far end of the square, opposite the clock tower, is the internet •*Café-restaurant Macedo*.

Pick up the arrows behind the **Igreja de S. Pedro** and continue on past the drinking font *Fontenário de S. Pedro* into rua Direita to •**Casa de Mattos [0.3 km]** ⓒ 919 822 398 directly on the camino (right) but not well signposted. 5 rooms and separate chalet with single from €40 incl. breakfast. Continue to the top of rua Dereita and turn **<left [0.1 km]** and **up for [0.1 km]** to:

3.9 km São Pedro Rates •**Albergue**
This wonderful pilgrim hostel was the first to open on the Portuguese side of the camino and was inaugurated on St. James Day 2004. 129 pilgrims comprising 6 nationalities slept here in its first full month of opening. The hostel was further renovated and extended in 2009 and now offers 50 beds in various small dormitories and ample shower

and toilet facilities. A cosy living room, laundry room and kitchen make up the amenities on the first floor. There is an extensive courtyard for clothes drying and relaxing and also provides access to a small museum displaying objects typical of rural life in the area. A veritable haven of peace and welcome from Nuno Ribeiro and his team of dedicated volunteers – you might even be lucky enough to experience the mystical ritual of the flaming *Queimada*. During the busy periods it is open from early afternoon but if it is closed you can obtain the key from the well-stocked and welcoming shop located 50m further on – no obvious shop sign but opposite the *Capela de S. António* where Dª Lurdes and her family will welcome you each day until 21:00.

Continue up past the albergue and shop and s/o over crossroads onto short stretch of asphalt road which becomes a delightful earth track **[0.7 km]** and veers right> down to a stream bed (wet) up through overhanging vines into eucalyptus woodland continuing along forest tracks up to a high point at Dead Woman's Peak *Alto da Mulher Morta* at which point we enter the administrative area of Barcelos. The natural path now undulates gently to cross over a road close to the village of Courel (left) **[2.2 km]**:

2.9 km **Cruce** continue up on track to through woodland ahead along a walled lane up to asphalt road and turn <left and then right> around high walls of quinta **[1.7 km]** (alto 130m) we turn right> off this road at next junction and then down <left onto rough track and wind our way to the busy **[!]** N-306 **[1.4 km]** turn <left along the N-306. Stay alert walking this stretch of road as it is narrow with little margin for the fast moving traffic with several blind bends. We pass the Igreja Pedra Furada **[0.2 km]**. Adjoining the church is the perforated stone *pedra furada* that gives this area its name. Opposite the church is the austere •**Quinta de Sta. Leocádia** © 252 951 103 AT *Ag.Turismo* with

single from €50 but you need to book ahead as the owner is seldom in residence. Continue s/o along the main road and at the start of the next village we arrive at a veritable pilgrim haven in Pedra Furada **[0.9 km]**

4.2 km **Pedra Furada** popular •*café-bar* and adjoining •*mini-mercado* with award winning restaurant to the rear •*Restaurant Pedra Furada* © 252 951 144 (rua Santa Leocadia 1415) specialising in typical home grown produce. The proprietor António Martins Ferreira [m] © 917 838 144 and his family have been welcoming wayfarers for many years and has recently made available a small •**Albergue** comprising one bedroom for 2 (max 4 sharing) with shower and toilet facilities solely for pilgrims – €10 for single occupancy and €20 for up to 4 sharing. Together with other concerned individuals in Barcelos António is part of an association formed in 2009 to co-ordinate efforts to improve the pilgrim infrastructure in the area. Initial projects

include planning for the safety of pilgrims walking this stretch of main road and the opening of the new albergue in Portela (see next stage). Continue up rua S. Leocadia •*cafés* to crossroads at the top and high point (Alto 150m) **Goios [0.6 km]** and **option** to visit [1] the panoramic viewpoint (290m) and chapel of Sta. da Franqueira [2] the remains of a Roman castrum [3] the Manueline Convento da Franqueira or [4] stay in the adjoining luxurious Quinta da Franqueira.

This **alternative route** via Monte Franqueria (a pilgrimage site in its own right) is *not* waymarked but easy to follow and adds 2.5 km to the recommended route. The strenuous uphill climb (an additional 140m) offers splendid views over the coast and some interesting historic sites along the way. Turn up <left at the crossroads and immediately right> up by side of timber yard to spiral up to the top of the hill at 290m to the 18th century **Capela de Sta. da Franqueira [2.9 km]** site of a pilgrimage held annually (2nd Sunday in August). Adjoining the chapel is a small cafe and in front is a panoramic **viewing balcony** with unsurpassed views west over the Atlantic. The route now starts its descent on the far side of the hill down to the *sign* (left) for **Castelo de Faria [0.5 km]**. Here there is a short **detour** of 100 metres along a sandy track to

this timeworn fortress, which fell into ruin as far back as the 14th century. It was built over a Roman *Castrum* and before that over a prehistoric settlement *Citania*. A brief climb up through the ancient woodland to the ruins built around a rocky outcrop evokes a sense of both history and mystery – this peaceful site is little visited. Continue down the asphalt road along the Stations of the Cross, past the **medieval tower [0.5 km]** and beyond it the Fountain of Life *Fonte da Vida*, which was renowned for its healing waters.

Turn off <left by picnic site and cantina to the **Convento do Bom Jesus do Monte da Franqueira [1.1 km]**. Built in the 16th century this is a fine example of the Manueline style although the interior is in partial disrepair. Adjoining the church is the splendid •**Quinta da Franqueira** © 253 831 606 lovingly restored by the Gallie family from England it offers a uniquely peaceful haven with private access to a balcony in the adjoining church. Single rooms from €50 includes use of the delightful gardens and swimming pool, but not the drinks cabinet where a slate is provided to record details of your imbibing. Continue down (steeply) over the

motorway **[0.6 km]** to rejoin the waymarked route in Carvalhal **[1.1 km]**.

To continue on the recommended route start the descent from the crossroads along the main road passing *Capela de Senhora da Guia* **[0.4 km]** set back from the road with •*fonte* and good views north/ east over Barcelos and the Cávado valley. Turn <left signposted Aldeia /Souto /Pedrêgo **[0.8 km]** off the main road and proceed down the cobblestones into Pereira **[0.7 km]**:

2.5 km Pereira *Cruce* •*Café S. Salvador* small hamlet with churrasquería, shop and small chapel at the crossroads. We continue along a maze of small roads but the route is well waymarked as we pass the ancient •*Fonte de Pontegãos* **[1.0 km]** s/o under the motorway and veer right> at T-Junction **[0.8 km]** •*café-mercado (left) (here the alternative route from Monte da Franqueira joins from the left).* Follow sign for Barcelos to the parish church in **Carvalhal [0.6 km]**.

2.4 km **Igreja Carvalhal.** Turn <left at church and 50m right> through Portocarreiro and over stream and up to Holy Cross chapel *Capela da Santa Cruz* **[1.3 km]**. We now approach the industrial area of Barcelinhos straight over **roundabout [0.6 km]** around side of car showrooms and through underpass (N-103 Braga to Viana do Castelo road) to rejoin the main road on the outskirts of Barcelinhos •*cafés (Here the ancient way went directly to the river to the medieval ferry point before the bridge was built).* Turn right> along main road to crossroads and turn down <left opposite ancient drinking font to the medieval bridge Ponte Barcelos in **Barcelinhos [1.2 km]**. Here (right) is the Chapel of Our Lady of the Bridge. The original chapel was built in 1328 to provide shelter for pilgrims (the stone benches and basins used for washing their feet can still be seen). 100m (left) along the riverside is •**Residencia Gallo** ⓒ 918 967 968 / ⓒ 917 204 587 a residence for traditional folk-dance groups where accommodation has recently been made available for pilgrims (€5).

❶ *Capela de Nª Sª da Ponte* [● *numbers refer to historical monuments on the town plan, those with an asterisk* are national monuments* ● *from the bridge to the central square is 800m.*] Cross over the medieval bridge ❷ **Ponte Medieval** built on the instructions of *D. Pedro* Earl of Barcelos in 1328. This acted as a great spur to the development and prestige of the town and facilitated early pilgrims to Santiago. *Note*: by taking your time along the following route you will pass most of the historic sites along the way. You can take time to visit them as you pass or return, perhaps, when you have found a place to stay for the night. Turn <left then first right> up past the 15th century ❸ **Solar dos Pinheiros*** manor house of the Pinheiro family (left) with its gargoyles of the bearded one *Barbadão*. Next we come to the remains of the 15th century Palace of the Counts ❹ **Paço dos Condes** now an open air archaeological museum *Museu Arqueológico* with the Pillory **Pelourinho*** portraying the legend of the Cock *lenda do Gallo* (photo right and legend next page) with the 14th century parish church ❺ **Igreja Matriz*** fronting onto the municipal square *Largo do Municipio*. This Romanesque church, with later Baroque additions, was built in the 12th century and has a fine display of glazed tiles *Azulejos*. On the opposite side of the square is the sumptuously restored town hall and council office ❻ **Câmara e Paços do Concelho*** formerly a hostel for pilgrims to Santiago de Compostela. Continue into ❼ *Largo do Apoio* the original town square around which the nobility built their houses with central fountain (1621). Turn right> into rua S. Francisco and the main pedestrian shopping street, rua D. António Barroso (rua Direita) to **[0.8 km]**:

3.9 km **Barcelos** *Largo da Porta Nova*. The attractive main square is the hub of this lively town with the helpful tourist office located *behind* the 15th century

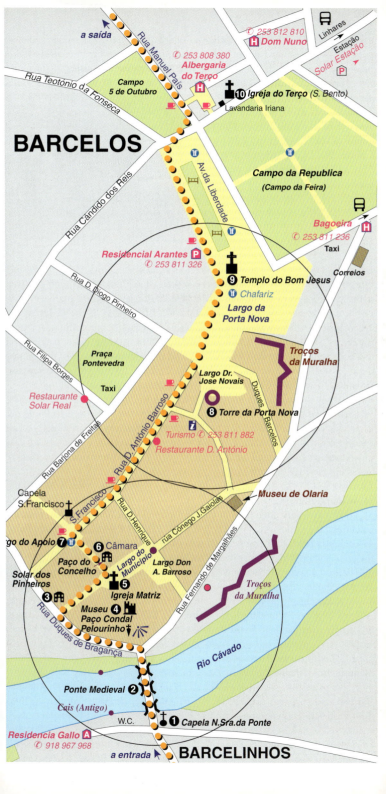

granite tower ❽ ***Torre da Porta Nova**** which is the only remaining medieval entrance into the town (formerly the tourist office and handicraft centre). At the other end of the square is a fine stone fountain with the interesting 18th century Baroque church dedicated to Good Jesus of the Cross ❾ ***Templo do S. Bom Jesus da Cruz**** *(Igreja de Senhor das Cruces)* built in 1704 in an octagonal shape over an earlier chapel. This is the venue of the 500-year-old Feast of the Crosses that takes place annually on 3rd May and is named after the miraculous appearance of a cross in the soil of the adjoining market square in 1504. Just behind the church is the centrally placed •Residencial Arantes on Av. da Liberdade and part of the camino.

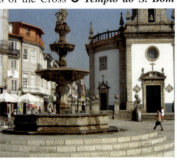

BARCELOS: Opening out from the Largo da Porto Nova is the extensive market square *Campo da Feira* otherwise known as *Campo da República*. The whole area becomes one of Portugal's best-known and liveliest markets *Feira de Barcelos* every Thursday. At the top end of the square is the ❿ ***Igreja do Terço*** built in 1707; its plain façade belies its rich interior and ceiling depicting the life of Saint Benedict *São Bento*. Adjacent to it is the new shopping centre and hotel in the Centro do Terço built around the original Convent of that name. Barcelos makes an excellent stopover and there are several parks and squares in which to rest and enjoy the local scene and a municipal swimming pool if you want to cool off. If you have walked from the new albergue in Rates you will have plenty of time to explore. However the next stage to Ponte de Lima is a long day so you need to be refreshed and ready for an early start (intermediate accommodation is now available). The tourist office has a list of accommodation, which includes the following (see town map for locations).

Turismo ✆ 253 811 882 Largo Dr. Jose Novais (handicraft centre + internet).
❏ **Accommodation:** •Residencial Arantes ✆ 253 811 326 rua da Liberdade, 35 good value with singles from €25 and centrally located above the popular restaurant and pastelaría. •Hotel Bagoeira ✆ 253 811 236 Av. Dr. Sidónio Pais, 495 recently renovated with single rooms from €45 central location overlooking the main square with popular restaurant attached. •Albergaria do Terço ✆ 253 808 380 off rua de São Bento with pedestrian entrance through shopping mall off rua Manuel Pais – stylish modern hotel on upper floors of the shopping centre with single from €40. •Residencial Dom Nuno ✆ 253 812 810) Av. Nuno Alvares Pereira, 76 modern hotel off road to rail station with 26 rooms from €37 single. •Residencial Solar da Estação ✆ 253 811 741 on Largo Marechal Gomes, 1 – opposite rail station on noisy roundabout with 10 beds from €15 single. **Restaurants:** There is wide range of cafes and snack bars around the main squares. Among the better restaurants are: •*Bagoeira* Av. Dr. Sidónio Pais, 495 (main square). •*Dom António* on the main pedestrian street rua D. António Barroso also known as rua Direita. •*Solar Real* Praça de Pontevedra on the first floor with splendidly atmospheric interior and fading murals. **Transport:** Rail station ✆ 253 811 243 with rail services along the Porto – Santiago line. Bus Av. Dr. Sidónio Pais (Campo da Feira) ✆ 253 808 300 Also Linhares ✆ 253 811 517 rua Dr. Julio Vieira Ramos. Both have regular services to Braga.

Barcelos is a delightful town occupying an elevated site above the river Cávado and was the first Portuguese County established by D. Dinis in 1298 but its origins go back to the Roman period. The town retains much of its medieval atmosphere, the oldest remaining structure being the original town walls and Torre da Porta Nova, which date back to the 15th century and to the first Duke of Bragança. There are several museums including the Ceramic Museum *Museu de Olaria* housed in the 19th century *Casa dos Carvalhos Mendanhas* which contains a large collection of ceramics from around the world, especially from this region and particularly of the famous brightly coloured cockerel which has become a national symbol of Portugal and logo for Portuguese tourism.

The Barcelos cockerel is based on the same story that we may have heard in Santo Domingo de Calzada on the Camino Francés. The cross in the Paço dos Condes portrays the miraculous story of the roasted cock that rose from the table of the judge who had wrongly condemned a pilgrim to Santiago to hang from the nearby gallows (located south of the river). The pilgrim had proclaimed his innocence and stated that if he were wrongly condemned to hang then a dead cock would rise from the judge's table in proof of his righteousness. The innocent lad was hanged and sure enough a roasted cock stood up on the judge's plate as he sat for dinner that night. The bewildered judge hurried from his table to find the pilgrim alive on the gallows – saved by the miraculous intervention of St. James and the Barcelos cockerel!

Detour – Braga: Buses run throughout the day and the journey takes around one hour. If you are planning to visit Braga and the nearby Bom Jesus (the most popular tourist site in Portugal) you will need to allow an extra day. The easiest way to do this is, perhaps, to book in to Barcelos for 2 nights and then you can travel to Braga without having to waste time looking for accommodation and carrying your rucksack to boot (the bus stop in Braga is 10 minutes walk west of the city centre). Braga is a city with a host of outstanding monuments. Sometimes referred to as the 'Rome of Portugal' it is the country's ecclesiastical capital with a somewhat pompous and grandiose atmosphere to match. Its name derives from the original Bracari Celts but Romans, Visgoths and Moors have all occupied it. Amongst the many historic buildings conveniently grouped around the city centre is the 11th century Romanesque cathedral *Sé* (see photo below) whose foundations go back to 1070 when they replaced an earlier mosque built by the occupying Moors and later underwent Gothic and Baroque embellishments. Access to the museum of sacred art is off a small cloister just inside the main entrance. Braga has more than 30 churches and several national monuments. The *Turismo* is housed in a prominent Art Deco building on the corner of *Praça da República* ✆ 253 262 550 and provides a useful map of the town and list of accommodation together with details of how to get to the famous **Bom Jesus do Monte** overlooking the city from its hilltop perch surrounded by ancient woodland and terraced gardens – a pilgrimage itself if you want to climb the steps to the chapel at the top.

I only went out for a walk... and finally concluded to stay out till sundown, for going out, I found, was really going in. John Muir

16 *186.4 km (115.8 miles) – Santiago*

BARCELOS – PONTE DE LIMA

▬▬▬	--- ---	15.7	--- ---	47%
▬▬▬	--- ---	15.8	--- ---	47%
▬▬▬	--- ---	2.1	--- ---	6%
Total km		**33.6 km (20.9 ml)**		

35.8 km (+^ 440m = 2.2 km)

Alto ▲ Alto da Portela 170 m (558 ft)

< A H > S.Pedro Fins – Portela 9.4 km / Lugar do Corgo 19.1 km

The Practical Path: This is the longest and most arduous of all the stages but arguably the most beautiful. It includes two hill passes *portelas* separating the two river valleys of Neiva and Lima. However, we have the beautiful natural landscape to lift our spirits and nearly half the route (47%) is on pathways through vineyards and woodland through the peaceful Neiva valley. From Portela (Vitorino) all the way is downhill into the beautiful Lima valley. The opening of a new albergue at Portela and the extension of bed spaces at Casa Fernanda's provides additional options if tiredness or nightfall overtakes.

The Mystical Path: The word hospitality comes from Medieval Latin *hospitare — to receive as a guest*. From this root we also find host, hospice, hospital and Hospitaller. The Knights Hospitaller provided welcome to the increasing numbers of pilgrims struggling across the remote landscape and now, centuries later, it is no different. The garb of the knight may have changed but the hospitality can still be found, "…ask and it will be given to you; seek and you will find; knock and the door will be opened unto you." *Matthew 7*.

Personal Reflections: "I heard there was the possibility of a place to stay in the area but had no idea where to start looking, it was getting late and I was exhausted. As if on cue 3 delightful children appeared 'out of nowhere.' Language was no barrier to their enthusiasm and insistence that I follow them… I sit under the starry sky and scribble these notes by the light of the fire lit from resinous pine needles. The fragrance now overtaken by the smell from the pork chops sizzling on the griddle. Framed in the light of the kitchen doorway is Mariana while her mother and father prepare the table in the background. The generosity of spirit that flows from this family leaves me humbled and filled with deep gratitude for the spontaneous hospitality offered to a total stranger."

0.0 km | **Barcelos** *Centro* pick up the arrows at the Igreja do Sn. Bom Jesus da Cruz and proceed up the tree-lined Av. da Liberdade past the fountain and s/o

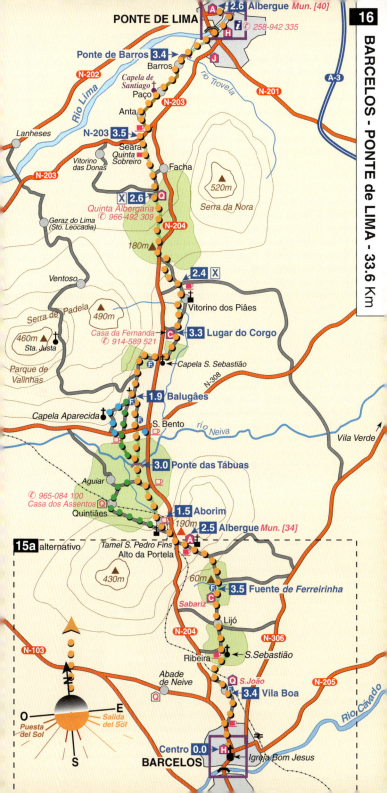

busy roundabout by *Centro Commercial Terço* cross over **by-pass [0.9 km]** and continue up wide avenue to **roundabout [0.5 km]** taking slip road to right> •*Café Olival* into rua de S. Mamede. Veer right> **[0.9]** and then up <left past **school [0.2 km]** and <left at **Igreja de Vila Boa [0.4 km]** with shaded porch, past concelho and turn right> **[0.3 km]** into rua do Espírito Santo *(Note: 100m s/o on main road •café-pastelaria opens early)* into village green **[0.2 km]**:

3.4 km **Vila Boa** extensive village green *Lugar do Espirito Santo* with •*fonte* (right) adjacent to the Quinta entrance. •**Quinta São João** ℂ 253 811 519 a well restored manor house with double rooms from €50 and swimming pool and large annex for wedding functions.

Detour: ●●●●● **Abade de Neiva** a small village 1.5 kilometres west of Vila Boa (sign posted) with 2 Quintas [1] •**Casa do Monte** ℂ 253 811 519 in Lugar do Barreiro. [2] •**Casa de Abade do Neiva** (ℂ 253 811 553 in Lugar da Igreja. The Romanesque church *Santa Maria de Abade do Neiva* has a niche in the form of a scallop shell and was founded by D. Mafalda, wife of D. Afonso Henriques in the 12th century and is now a National Monument.

We continue down over **railway [0.3 km]** onto a lengthy stretch of sand road through eucalyptus woods on the original caminho de Santiago over bridge **Ponte de Pedrin [0.9 km]** through Lugar de Ribeira with welcoming •*Cafe Arantes* **[0.4 km]** and chapel of St. Sebastian *Capela de S. Sebastião*. We then pass another chapel dedicated to the miracle of the Holy Cross **Capela de Santa Cruz [0.2 km]** in the area of Lijó s/o over road onto a short stretch of cobble-
lane onto track and then cross over **road [1.3 km]** into mixed woodland of pine and eucalyptus continue to end of the asphalt **road [0.3 km]** and here on the left corner is •**Casa do Sabariz** ℂ Fernanda Cunha 964 751 844 a quinta-style country house with 2 double apartments with all facilities generally available for weekly let but may be available for overnight stay. Proceed down gravel track to wayside **fonte [0.1 km]**:

3.5 km **Fonte da Ferreirinha** •*fonte* ancient spring offering cool refreshing water. Track meanders through vineyards over stream past the gates of *Quinta de Revorido* (dogs) to join asphalt road **[0.7 km]** in the parish of *Tamel S. Pedro Fins* and we start a steep climb past •*Fonte Rua da Cruz (quality no longer monitored)* and continue the climb to junction with the main road and wayside cross **cruceiro [1.2 km]**. We have another steeper climb up past
the parish council offices *Freguesia de Tamel S. Pedro Fins* and *Capela Sra. da Portela* with ancient wayside cross with interesting pilgrim motifs of staff and gourd on the shaft and, adjoining is the new pilgrim hostel **[0.6 km]**:

2.5 km **Portela** •**Albergue** new hostel (opened in 2010) in the former *Casa da Recolecta* a fine stone building adjoining the church. 31 bed spaces in 3 dormitories with modern shower and toilet facilities, a fitted kitchen and lounge. Opposite the hostel is the •*Bar-Restaurant 2000*.

Continue up to a high point of today at the Portela (195m) and the junction with the main Barcelos to Ponte de Lima road [!] **N-204** and turn right> along the crest of the pass (caution on the dangerous bend in the road [!]) as we now start heading downhill into the Rio Neiva valley past Fonte da Portela (dry) and first <left (signposted *Quintiâes*) right> onto track over river and past the modern parish church down steps and turn right over the rail line in:

1.5 km **Aborim / Option:** The main waymarked route now turns right> and immediately <left onto a sand road. **Note:** take care around Aborim as there are several other waymarked paths in the area. One is an alternative route in case the main camino is flooded (it is low lying). The Camino del Norte via Lanheses is also close by and you don't want to inadvertently stray onto it. The safest way to avoid confusion is to make sure you enter Aborim by the modern parish church and leave over the railway line. 100m (s/o) along the rail line and opposite the station *Estação Aborim Tamel* is the pleasant •*Café Oliveira*.

Detour ● ● ● ● ● **Quintiâes.** If you need accommodation you can take a short detour into Quintâes [1.5 km] by asphalt road from Aborim (signposted s/o left before crossing the railway). The House of Agreements •**Casa dos Assentos** ✆ 253 881 160 (Júlia Novais Machado) is a beautiful historic manor house dating back to the 16th century

offering 6 rooms, 3 separate apartments, 2 swimming pools and with single from €50. On the way you pass by the old parish church of Aborim *Igreja Velha de Aborim* located down to your right (which offers an alternative route to the recommended one in very wet weather). *[The dense woods (right) just before crossing the railway at Quintiâes hide the ruins of a medieval castle and chapel. A visit is only recommended for the seriously adventurous as the area is very overgrown and close to the steep rail cutting.]* Waymarks (to the Northern route) will lead you behind the cemetery (right) but the Quinta is located behind the parish Church located at the end of the road to the left. There is a basic •*bar-cafe* and *mini-mercado* adjacent.

To rejoin the recommended route make your way down past the bar to the T-junction and shop in Gândara [0.8 km] and veer right> signposted Barcelos (Note: this is the opposite direction to the arrows which are for the Camino do Norte via Aguiar, Vilar Nova and the Ponte de Nova). Continue to the bridge over the small stream [0.6 km] and veer <left immediately over the *Ribeiro do Pico* to rejoin the waymarked route from Aborim by the pipe factory.

From Aborim the path continues along alternating stretches of sand-tracks and cobblestone laneways (often wet as this is a low lying area) turning right> on asphalt road **[1.0 km]** (winter route in wet weather) to T-Junction **[0.5 km]** where we turn <left onto the Caminho de Santiago in the Quintiâes district *(100m right off the waymarked route is •Café Gandera on the main road).* The waymarked route now meanders

through an ancient hamlet to turn right> by factory **[0.5 km]** (Alternative route from Quintiâes joins from left) onto a cobble lane leading to the beautiful medieval bridge over the river Neiva **[1.0 km]**.

3.0 km **Ponte das Tábuas** 'Bridge of Boards' a reference to an earlier wooden bridge over the rio Neiva dating to the 12th century. The present medieval stone structure is very emblematic of the pilgrim way. Up ahead, just visible in the distance, is the Capela da Aparecida (see detour). On the far side of the bridge is a small sandy beach by the weir, an idyllic spot for a picnic or a swim.

Option: There are several options through the straggling village of Balugâes ahead. ❶ The main waymarked route continues to the right and takes a 'middle' course, with drinking fonts only *(just before entering Balugâes there is the possibility to turn down right to the crossroads at São Bento (300m) with cafe)* ❷ Just over the Ponte das Tábuas an alternative route veers up to the left through woodland to join the N-308 by café and timber yard for a detour to Capela da Aparecida *or* continue s/o to rejoin the main route at caminho signboard ■.

Detour ●●●●● **Capela da Aparecida:** Just beyond the Ponte de Tábuas turn up <left sign for GR 11/ E9 onto a path that winds its way up through pine trees to cross over [!] main road N-308 [900m] with •*Café Aldeia* on the corner. The detour to the 18th century sanctuary of the Apparition of the Virgin *Santuário da Senhora da Aparecida*, site of a miracle where a devout deaf and dumb penitent

regained his hearing and speech after the appearance of the Virgin. The sanctuary is the venue for a pilgrimage held annually on 15th August and the detour will add an extra 1 kilometre to the waymarked route – but allow yourself an extra hour to refresh yourself by the shaded drinking font, to visit the peaceful chapel and to climb underneath it to wash your sins away forever – according to the local tradition! Not a bad exchange for one hour of your time? However, if you started in Barcelos and intend making it to Ponte de Lima tonight then you may need to leave remission for some future date. ***Directions***: turn up <left on the main road and then right> [400m] and wind up past drinking font and up the steep steps to the Sanctuary [300m]. Access to the tunnel under the chapel is at the side by iron railings. Climb underneath and out the other side – if you can't make it around the boulder you will have to back-out and reflect some more on the errors in your life! Return downhill by the asphalt road ahead (no need to return to the main road) ignoring any side roads to left and right and rejoin the recommended route at junction with drinking font and camino signboard [600] ■.

❶ For the main waymarked route veer right> on newly surfaced track along this low-lying area through vineyards veer up <left at fork up to main road [!] **N-308 [1.2]** *(At this point café Aldeia on alternative route 2 is 400m up left while the main crossroads at São Bento is 200m down right with shops and •café-pizza. To return to the waymarked route either continue along the busy N-204 Barcelos to Ponte de Lima road and rejoin the waymarked route at the crossroads at Capela de S. Sebastião 1½ km or return back up the N-308 for 200m to rejoin the waymarked route there)*. To continue on the waymarked route cross N-308 onto track (noisy dogs) which leads into Balugâes and •*fonte* **[0.5 km]** and up to road junction with another •*fonte* and caminho **signboard [0.2 km]** ■.

`1.9 km` Balugâes *Cruce* at this point the alternative route from the Santuário da Aparecida joins from the upper road (left). Continue downhill along the Stations of the Cross (that lead back up to the sanctuary) to a modern

fountain **fonte [0.2 km]** and optional detour: *Short (½ km) detour* ● ● ● ● ● *to the Romanesque church Igreja Velha de Balugâes with covered portico and medieval cruceiro in a small park.* ***Directions***: *At the fountain veer up <left to follow a quiet country lane to the church. To rejoin the waymarked route continue along the road which curves back to the camino.* The waymarked route continues past the return loop from the Romanesque church (left) and bus-stop onto a delightful path through pine woods **[0.6 km]** veering right> back onto minor road down to crossroads **N-204 [0.6 km]** •*fonte* (right) by bus shelter. Cross over by wayside chapel *capela de S. Sebastião* also dedicated to Fátima. The route now follows peaceful laneways along a small river valley *ribeira de Nevoinho (that flows into the Neiva just above the Ponte das Tábuas)*. We finally enter a small hamlet with **crossroads [1.9 km]** in:

3.3 km **Lugar do Corgo** in the parish of *Vitorino dos Piâes* although we are still several kilometres from the Parish Church and village of that name. Here on the left is the ever popular •**Casa Fernanda** Ⓒ 914 589 521 the modern bungalow of Fernanda and Jacinto Gomes Rodrigues who have welcomed pilgrims to their home over many years providing bed and board. This facility  has recently been extended to accommodate 14 pilgrims in a new timber chalet. This is a long day's stage and if you started in Barcelos you have already walked for 19.3 kilometres (before adjusting for height climbed and possible detours) and we have another 14.4 kilometres before we reach Ponte de Lima.

Continue s/o in Lugar do Corgo and turn off <left onto **track [0.1 km]** we now crisscross over several roads turning right along an avenue up to the parish church **[2.2 km]** *Centro Paroquial* in *Vitorino dos Piâes* with interesting carvings and collection of sarcophagi in the forecourt. Continue up to the **crossroads [0.1 km]**.

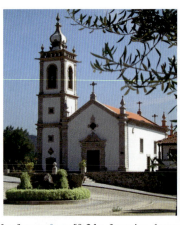

2.4 km **Cruce / Vitorino dos Piâes** with •*Café-Restaurante Viana e mini-mercado* (50m down right). Last chance to buy food or drink before we reach Ponte de Lima. At the crossroads continue s/o *up* the hill turning <left **[0.3 km]** past •*fonte* **[0.3 km]** turning down <left and then up steeply right> onto **path [0.2 km]** through eucalyptus woods turning <left to junction with the main road at Portela **N-204 [0.4 km]** and our 2nd high point of the day at 190 m. We now turn right> by cement works along main road **[!]** and turn off <left onto **track [0.2 km]** (opposite sign for Facha). Lovely views now open up ahead over the Rio Lima valley as we proceed down through eucalyptus woods to quiet country lane **[1.2 km]** and:

2.6 km **Facha** •**Quinta de Albergaria** Ⓒ 258 942 241. Continue past statue of Santiago in niche and s/o *up* asphalt road turning <left at sign for **Leiras [0.6 km]** over the road onto cobblestone lane past wayside cross with tile image of Santiago peregrino opposite wayside chapel *capela de S. Sebastian* **[0.8 km]** continue s/o past •**Quinta do Sobreiro** Ⓒ 258 931 070 (2 night minimum stay) **[1.6 km]** continue through vineyards and apple orchards to the main road **N-203 [!] [0.2 km]**.

STAGE 16: 143

3.5 km N-203 Turn right> along the busy main road (between Viana do Castelo and Ponte de Lima) in Seara with popular restaurant and Pensão •**Pinheiro Manso** ⓒ 258 943 775 and then <left **[0.2 km]** [!] cross over main road •*Café-Pastelaria O Farinheiro (we now follow quiet country lanes parallel to the rio Lima through the hamlets of Anta, Bouça, Paço, Periera, Barros which all merge one in to the other all the way into Ponte de Lima)* pass •*fonte* **[1.2 km]** s/o over several small crossroads and veer <left **[0.8 km]** at Wayside shrine to S. Antonio. At the top of the gentle rise ahead in **Lugar do Paço [0.3 km]** we come to the Capela de Santiago which lies in ruins behind the private house on our left.

Note: Here in the townland of Correlhã is the only chapel dedicated to San Tiago that lies directly on the route in Portugal. It is somewhat difficult to locate and incongruously situated just inside the privately owned yard (50m left off the road). The dilapidated Capela de Santiago has an interesting connection with the camino as the lands here at Correlhã were bequeathed to the city of Santiago de Compostela in the year 915, this bequest being ratified by D. Henrique and D. Teresa on their pilgrimage to Santiago in 1097. It may be possible to visit the chapel and to see the remarkable 18th century statue of *Santiago de Peregrino*, which is now kept in the house adjoining the chapel (on the road), which is in the private ownership of Fátima and her brother José Begerra Silva e Sousa.

Proceed along the quiet country lane through Pedrosa with the ancient *Cruceiro da Pedrosa* (left) and •*Bar* **[0.5 km]** and the tiny Capela de S. Francisco into Barros to the medieval bridge *Ponte de Barros* over the **rio Trovela [0.4 km]**:

3.4 km **Ponte de Barros** we now turn <left by bandstand and chapel to Our Lady of the Snows *capela da Sra. das Neves* and continue along the earth track parallel to the river Lima to junction with viewpoint and boulders **[1.2 km]** *(Note: If you plan to stay in the Youth Hostel Pousada da Juventude the quickest way is to take the short-cut up the narrow lane (right) to the main road. The YHA is on the opposite side of the main road – 250m).* Continue under road bridge **[0.2 km]** past the *Capela de N. Sra. da Guia* and along the lovely tree-lined Avenida D. Luis Filipe past the popular •**Hotel Império do Minho [0.4 km]** (pilgrim discount) and along the river front to the central square Largo de Camões to the medieval bridge Ponte de Lima **[0.4 km]**. For the new pilgrim hostel cross the bridge past the church to the hostel entrance **[0.4 km]**.

2.6 km **Ponte de Lima** •**Albergue** *Casa do Arnado* this wonderful new pilgrim hostel (pictured above) opened in 2010 in a central location by the bridge.

Ponte de Lima: A delightful market town that retains a sleepy medieval atmosphere. Take time to amble around its narrow cobbled streets and historic buildings. This is an ideal place to take a rest day – if your schedule allows. The town has several museums and there are lovely walks along the Rio Lima itself. It prides itself on being the 'oldest' town in Portugal and there is certainly little doubt that it occupies one of the most beautiful riverside settings to be found anywhere. The Lima valley is outstanding in its natural surroundings and even the A-3 motorway is far enough away not to disturb its tranquillity. However, a fortnightly market, reputedly the oldest extant market in Portugal (Barcelos claims to be the most popular) spreads itself along the sandy beach and creates a great deal of activity and several annual fiestas add to the action such as the *Vaca das Cordas* where a roped cow is led around the parish church before being maddened by darts and led down to the beach for slaughter to become part of this annual feast. It all harks back to ancient pagan fertility rights (whatever one thinks about animal rights) and takes place in June, the day before Corpus Christi *Corpo do Deus* when the town streets are covered with incredible floral displays. August generally sees a 'medieval' market arrive with juggling, jousting and joviality. The *Feiras Novas* takes place during the third weekend in September when a sea of humanity floods the town in the biggest party of the year that goes on 24 hours a day for 3 days.

❏ **Historic Buildings and Monuments:** The main sites and buildings of historic interest are clustered around the town centre area and are therefore easy to visit and include (from the start on the way in) ❶ **Igreja de S. Francisco e S. António dos Capuchos** XVI **e Museu dos Terceiros** (adjoining Hotel Império de Minho) with impressive baroque façade and museum of religious art and artefacts. ❷ **Torre da Cadeia** XIV the original prison tower now housing a library with free Internet access with entrance from the intimate square situated *behind* the esplanade which also has an evocative 18th century granite statue of a local woman carrying a water jar *Estatueta uma Cantareira*. ❸ **Igreja Matriz** XVthc parish church on the main street opposite **Igreja da Misericórdia** XVIthc ❹ **Paço do Marquês** now the tourist office with viewing gallery from the roof. ❺ **Torre de S. Paulo** part of the original 14th century defensive walls of the town and adjacent to the **Chafariz** the beautiful fountain fashioned in 1603 and occupying pride

PONTE DE LIMA 145

of place in the centre of the main square *Largo de Camões* with its popular
•*cafés and bars* overlooking the river. ❻ **Medieval stone bridge** rebuilt in 1368
on Roman foundations. This handsome bridge is just 300 metres in length and
4 metres wide. It forms the pedestrian link between the busy southern town
and the quieter northern quarter. ❼ **Capela do Anjo da Guarda / S. Miguel**
an intriguing stone shrine dedicated variously to the Guardian Angel or Saint
Michael. It is an open vaulted structure with interesting motifs located on the
riverbank and adjoins the **Capela de Sto. António da Torre Velha** XIXthc. Just
beyond the church is the new pilgrim hostel behind which are the beautiful ●
Thematic Gardens *Jardims Temáticos* with their peaceful and well maintained
sections each having a separate theme. Further down the river (adjacent to the
road bridge) is the ● *Clube Náutico* with canoe hire and restaurant. Ponte de
Lima is the headquarters of the *Solares de Portugal* part of the TURIHAB
organisation that offers over 1,000 luxurious beds in historic Quintas and
Manor houses in Northern Portugal and also the headquarters of the Friends of
the Portuguese Way to Santiago *Associação dos Amigos do Caminho Português
de Santiago*. This latter organisation is sponsored by the government's rural
development programme, which provides it with an office in rua do Carrezido,
7 adjoining the TURIHAB offices (opposite the Post Office).

❏ **Accommodation:** *Turismo* Praça de República ✆ 258 942 335
New pilgrim hostel in restored former *casa da musica* •**Albergue** *Casa do Arnado* on largo da Alegria (adjoining the bridge). On the far side of town on rua Agostinho José Taveira located off the N-203 is the modern Youth Hostel •**Pousada da Juventude** ✆ 258–943 797 / 605. •**Hotel Império de Minho** ✆ 258–741 510 Av. 5 de Outubro with 40 air-conditioned rooms, restaurant, swimming pool and bar in secluded gardens to the rear – single from €40 with pilgrim discount on production of credencial, includes buffet breakfast. •**Pensão São João** ✆ 258 941 288 near the bridge (entrance from side street, rua do Rosário off Largo de S. João) 8 rooms from €30 single, also popular restaurant on ground floor. •**Pensão Beira Rio** ✆ 258 944 044 located above the Pizzeria on Passeio 25 de Abril – front rooms overlook the river with single from €25. •**Pensão Morais** ✆ 258 942 470 on rua Matriz with basic rooms from €25. For old-style luxury at the top end: •**Casa das Pereiras** ✆ 258 942 939 adjoining the 18th century capela das Pereiras with access off rua Fonte da Vila just above the town centre with swimming pool and shaded gardens. 6 rooms, single from €60. There are also a limited number of first and second floor rooms available that are not listed with the tourist office. A walk around town will give you a flavour of what's on offer. On the far side of the river, in the vicinity of the new albergue in Arcozelo is •**Quinta Casa do Arrabalde** ✆ 258 742 442 and •**Quinta do Arquinho** ✆ 258 742 306 a converted 18th century mill directly on the original Roman road.

Pilgrim hostel *(above)* **Youth hostel** *(below)*

The town has a variety of **restaurants** (booking generally not required). Overlooking the river eastwards from Hotel Minho along Passeio 25 de Abril are: •*Encanada* ✆ 258 941 189 with terrace above the road. •*Manuel Padeiro* ✆ 258 941 649 on rua Bonfim set back from the busy *passeio* but with outside tables that get the evening sun. Along the *passeio* are: •*Parisiense* ✆ 258 942 159 with ground and first floor tables, pizzeria •*Beira Rio* and just beyond it is the basic •*Catrina*. Various snack bars spill out onto the central square *Largo de Camões* with its lovely central fountain *Chafariz* and behind the square in *Largo Feira* •*S. João* ✆ 258 941 288 and at the far end is the popular •*Alameda* ✆ 258–941 630 whose small dining room overlooks the river. On the far side of the river in the vicinity of the pilgrim hostel and themed gardens are a number of cafés.

Themed Gardens *Jardims Temáticos*

PONTE DE LIMA 147

REFLECTIONS:

❏ **I dwell in the high and holy place, with they who have a contrite and humble spirit.** *Isaiah 57:15*

17 *152.8 km (94.9 miles) – Santiago*

PONTE DE LIMA – RUBIÃES

▬▬▬ --- ---	10.3 --- ---	57%
▬▬▬ --- ---	7.8 --- ---	43%
▬▬▬ --- ---	0.0 --- ---	0%
Total km	**18.1 km** (11.2 ml)	

▰▲▰ 20.4 km (+^ 460 m = 2.3 km)
Alto ▲ Portela Grande 405m (1,329 ft)
< 🅰 🅷 > None

The Practical Path: We now have our first glorious day where natural paths account for over half the route and there are no main roads at all. This stage also marks our steepest accumulative climb almost entirely encountered in the one ascent up the Labruja valley to the high pass through the mountain ridge and into the Coura valley via the Alto de Portela Grande. Facilities along the way are limited but there is reasonable shelter amongst the pine woods on either side of the pass and a number of drinking fonts along the way – you will need to use them. **Intermediate Accommodation:** None.

❏ **The Mystical Path:** With all the great discoveries made within the sense-perceptible world of science we have never been able to see the super-sensible. Not even the most powerful telescope on earth has been able to glimpse even the tiniest fragment of God. Knowledge of Higher Worlds does not come from exploring the physical universe within the laboratory of the mind but in diving into the mysteries. Paradox is at the heart of the spiritual quest and so the top of the mountain becomes a symbol of the wisdom often found at the lowest point of the journey and within the humblest of hearts.

❏ **Personal Reflections:** "The steep climb is rewarded by stunning views back over the incomparable beauty of the Lima valley while the unexplored country to the north invites discovery. I drink deeply from the clear cool waters that flow from the mountain spring while all around me are the harmonious sights and sounds of nature. There is no sign of human activity apart from a vacant mountain hut… I like the idea that high places reflect Higher Mind – that place where clutter and illusion seem to evaporate in the rarefied air of the mountains. While fog hangs in the valleys, clarity abounds amongst the peaks. The wounded ego is nowhere to be seen and the mundane commitments fashioned in the lowlands all pale into insignificance from these lofty heights."

17 PONTE de LIMA – RUBIÃES – 18.1 km

RUBIÃES
- **1.3 Albergue** — Milário, S.Pedro Rubiães
- Pensão São Roque ✆ 252-943 692
- **3.7 São Roque** — Agualonga
- *Ponte Romano*
- N-201 — Cabanas, Antigo molinho
- Morgado, Romarigães
- Coura
- 405m — **3.0 Alto** *Portela Grande*
- 435m
- *Cruz dos Franceses*
- 530m
- 520m
- Santuário, Labruja, EN-306
- 135m — **1.9 Fonte** *Três Bicas*
- Capela N.S. Nieves — **2.9 Café** *Nunes*
- Revolta — Ponte do Arco
- **A-3 Ponte 2.6** — S. Pedro
- 720m
- *rio Labruja*
- N-201 — EN-306 — café 200m — Calheiros
- *Ponte Arco da Geia*
- **2.7 Igreja** — Arcozelo — EN-306
- A-27
- O — o por do sol
- E — o nascer do sol
- S
- *Casa de Sabadão*
- *Quinta Arquino*
- **0.0 Albergue** — **PONTE de LIMA**
- A-3

0.0 km **Ponte de Lima** from the albergue on the north side of the river Lima turn right> past the •café (right) in the square (signposted Quinta do Arquinho). We now make our way around the back of the themed gardens *Jardims Tematicos* veering <left and <left again onto a **track [0.4 km]** beside the entrance to •Quinta do Arquinho Ⓒ 258 742 306. We follow the low-lying track to cross over the **N-202 [0.8 km]** onto a cobbled lane past the fading opulence of •Quinta de Sabadão Ⓒ 258–941 963. *(In winter this whole area can become marooned from the overflowing rivers Lima and Labruja).* We now head out under the A7 **motorway [0.7 km]** along quiet country lanes to pass the Centro Social **[0.8 km]** in:

2.7 km **Arcozelo** with church and •*fonte* onto track over the Rio Labruja by the medieval bridge (asphalted) **Ponte da Geira [0.9 km]** continue up and turn <left onto path **[0.2 km]** *[Detour* ● ● ● ● ● •*café 200m s/o on main road]* we now meander along lanes and earth tracks through the natural environment of the Labruja valley (disturbed only by the A-3 motorway that snakes above us). We pass (left) a newly renovated mill *Casa do Caminho da Beira Rio* to climb along a pathway that summits just above the A-3 •*fonte* (right) and then descend to an option point underneath the motorway **[1.5 km]**.

2.6 km **Option / A3 Underpass.** Up to the right is the road route while the recommended route lies over a partially collapsed metal bridge over the river Labruja and up a steep pathway that climbs up around the motorway to the Ponte do Arco where the other route joins from the right. Consider using the alternative route if the river is in torrent.

For the alternative route ● ● ● ● ● take the track to the right that climbs above the A-4. From here a wide farm track takes you to the main road [0.5 km] turn <left and continue along main road turning off <left [1.3 km] (signposted Labruja/ Sanctuario do Socorro) to cross the rio Lubruja over the Ponte do Arco [0.3 km] where the recommended path joins from the left. (Total distance similar at 2.1 km as compared to 2.3 km via recommended route).

For the recommended route continue straight on over the rio Labruja which flows rapidly through a narrow gorge at this stage. Scramble up the far side underneath the A-4 flyover onto a narrow path that climbs up through scrubland at the edge of pine woods away from the A-4 as it flattens out and follows the contours around the side of the *Vale do Inferno*. We now rejoin the asphalt **road [2.3 km]** at the Ponte do Arco at the point where the alternative road route joins from the right. Continue past the capela de São Sebastião •*fonte* (left) in the area of Devesa / Revolta, veering <left (signposted Valinhos Valada) to cafe **[0.6 km]** in:

STAGE 17: 151

2.9 km Revolta •*Café Cunha Nunes* welcoming cafe and shop run by Marcia and Manuel adjoining the chapel to Our Lady of the Snows *Capela de N. S. Das Neves* with wayside cross. This is the last chance to acquire food or drink (apart from water at drinking fonts) on this stage. We now start climbing alternating between paths and lanes with the village of Labruja and its distinctive

parish church visible over the valley to our right (with the Santuário do Senhor do Socorro in the far distance, behind it) and the ominous A-4 motorway over to our left to:

1.9 km Fonte des Três Bicas •*fonte* where clear water gushes from 3 channels *três bicas* carved into the stone. Fill up your bottles with the cool and refreshing waters for the long climb ahead. Continue over bridge and turn up sharply <left past Casa da Bandeira and over road onto track through the pine woods ahead, much of which has

recently been felled *(the tiny Capela Santa Ana is visible below in the valley floor)*. The path becomes a forest track and then turns up again <left onto another path passing wayside cross *cruz dos Franceses* **[2.2 km]** where pilgrims to Santiago have placed stones to mark their passage and prayers. It is otherwise referred to as *cruz dos Mortos* a reference to the ambush that took place here on Napoleon's troops during the peninsular war (1808 - 1814). Cross over track back onto path by drinking tap (dry) and beehives and as we summit we have a magnificent view back over the Lima valley to the south. We make our way around the paddock ahead to finally reach our **high point [0.8 km]** at:

3.0 km Alto da Portela Grande (405m). Adjoining the entrance to the forester's lodge is a drinking font •*fonte* (50m *off* route). A view north over the heavily wooded rio Coura valley now opens up as we start our descent over a rough stony path **[!]** through pine woods, the terrain flattening-out as we cross

a small stream with a series of ancient millwheels running above and below the path **Moinhos de Cabanas [1.0 km]** This line of unusual wheels were used to mill grain, particularly maize (for the delicious maize bread found in these parts). A little further on we pass Quinta de Matos. The path now drops down into the hamlet of **Cabanas [0.5 km]** onto asphalt road s/o past **wayside cross [0.5 km]** s/o past •*fonte* (left) down to the ancient Roman bridge

Ponte Águalonga [0.9 km] the track now meanders through Águalonga and over 2 roads to emerge onto the main Ponte de Lima to Valença road (N-201)

in São Roque **[0.8 km]** with the hostel directly opposite:

3.7 km **Rubiaes** •*O Repouso do Peregrino* ⓒ 251 943 692 were Silvia Castro has been welcoming pilgrims for many years and can arrange transfer to a restaurant nearby. 7 double rooms all with shower en suite from €15 with simple breakfast. Adjacent is a modern pharmacy and there are 2 basic bars within 100m *off* route. Continue downhill passing **Quinta S. Roque** and veer right> onto **path [0.3 km]** and continue through woodland to derelict *cruceiro* **[0.7 km]** and **option**: turn down (left) 100m to visit the enchanting 12th century Romanesque church dedicated to St. Peter *Igreja de São Pedro de Rubiães* and *miliario* the historic Roman mile marker on the Via XIX has been hollowed out to form an

ancient sarcophagus. Continue down the main road to **albergue [0.3 km]**.

1.3 km **Rubiães** •**Albergue** *Escola* ⓒ hospitalero 917 164 476 / 251 943 472 delightful pilgrim hostel opened in 2007 in a former schoolhouse. The converted accommodation is modern and spacious with good kitchen and dining area and extensive lounge and outside patio area. One large dormitory sleeps 34 in bunk beds with ample ladies and gent's toilets and showers with additional room on the top floor. ½ km further down the road by the bridge (just *off* route) is a useful bar and restaurant •*Bom Retiro* ⓒ 967 552 716 which also holds a key to the hostel. On the far side of the road bridge is •*Café Ponte Nova* with well-stocked shop to the rear – the camino passes by this café via a Roman bridge on the next stage, a useful place for breakfast if you are staying the night in this albergue.

REFLECTIONS:

❏ **Do not seek to follow in the footsteps of the men of old;**
Seek what they sought. *Matsuo Basho, 16th century Japanese pilgrim poet.*

---

18 *134.7 km (83.7 miles) – Santiago*

RUBIÃES – VALENÇA / TUI

▬▬▬ --- ---	9.1 --- ---	54%
▬▬▬ --- ---	8.8 --- ---	7%
▬▬▬ --- ---	1.4 --- ---	39%
Total km	**19.3 km** (12.0 ml)	

🔺 20.3 km (+^ 200 m = 1.0 km)
Alto ▲ S. Bento 270 m (886 ft)
< Ⓐ Ⓗ > Valença 16.3 km.

The Practical Path: Apart from the short stretch of main road into Tui the rest of this stage is split between natural pathways and quiet country roads through woodland affording both shelter and shade. With the exception of a modest climb out of the Coura river valley into the Minho basin the majority of this stage is downhill from São Roque. The Minho now becomes the Miño and our clocks may also need adjusting one hour as we make our way over the border from Portugal into Spain. Most pilgrims head straight for Tui and the first of the Spanish pilgrim hostels adjoining the cathedral. However you have an option (recommended) to visit the historic old walled town of Valença and / or stay in in the atmospheric old town or the modern hostel just outside it.

❏ **The Mystical Path:** *'All roads lead to Rome'* was a truism in the time of the Caesars but now we begin to understand that *'All roads lead Home'* and are assured that all we need to do to realise the truth of this simple statement is to: *'Render unto Caesar the things which are Caesar's; and unto to God the things that are God's.' Matthew 22:21.* To whom do you pay tribute? Whose footsteps do you follow? What is it you seek?

❏ **Personal Reflections:** "The dark grey clouds had been gathering all afternoon but nothing could have prepared me for the downpour the moment I set foot in Galicia. The ensuing deluge was so powerful that within minutes I was wet from head to foot and the road turned to a river… The hot shower restored some heat to my body. There is only one other pilgrim in this spacious hostel – a young Japanese girl who walked to Santiago from France and just kept going! She follows the blue arrows now towards Fátima but she has no destination in mind. What are the hidden forces that drive us on, through the blistering heat, the bitter cold and the torrential rain? It is not a physical destination that draws us but something metaphysical…"

0.0 km **Albergue** we leave the albergue and turn right> downhill and turn off sharp <left **[0.3 km]** onto a muddy path that follows the bed of a stream to an exceptionally well preserved Roman bridge *Pons Romana* over the rio Coura whence we follow the surface (clearly visible) of the original Roman road to cross the N-201 at Ponte Nova **[1.0 km]** with •*café* and shop onto a track alongside the river Coura with old millrace and weir. The camino now alternates between quiet country lanes and earthen tracks up through a wooded valley to crossroads at the high point of this stage at 270m **[3.2 km]**

4.5 km **São Bento da Porta Aberta**. Major crossroads •*café* with adjoining shop. The camino now crosses over behind the church *Santuario São Bento XVII* onto a path with distant views over the Minho valley as we begin our descent towards Valença along delightful woodland paths through pine, eucalyptus, holm oak and the occasional cork tree (Portugal is one of the world's largest producers of cork). The path alternates between these woodland paths, cobblestone laneways and short stretches of asphalt road (all well waymarked) into:

3.3 km **Fontoura** with •*Café Central* (right) up past chapel and pilgrim memorial plaque *Peregrino Caminhante* adjoining •*fonte* (left) and access road to the parish church *Igreja de São Miguel*. The route alternates again between road and pathways on level ground through woodland into Paços and Pedreira •*café-mini-mercado* and then over the river Pedreira via the Roman bridge.

3.2 km **Ponte Romana da Pedreira** up past Quinta da Bouça **[0.6 km]** and s/o through woodland and along quiet country lanes up to the N-13 **[1.7 km]**.

2.3 km **Tuido** cross over the main road **[!]** to a selection of •*cafés-restaurantes* on the far side where the camino continues on a secondary cobblestone road parallel to the busy N-13 (signposted Arão) past •*Café A Toca* to turn <left at the Capela do Senhor de **Bonfim [0.7]** and down past the •**Casa do Diogo** © 251 822 306 in **Arão [0.5 km]** turning down right> with roadside cross, lavandero and •*fonte* (left) into rua da Cruz continuing along asphalt road, past •*Café* under **rail [0.6 km]** to veer right across the modern outskirts of Valença, passing the bus station and turning up <left into Valença by rail bridge up to main **roundabout [1.1 km]** *Largo da Trapicheira* and:

2.9 km **Valença Option.** The bridge into Tui and Spain lies straight ahead with the first Spanish albergue only (3.1 km distant) or up to the left along Av. Bombeiros Voluntários is the last pilgrim hostel in Portugal •**Albergue de São Teotónio** © 918 234 938 *(not to be confused with the luxury Pousada São Teotónio in the old fort)* with 40 beds and all modern facilities (photo right).

The Portuguese hostel adjoins the fire station *Bombeiros* on the roundabout directly opposite the main entrance to the Fortaleza. The decision is whether to leave Portugal without first seeing the old quarter of Valença and the magnificent Fortaleza. Allow 2 hours to visit and soak up some of the atmosphere with a stroll through the colourful streets and a brief visit to the main historic buildings. The tourist

buses tend to leave around 5 p.m. when the old fort reverts to a more relaxed mode and is a pleasant place for a drink or supper in the evening sunshine.

❏ **Accommodation:** *Posto de Turismo* Av. de Espanha (summer only). There are a number of modern hotels in the new town and several close to the main entrance to the Fortaleza in rua de São Sebastião. •**Hotel Lara** ✆ 251 824 348 single from €35 and adjacent •**Val Flores** ✆ 251 824 106. The best value in the new town is, perhaps, the •**Residencial Rio Minho** in Largo da Estação ✆ 251 809 240 opposite the rail station from €20. •**Pousada de S. Teotonio** ✆ 251 824 392 expensive and disappointing in its stark modernity with single room from €90. For a real treat try the adjacent •**Casa do Poço** ✆ 251 825 235 on Travesa da Gaviarra where a similar price will buy luxury in more authentic surroundings. At the other end of the scale are a variety of rooms to let above the bars and shops in the old quarter. Radio Táxis ✆ 252 822 121. **Rail station** *Estação Caminhos do Ferro* for services to and from Santiago ✆ 252 821 124. Bus *Autocarro* ✆ 251 809 588.

Valença Detour: The main attraction is the huge fortress *Fortaleza* standing guard over the Rio Minho. The narrow cobbled streets are lined with souvenir shops, bars, restaurants, hotels and pensions. It is very busy during the day with bus tours but worth a walk through if you have the energy. Alternatively, stay the night and take a whole day to explore both Valença and Tui. There is

much of interest in both towns and pleasant walks along the Minho. A ferry operated between these border towns until the rail and road bridge was opened in 1886. Occupying an elevated position on the border of Portugal and Spain it has been a major military defensive establishment from the earliest times and more recently modelled on the design of the 17th century military architect Vauban. In 1262 The town received a royal charter from D. Afonso III and was renamed Valença (formerly Contrasta). In 1502 D. Manuel I stayed in the town on his royal pilgrimage to Santiago.

Among the sites worth visiting (see town map) are: ❶ **Portas da Coroada** the main entrance to the fortress town opposite the pilgrim hostel. This leads directly to the tiny ❷ Capela de São Sebastião on the wide Largo Dr. Alfredo Guimarães. Next we come to ❸ **Capela do Bom Jesus** with its harmonious proportions in front of which is the statue to the illustrious son of Valença, S. Teotónio *(and in the square is the popular restaurant •Bom Jesus which serves good value food throughout the day and has an outside terrace that gets the last of the evening sun.)* Down to the right is the alternative way to access (or leave) the fort through ❹ **Porto do Sol** also known as Porto de Santiago. Straight ahead over the dry central moat we come to the inner gate ❺ **Portas do Meio** which leads into the main square ringed with more shops and cafés in the busy *Praça do Republica*. Continue due North to ❻ **Igreja de Santo Estevão** 12th century and the adjoining ❼ **Roman Miliario** dating back to Emperor Claudius c.47 A.D. (National Monument). In the next square is the venerable ❽ **Iglesia Santa Maria dos Anjos** a fine 12th century Romanesque church and adjacent ❾ **Capela da Misercórdia** 18th century with sculpture by master Teixeira Lopes *'O Senhor Morto.'* Beyond this church (left) we find •**Pousada de S. Teotonio** and beyond it the viewpoint over the Minho ❿ **Baluarte do Socorro.** Return to the Capela da Misercórdia and go behind it to the delightfully restored •**Casa do Poço** (photo right) below which is a little used side exit that brings you directly down to the international bridge via stone steps. To access these (to save you having to walk all the way back to the Porto do Sol) take the second *lower* gate out of the fort and make your way down the stone steps which lead to the bridge.

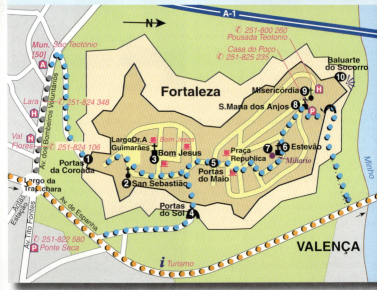

To proceed into Spain *España* from the main roundabout *Largo da Trapicheira* continue down hill passing the tourist kiosk (left) and over the International Bridge into Spain. ***Note:*** *Spain is 1 hour ahead of Portugal and GMT, so you may need to adjust your watch. You will also need to switch from asking directions in Portuguese to Spanish not forgetting that many signposts will now appear in a mixture of Galician* Galego *and* Castellano. *Some similarities remain: esquerda – izquierda, direita – derecha.*

Turn right> *gira a la izquierda* along the main road and right> again at crossroads passing Tui •**Parador** and down to the Rio Miño where we pick up the first of the official markers in Spain – PK 115.454 (unfortunately the camino is changing constantly so these signs, supposedly accurate to 1/100m, can no longer be relied on for accurate distances but are useful as waymarks). It was here at *Praia de Fábrica* that the ferry carrying pilgrims and merchants from Valença would land and this is the Camino starting stage in Spain. You also have an option here:

Option. Instead of the waymarked route up to the main road you can take the path (right) along the river for a delightful 1 km until you reach the steps opposite the marina. Ascend to the Praza da Estrela and on up the rua Bispo Castañon to its intersection with rua S. Telmo and turn <left under the arch to the Church of S.Telmo and then up right> to the entrance to the albergue (situated just below the cathedral). The distance is the same as the waymarked route but you enter along the river instead of the main road.

The waymarked route (left) winds its way up to the cathedral passing a handsome •*fonte* built into the side of the cliff. There is now a steep climb up into Tui onto the main road and turning off right> into the medieval heart of this border town passing the 16th century prison (now the Obradoiro school of Restoration) up to the west door of Tui Cathedral. Pass around the side of the cathedral into Praza do Concello and head down right> past the police station to:

3.1 km Tui •**Albergue** © 619 455 936. The pilgrim hostel occupies a well-restored period building just below the cathedral. 2 main dormitories sleep 40 in bunk beds. Separate ladies and gents toilets and showers. On the ground floor is a large lounge and kitchen / dining area. To the rear is a pleasant open patio with space to wash and dry clothes. Well located in the heart of the historic centre although a nearby nightclub can be noisy at weekends.

TUI: Historical border town with a population of around 15,000. It has a more interesting modern profile than Valença but at its heart is still the well-preserved medieval town. ❶ **Obradoiro** XVIthc the original prison where the date of construction 1584 can still be seen over the door. ❷ **Museo Diocesano** XVIIIthc originally a pilgrims hospice, now the Diocesan office and museum with an interesting display of Celtic, medieval and religious artefacts and well worth the small fee just to savour an original pilgrim hostel with its central courtyard. Here also is the sarcophagus in which lay San Telmo's body after he died at the Bridge of Fevers in 1251 (which we pass on the next stage). On the opposite side of the square *Plaza San Fernando* is Tui's centrepiece the impressive Romanesque cathedral ❸ **Catedral de Santa María** XIIthc dating from 1120 but with later Gothic additions, most notably the fine portico. The cathedral has a handsome cloister, reputedly the only remaining example of a medieval cathedral cloister in Galicia. Off the cloister are steps down to a delightful garden overlooking the Miño (see photo next page) and overlooking the gardens is the medieval tower with access off the far corner of the cloisters (light switch on wall to illuminate the spiral staircase). The interior of the cathedral itself is no less outstanding with a  chapel dedicated to St. James 'the Moor Slayer' *Santiago Matamoros* and an interesting statue to the first black saint from Africa *Sta. Ypiîgenía*.

Below the Cathedral is the chapel of Mercy *Capela de Misericordia* and ❹ **Igrexa de San Telmo** XVthc built over the crypt that housed the relics of S. Telmo. The waymarked route leaves town via the handsome town hall *Concello*, opposite the popular •*Jamonería Jaqueyi* past the •*Café Central* to the evocative Nuns Way *Rua das Monxas* with ❺ **Igrexa Santa Clarisa** XVIIthc (the work of master mason Santiago Domingo de Andrade with fine Baroque altarpiece) and opposite is the **Convento de Clarisas** XVIthc surrounded by the walls of the convent of the enclosed order of nuns of St. Clare *Convento das Clarisas Encerradas*. The waymarked route continues through an arched passage below the convent known as the nuns tunnel *Túnel das Monxas* to leave the medieval city through the *Porta Bergana,* today nothing more than a memory.

If you are staying the night in Tui then take a stroll along the Paseo de Calvo Sotelo may entice you to linger in its lively pavement cafés and bars. At the far end is the handsome 'wild horse' statue with a balcony overlooking the Troncoso gardens built around the old medieval city walls – or take a 'sundowner' on the balcony of the adjoining bar and restaurant. Midway along the Paseo is the 18th century Church of St. Francis.

❏ **Accommodation:** *Turismo* ⓒ 986 601 789 rua Augusto González Besada A walk around the old quarter will reveal a number of discreet signs for beds *camas* from €15. •**Hostal La Generosa** ⓒ 986 600 055 basic and old-fashioned on the busy and central Paseo de Calvo Sotelo single from €20. •**Cafe Scala** ⓒ 986

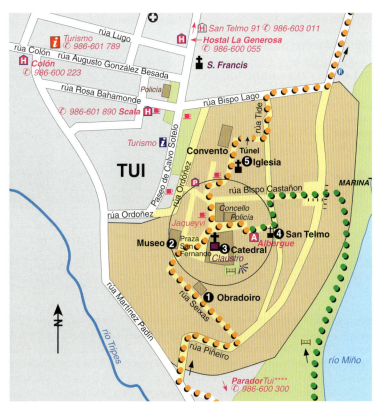

601 890 c/Rua Rosa Bahamonde, 5 above the cafe-restaurant of the same name •**Habitaciones** 627 072 332. •**Hotel Colón** ⓒ 986 600 223 modern rooms from €35. •**Hostal San Telmo** ⓒ 986 603 011 on Av. de la Concordia (past the Jardim Troncoso) and at the lower end of town on the way in (top price bracket) •**Parador de Tui** ⓒ 986 600 300 from €75. There are several restaurants (expensive) in the old town near the cathedral •*O Novo Cabalo Furado* on Praza do Concello is one of the best, but like most restaurants in Spain it doesn't open till 20.00 or later. The adjacent wine bistro •*Jamonería Jaqueyi* has terraced seating in this elegant square. For less expensive fare and earlier options try around Paseo de Calvo Sotelo or •*Cafe Scala* on c/Rua Rosa Bahamonde which serves food all day.

❏ **Death – the last sleep? No, it is the final awakening.** *Walter Scott*

19 *115.4 km (71.7 miles) – Santiago*

VALENÇA / TUI – REDONDELA

▓▓▓▓▓▓	--- ---	6.2	--- ---	20%
▬▬▬▬▬▬	--- ---	19.6	--- ---	63%
▬▬▬▬▬▬	--- ---	5.3	--- ---	17%
Total km		**31.1 km** (19.3 ml)		

▲▲ 32.6 km (+^ 300 m = 1.5 km)
Alto ▲ Alto Cornedo 235 m (771 ft)
<[A] [H]> Porriño 16.2 km / Mos 21.5 km

The Practical Path: Most of this stage is along quiet country roads (63%) and woodland paths that follow the rio Louro valley. There is good shade and several drinking fonts along the way. The challenge today is the stretch of main road both entering and leaving the industrial town of Porriño and the slog through its industrial estates (it also provides a half-way stopover with albergue). The busy N-550 runs parallel to our path and we crisscross it and the railway line several times on our way to Redondela. There is also a steep climb from Mos up the Road of the Knights *Rua dos Cabaleiros* around Monte Cornedo. However, this is rewarded by our first views of the sea since leaving Porto, the beautiful Ría de Vigo. The final part of the day is then all the way downhill into Redondela, an attractive town with good facilities and a superbly restored pilgrim hostel.

❏ **The Mystical Path:** 'when you live your life as though you're already dead, life takes on new meaning. Each moment becomes a whole lifetime, a universe unto itself… Our priorities change; our hearts open, our minds begin to clear of the fog of old holdings and pretendings. We watch all life in transit and what matters becomes instantly apparent: the transmission of love, the letting go of obstacles to understanding, the relinquishment of our grasping, of our hiding from ourselves.' Who Dies? *Stephen and Ondrea Levine*

❏ **Personal Reflections:** "… around me everything is silent but for the babbling of the brook whose waters make their way inexorably back to the ocean. The isolated cross marks the spot of a saint's death and the inner silence is broken with thoughts of death and dying. Like the busy waters of the brook, I too, will return to the Source. My body, like the Earth's, is already half way through its physical lifespan. Body and Earth, both will dissolve back into the dust from which they were made. Only what is perfect and formless is eternal and created by the Love of God. All else is impermanent and ephemeral. How could I ever have believed that God created what was transitory? Even the sun will die…"

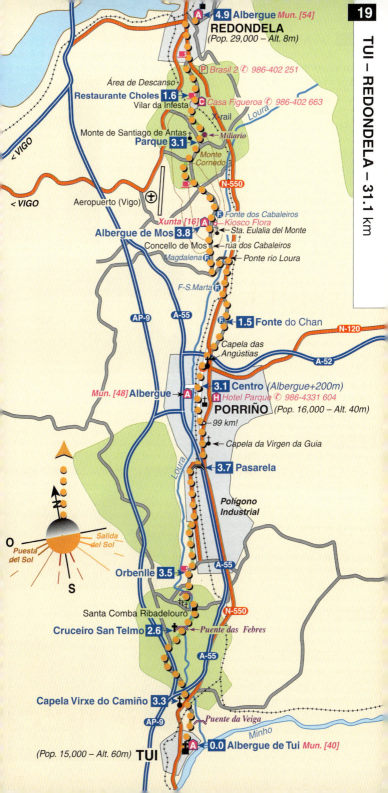

0.0 km **Tui Albergue** Leaving the hostel in Tui turn <left up the steps and right> into Praza do Concello veering right> by •*Café Central* into rua das Monxas past the convent of the St. Clares *Convento das Clarisas* and through the nun's tunnel *Túnel das Monxas (photo right)* turning down rua Antero Rubín to the ancient •*fonte* (right – below the overpass) to the 14th century **Convento Sto. Domingo [0.7 km]** *(the Dominicans have been associated with this site since 1330).* Continue past the adjoining *Museo Municipal* under the archway (simulating an earlier medieval gateway) turning right> (sign Praia da Areeira) into Praza San Bartolomé one of the oldest suburbs of Tui with the 11th century Romanesque monastic church of St. Bartholomew **San Bartolomé de Rebordáns [0.6 km].** *(Recent excavations in the area have unearthed Roman and Visigothic ruins. The finely carved cruceiro dates from 1770).*

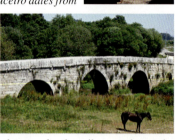

We now leave the town behind us turning down onto a path continuing to the medieval bridge *(photo right)* over the rio Louro **Ponte da Veiga [0.6 km]** which we don't cross but turn <left onto a wide earth track (waymark 112.761) along the ancient Via Romana XIX. The camino is somewhat obscure here and has been realigned (to avoid having to cross rail tracks) and now does a wide loop *under* the railway and over the main road [!] **N-550 [1.1 km]** (sign to Rebordáns) to the Virgin of the Way **Chapel [0.3 km].**

3.3 km **Capela da Virxe do Camiño.** The camino now crosses *over* the new motorway A-55 where a red asphalt 'pilgrim' track replaces the earth path but at least it has an attractive timber covered safety barrier. We follow this all the way *under* the A-9 **[1.8 km]** and 200m later we turn right> **[0.2 km]** [!] back *over* the motorway to enter a densely wooded section that is low-lying and can be wet and muddy after rain to emerge at an isolated glade by the river and wayside **cross [0.6 km].**

2.6 km **Cruceiro San Telmo** – also known as the bridge of Fevers *Ponte das Febres.* Here San Telmo fell sick and died of a fever in 1251 on his way back from a pilgrimage to Santiago de Compostela. A cross marks this mournful spot *Aqui enfermo de Muerte San Telmo Abril 1251*. Turn <left over the bridge along a woodland path parallel to the river (there are several local walking routes around the river valley but stick to the yellow arrows to avoid confusion). We wind our way up

onto the asphalt road through a straggling hamlet up to **A Magdalena [1.8 km]** recognisable by the roadside crosses marking the Calvario de la Magdalena to the church of Santa Columba de Ribadelouro. *[Note: 100m right off route •café – often closed]* turning <left by cruceiros and then immediately right> down onto a path to cross over the river again via a medieval stone **bridge [0.3 km]**. Shortly afterwards the scars of the open cast mines of Porriño appear on the horizon warning us of the intense industrial activity ahead. We continue along a quiet country road to a extensive village square **[1.4 km]** in:

3.5 km Orbenlle •*Bar O Novo Cazador* and a welcoming •*Café* less obvious but directly ahead. This is the last chance to fortify us for the long and soulless trek through the industrial park that awaits around the corner. We now enter the industrial estates *polígono industrial de Porriño (based largely on the cutting and sanding of the pink granite from the quarries in the surrounding hills)* and make our way up the dauntingly straight industrial avenues (the concrete surfaces can be alleviated somewhat by using the grass verges and one section of track – left of the road (see photo right) alongside the nature reserve *Refuxio de Fauna)* to:

3.7 km Pasarela cross the footbridge (photo right) over the rail line then under motorway flyover along the N-550 past the chapel to the Virgin of the Way *Capela A Virxe da Guía* **[1.6 km]** turning <left at next traffic lights **Semáforo [0.5 km]** (waymark 99.408!) over rio Couro into Porriño town centre passing the 16th century Capela San Sebastian with •*fonte* (right) and Capela San Benito and •*fonte* (left) past the Igreja Santa María into the main street *la calle principal Ramón González* and past the impressive stone façade of the Casa Consistorial to the central fountain *Fonte y Parque do Cristo* and the steps leading up to the Igreja Bom Cristo (right) and s/o past the minerals museum *Museo Municipal de Minerals* to the central roundabout *Praza Central*. Plaza **[1.0 km]**:

3.1 km Porriño Option •Albergue To access the pilgrim hostel (300m) turn <left down Av. Buenos Aires over the rail line and river Louro to the modern purpose built hostel overlooking the river and park. (Immediately to the rear is the noisy A-55 motorway). 48 bunk beds in 2 dormitories with all modern facilities kitchen and lounge overlooking the river.

❏ **Other accommodation** includes: •**Hostal Louro** ✆ 986 330 048 on Av. Buenos Aires. •**Hotel Azul** ✆ 986 330 032 on rua Ramiranes the central •**Hotel Parque** ✆ 986 331 604 on Servando Ramilo, off the Parque Cristo. The central area has a multitude of bars and restaurants. Porriño is a sprawling industrial town of 15,000 sandwiched between the río Louro and the steep cliffs to the east where granite quarries provide much of the raw material for the intense industrial activity. It is crossed by the main line rail, the N-550 and 2 motorways, the Autovía del Atlántico A-55 and the Autovía de las Rias Baixas A-52. To continue (from the central roundabout in Porriño) keep s/o

Porriño *Casa Consistorial*

along rua Ramiranes passing the rail station (left) and cross over [!] the main roundabout by the Capela das Angustias •*fonte* under **motorway [0.8 km]** and up to a small hamlet with •*fonte* **[0.7 km]**.

1.5 km **Fonte do Chan** *(rest area with giant granite boulder that forms a dedication to local mountaineers and the first Galician to summit Mount Everest)*. Continue back down again to cross the busy **N-550 [0.4 km]** which we have to join for several short stretches. *(Note: A short detour along the Via XIX crosses the rail line here* [!] *and rejoins the official route beyond the timber yard where the Via XIX veers off up left again to rejoin the main route at Mos)*. Continue along the left verge of the N-550 under rail bridge and past the petrol station and shop (opposite side of the road) to turn off <left for a brief respite and refreshment at the •*Fonte de Santa Marta* **[1.2 km]** to emerge once more onto the N-550 before finally turning off <left to cross **Ponte Rio Loura [0.5 km]** which we cross for the last time (local river walk right). Continue s/o up along a quiet asphalt road passing a picnic area and •*Fonte Magdalena* **[0.7 km]** and shortly afterwards we pass new school building *Concello de Mos* as we start the steep climb up the road of the Knights *rua dos Cabaleiros* over crossroad into the part pedestrianised hill village of Mos past the Iglesia de Santa Eulalia del Monte and the newly renovated Pazo de Mos to arrive at the pilgrim hostel **[1.0 km]**.

3.8 km **Mos** •**Albergue** *Casa Blanca* maintained by the local association *asociación vecinal* with 16 bunk beds and all facilities including kitchenette. The key is held by Flora in the welcoming •*Cáfe Flora* opposite she also provides simple meals and a shop. Continue up passing •*Fonte dos Cabaleiros* to •*Cáfe-Bar Victoria* **[0.8 km]** alternating between

road and path through woodland climbing all the time to reach our high point of this stage (235m) at Monte de Santiago de Antas and extensive park **[2.3 km]**

3.1 km **Parque** with chapel dedicated to *Santiago Caballero* his mounted image carved above the door *Capela de Santiaguiño de Antas* 50m off route to our right and 50m further on •*cáfe* on the main road. We now start our long descent towards the Ria Vigo which lies hidden by the woodland around Monte

Cornedo but we can hear the aeroplanes landing at Vigo airport only 2 km to the West. We pass a Roman milestone *Marco Miliário* marking the military route Via XIX – evidence that we are directly on the original pilgrim way to Santiago. Shortly afterwards we pass O Loureiro and Vilar •*Pastelería O Parque* **[0.8 km]** and •**Casa Figueroa** **[0.5 km]** ⓒ 986 402 663 turn <left **[0.3 km]** to:

1.6 km **Restaurante** •*Churrasquería Choles* we now alternate between path and road through woodland with our first (distant) views of the Ria de Vigo as we descend to a small rest area *Área de Descanso* and follow a maze of small country lanes very steeply **[!]** down to level out where the AVE rapid rail from Vigo to A Coruna crosses (up to our right is •**Pension Brasil 2** ⓒ 986 402 251 and we continue to the busy main road N-550 **[3.6 km]** •*cáfes* to junction **[0.6 km]** and veer right> signposted Redondela town centre and continue to major junction with pilgrim hostel straight ahead **[0.7 km].**

4.9 km **Redondela**•**Albergue** beautifully restored pilgrim hostel was originally a 16th century manor tower house *Casa da Torre*. 54 places in bunk beds with ample modern male and female toilets and shower rooms. As if to compensate for its tiny kitchenette, it has an enormous lounge area with extensive books and magazines on the camino. There is a council library upstairs and some museum pieces including a splendidly preserved Roman Miliário. The albergue is located just off the main

paseo and alongside a culvert of the río Pexeiro and provides an atmospheric and welcoming environment, somewhat diminished by the proximity of the busy traffic roundabout.

❏ **Accommodation**: There are no other hotels in the town but limited hotels on the outskirts include: •**Pension Brasil 2** ⓒ 986 402 251 Quintela 1.9 km back along the N-550, 13 rooms from €27. Directly on the camino 3.1 km out of town (see next stage) •**Hostal Jumboli** ⓒ 986 402 251. •**Hotel Antolín** ⓒ 986 495 409 from €30 single on the beach at Outeiro das Penas, Cesantes 3.9 km overlooking the Isla de San Simón.

Redondela Town: built at the top end of the ría de Vigo but not visible from the town itself. The albergue is located in the centre 100m from the lively •*cafés bars and restaurants* lining the paseo while adjoining the albergue is the popular up-market restaurant •*O Migas*. The 15th century **Iglesia de Santiago** is located up the cobbled rua do Adro only 200m from the albergue and just off the waymarked route. The church is very emblematic of the camino with a statue of Santiago Matamoros above the equally fine rose window circled with shells and other Santiago motifs. There is a regular mass at 8.30 p.m. (check times at the hostel).

❏ *Words are but symbols of symbols and therefore twice removed from reality.* A.C.I.M.

---

20 84.3 km (52.4 miles) – Santiago

REDONDELA – PONTEVEDRA

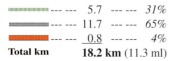

▬▬▬▬▬ --- ---	5.7 --- ---	*31%*
▬▬▬▬▬ --- ---	11.7 --- ---	*65%*
▬▬▬▬▬ --- ---	0.8 --- ---	*4%*
Total km	**18.2 km** (11.3 ml)	

▲ 20.0 km (+^ 360 m = 1.8 km)
Alto ▲ Alto da Lomba 153 m (502 ft)
< Ⓐ Ⓗ > Arcade 6.9 km

The Practical Path: We now encounter an interesting stage along the coastal inlet of the Ría de Pontevedra. We start at sea level then climb up through mixed forest around the Alto de Lomba before dropping down again to the sea at Arcade and Pontesampaio, both of which offer the opportunity for safe swimming (with beach showers). We then start the 2nd uphill stretch of the day to climb the ancient stone paths of the Verea Vella da Canicouva to the next high point around the Cruceiro Cacheiro before descending finally to the provincial capital of Pontevedra. The route is delightfully varied with several drinking fonts and cafés and shops to buy refreshments and a third is along paths through woodland offering shade and tranquillity. The remainder is largely along quiet country lanes, apart from a brief but dangerous uphill stretch of the N-550 into Arcade. Note that the modern and well-equipped pilgrim hostel is 1½ kilometres *this* side of the town centre in Pontevedra.

❏ **The Mystical Path:** 'Words will mean little now ... we seek direct experience of truth alone. For we wait in quiet expectation of our God and Father. We have come far along the road, and now we wait for Him. We look ahead, and fix our eyes upon the journey's end.' A Course In Miracles. *Workbook Part II Intro.*

❏ **Personal Reflections:** "I surround myself in the silence of nature endeavouring to empty my mind of its constant stream of thought. To write these reflections I must engage my mind. I will close this notebook and I will wait… and see."

0.0 km **Albergue** Leaving the hostel in Redondela head into rua Isidoro Quemalinos past the narrow connecting street (right) which leads to rua do Adro and the Church of Santiago pass under the rail viaduct and over the **N-550 [0.7 km]** at the 18th century Capela de Santa Mariña / Capela das Angustias (right). We now follow a narrow asphalt road into Cesantes veering right> up into **rua de Torre [1.4 km]** and shortly after turn <left onto path just over rail line. We now make our way up to the **N-550 [1.0 km]** to:

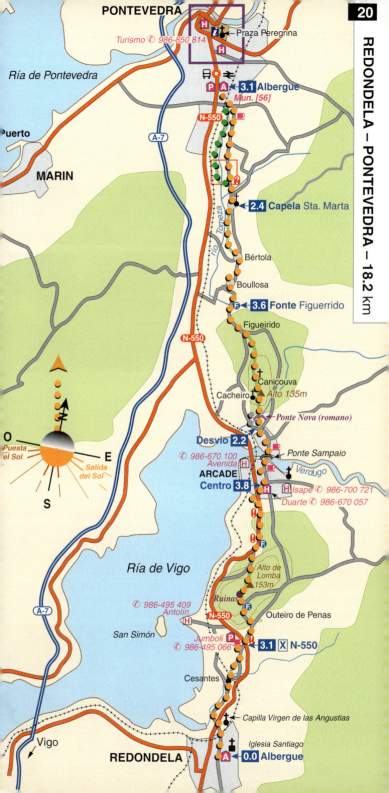

3.1 km N-551 •Hostal Jumboli ✆ 986 495 066 rooms from €15 and •*café* on main road serving early breakfast. Cross the busy N-550 [!] and turn up steeply <left **[0.4 km]** to •*fonte* **[0.2 km]** with motifs of the pilgrimage and cool water to refresh after the steep climb. Just above the drinking font turn off <left onto a forest track through the eucalyptus woods around *Outeiro de Penas* passing the ruins of an ancient wayside Inn **[0.7 km]** *Hostal da Malaposta* to reach the high point of this stage Alto de Lomba (155m). The otherwise peaceful surroundings disturbed by occasional air traffic on the flight path to Vigo. Views over the distant ría de Vigo and its iconic bridge now open up as we descend back to the **main road [1.3 km]** •*fonte* (right). We now join the N-550 for a noisy and dangerous [!] 700m stretch (take extra care as the verge is narrow, unprotected and on a bend) to arrive at the Arcade tourist kiosk *turismo* **[0.7 km]** (summer only). The waymarked route turns <left off the main road for a short circuitous detour past *Fonte do Lavandeira* (*not* drinking water) and back to the main road, which we cross over again **[0.5 km]** to:

3.8 km Arcade •Hotel Duarte ✆ 986 670 057 single from €15. We now make our way down the narrow rua Barronoas through Cimadevila to crossroads with **rua Rosalia de Castro** ❖ **[0.7 km]** •*Café Flora* and •*mini-mercado* at this point the waymarked route proceeds s/o and we have various options in this small seaside town with several hotels, shops, cafés, restaurants and beaches.

Detour Arcade: ●●●●● **[1]** To access •Hotel Isape [0.8 km] ✆ 986 700 721 single from €25 and popular bar and restaurant. *Directions:* ❖ turn right and up right again into Av. Xosé Salla [200m] and take the first left into rua Escalinata de Soutomaior [300m] up to the church of St. James *Iglesia de Santiago de Arcade* (see photo below) with viewing platform overlooking the ponte Verdugo – opposite the church is Isape, the quietest hotel location in Arcade. **[2]** To access •Hotel Avenida [0.4 km] ✆ 986 670 100 on the main road with modern rooms from €30 single. *Directions:* ❖ Turn left and then right at traffic lights [100m] over rail line [100m] to hotel [200m]. **[3]** To access the beach for safe swimming *Directions:* ❖ Turn left s/o at traffic lights [100m] past taxi rank and over rail line [100m] to roundabout near the seafront [200m] with statue to a shell fisher-woman *Mariscadora* pass the popular and in-expensive bar and restaurant •*O Recreo* (mariscos) to the sandy beach *Praia do Peirao* with beach showers. Along the main street in Arcade are several seafood restaurants including the Michelin recommended •*Restaurant Arcadia*.

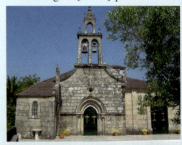

STAGE 20: 171

To continue on the waymarked route ❖ keep s/o and make your way through *A Calle* to **Pontesampaio [0.4 km]** the handsome stone bridge over the río Verdugo built in 1795 over earlier foundations *(it was here that local militia inflicted a significant rout on Napoleon's troops during the War of Independence, witnessed by a memorial at the far side).*

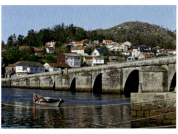

A delightful spot for a rest with a fine sandy beach for swimming (beach and showers over the bridge right). **(Detour:** ● ● ● ● ● *to view the 13ᵗʰ century Romanesque Igrexa Santa María de Pontesampaio continue up the main road for 300m).* The waymarked route now branches off steeply <left just past the memorial and •*café-bar* to take a detour away from the main road passing the *cruceiro de Ballota* and winding its way up and down again before crossing back over the main road **[1.1 km].**

2.2 km **Desvio** *[A 500m detour over a road bridge maybe in operation here to avoid the original bridge which was destroyed in recent floods].* Unless the river is in spate it easy to follow the original route and cross the rio Ulló by the remains of the medieval bridge **A Ponte Nova** *(built on Roman remains as this was part of the calzada Romana XIX)* and continue up the far side by picnic area in the woodland glade to wind back up to the side of a fish farm **[0.5 km]** where the temporary detour joins from the left. Continue up the ancient stone paved pilgrim way *Verea Vella da Canicouva* up to the crossroads and wayside cross *cruxeiro Cacheiro*. This section alternates between paths and quiet country lanes and just past the hamlet of Boullosa we begin to descend towards Bértola and Pontevedra and

here on our right we can refresh ourselves at a •*fonte* **[3.1 km]:**

3.6 km **Fonte de Montes de Figueirido**. Drinking font and picnic area by side of the road. We alternate again between quiet asphalt roads and green pathways until we enter the municipal area of Pontevedra *Concello de Pontevedra* at Capela da Sta. Marta **[2.2 km]** and proceed up to the main road where we turn left over rio Pobo towards Pontevedra and option for riverside walk **[0.2 km].**

2.4 km **Tio Tomeza / Option**. From here the waymarked route is all by the side of the busy main road into Pontevedra. However there is a wonderful alternative route (yellow and white signs) along treelined river valley all the way to the outskirts of the city 200m from the pilgrim hostel. This alternative is highly recommended where birdsong song replaces the the noise of traffic.

Alternative River Route to Albergue 4.2 km: ● ● ● ● ● Turn <left at sign for Ponte Rebón s/o over bridge and turn <left onto path into woodland and right> over the river **[0.5 km]** which we now follow north all the way into Pontevedra. This shaded river route crosses several small tributaries and is well maintained with panels explaining the names of the trees and areas we pass through. Continue over lane (new railink under construction) by the Ponte da Condesa **[1.3 km]** passing the Poza da Moura (mill race) and the Ponte Valentín **[0.8 km]** up to (but not over) railway and under road bridge tunnel **[0.7 km]** and then under rail bridge tunnel **[0.2 km]** to rejoin the waymarked route on the main road where we turn left up to the Albergue in Pontevedra **[0.2 km]**.

For the waymarked route continue s/o along the main road to •*Casa Mella café-restaurante* **[2.5 km]** continue s/o over the Avenida de Marco at traffic lights. The traffic now intensifies as we enter the suburbs of Pontevedra, turning up <left at roundabout to •**Hostal Peregrino** Ⓒ 606 794 890) where directly opposite is a ramp up to the hostel **[0.6 km]**:

3.1 km **Pontevedra** *South* •**Albergue**
Modern pilgrim hostel Ⓒ 986 844 045 somewhat incongruously sandwiched between road and rail line, adjoining the main rail station and opposite the bus depot. However, what it lacks in romantic ambience it makes up for in its excellent facilities and warm welcome. 56 bunk beds with ample male and female toilets and showers, extensive  entrance lobby, kitchenette, dining and lounge area. **Note:** the hostel is located 1½ kilometres south of the medieval city centre which the camino passes through on the way to Santiago (see next stage). Depending on arrival time you can visit the city centre after a rest and shower or spend time in the centre on the way through in the morning. The opening hours for the hostel can be inconsistent and somewhat restrictive so another option is to continue to the city centre and find a more central hotel or pension. Allow a leisurely 30-minute walk to the Praza da Peregrina at the start of the old town – alternatively, there are buses or taxis from the rail station or the main bus station opposite. Whatever you do, don't miss exploring this wonderful city with its many fascinating monuments and historic buildings, many of them directly associated with the pilgrimage.

❏ **Turismo** Ⓒ 986 850 814 calle Xeneral Gutierrez Mellado, 3. A tourist kiosk on the Praza España is open during summer. Radio **Taxis** Ⓒ 986 868 585.

❏ **Alternative Accommodation:** All hotels listed are centrally located in or adjoining the old quarter. *(€20-40 individual)* •**Fonda Chiquito** Ⓒ 986 862 192 rua Charino 23. •**Casa O Fidel** Ⓒ 986 851 234 above lively pulpería, rua San Nicolás 7. •**Casa Alicia** Ⓒ 986 857 079 Av. Santa Mariá 5, adj. praza España. •**Casa Maruja** Ⓒ 986 854 901 rua Alta, close to Casa Alicia. •**Hospedaje Penelas** Ⓒ 986 855 705) rua Alta 17. For good location and value try •**Hotel Ruas** Ⓒ 986 846 416 rua do Padre Sarmiento. *(€40-60 individual)* •**Hotel la Peregrina** Ⓒ 986 866 249 rua Eduardo Pondal. In the luxury bracket (good value indulgence from €90) •**Parador Casa del Barón** Ⓒ 986 855 800 a fine

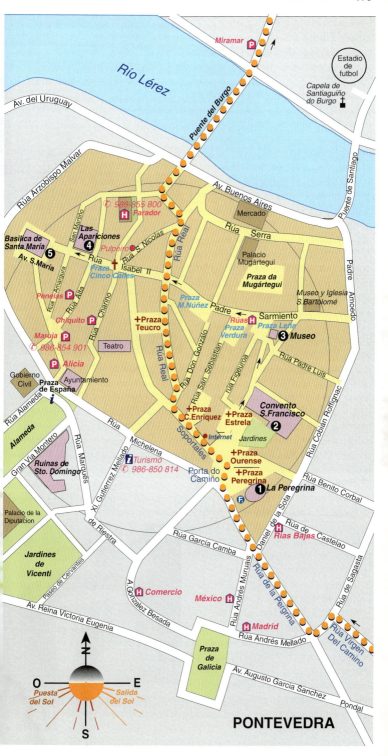

baronial house in the old quarter close to its exit over the Puente del Burgo. The majority of the other accommodation is in expensive modern hotels along the main road from the rail and bus stations such as: •**Hotel Virgen del Camino** ⓒ 986 855 900 directly on the camino. •**Hotel Vedra** on Filgueira Valverde, 10 close to the rail station. There are also 2 reasonably priced hostels on the far side of the river Lérez: the somewhat run-down •**Hostal Miramar** ⓒ 986 851 238 on the busy corner of Av. da Coruña, or the •**Hostal Corinto** ⓒ 986 870 345 rua da Alba-Touceda just off the camino beyond the football stadium.

Pontevedra is the regional capital and a lively commercial and tourist town with a population of 75,000. At the heart of its modern suburbs is a delightful medieval core *zona monumental / barrio Antigo*. The waymarked route follows the original camino *Rua Real* that goes right through the centre of the ancient quarter but the following walking tour takes in most of the historic sites: We approach the centre via ruas Virgen del Camino and Peregrina and the *Porta do Camiño* into 4 interconnecting squares, the first (highest) of which is ✣ *Praza de la Peregrina* and location for the

unequalled elegance of the pilgrim chapel ❶ **Santuario da Peregrina** (photo above). This beautiful 18th century chapel was conceived by the architect Arturo Souto and built in the Baroque style to a floor plan in the shape of a scallop shell – one of the great treasures of the camino. The route leads into ✣ *Praza de Ourense* with its delightful gardens *Xardíns de Castro San Pedro* and cheerful cafés and bars forming part of the nightly *paseo* with the imposing edifice of the 14th century ❷ **Convento de San Francisco** in the background. The lower section of this extensive open area is known as ✣ *Praza da Herrería*✣ and ✣ *Praza de Estrela* which provide an option (recommended) to take a short 100m detour to one of the city's most emblematic squares and best museums ✣ *Praza de Leña* ● ● ● ● ● To take this detour continue past the Convento

de San Francisco and s/o 'out' the far side of Praza de Estrela and turn left directly to the intimate square with its squat granite arcades and central *cruceiro* so typical of Galicia. Several cafés and the hotel Ruas give it a lively atmosphere and here we also find the excellent provincial museum ❹ **Museo de Pontevedra** housed in several adjacent historic buildings with a connecting stone bridge. Casa García Flórez houses exhibits of the famous

jet-black jewellery from Santiago and an interesting collection of images of St. James dating from as early as 12th century. There is also an entire floor dedicated to the famous Galician writer and philosopher Alfonso Castelao who, along with Rosalía de Castro, did so much to preserve the unique Galician culture that we can enjoy today. Return to pick up the camino in Praza da Herrería or continue into rua Padre Sarmiento passing ❖ *Praza da Verdura* and ❖ *Praza Méndez Núñez* (also accessible via the colourful rua de Don Gonzálo (see photo right) either of which leads back to the camino in rua Real.

From Praza da Herrería❖ continue along the waymarked route via the ancient arcaded street *rua dos Soportais* that leads into ❖ *Praza Curros Enríquez* and thence along the ancient Royal Road *Rua Real* passing through ❖ *Praza do Teucro* to its junction with rua Padre Sarmiento (from the museo) which provides another detour (recommended) to visit the cathedral. ● ● ● ● ● To take this detour turn left up rua de Isabel II to ❖ *Praza y Cruceiro das Cinco Ruas* the meeting point of five of the timeworn cobbled lane ways. A magical spot with an intriguing *cruceiro* depicting the temptation of man with a snake coiled around the shaft watching a naked Eve offering the apple to Adam. Continuing up rua de Isabel II we pass ❹ **Santuario da Aparicións** where the Blessed Virgin appeared (again) to sister Lucía and just beyond we arrive at ❺ **Basílica de Santa María A Grande** the celebrated 16th century Basilica dedicated in her name. Either side of the main entrance are statues of the founding fathers of the church, St. Peter and St. Paul, while the rose window portrays the Assumption and Coronation of the Virgin Mary. But the real celebration is the southern façade and the mystery and mastery of Flemish sculptor *Cornielles de Holanda* and the Portuguese artist *João Nobre* together with the stonemasons who created this 'storybook in stone' displaying the unfolding drama of the church ending with the Passion of Christ and the promise of redemption – reminiscent of the craftsmanship that created the Pórtico da Gloria in Santiago cathedral.

If you have followed this itinerary you are probably in need of refreshment. Help is at hand as the cobbled lanes of the old quarter are bursting with *tapas* bars and cafés. Immediately behind the Basilica on the narrow rua Isabel is the atmospheric *O Cortello* with a selection of smoked hams hanging from the ceiling – a reference, perhaps, to its Galician name that translates as pigsty! If you head back towards Praza España along Avenida de Santa María you come to a shaded triangular Praza, site of a medieval Jewish cemetery Lampán dos Xudeus around which are several cafés and pensions and the *Meson Santa María*. Continuing along Avenida St. María you reach ❖ *Praza de España* the main square that divides the modern city from its ancient heart. Here we find the main government buildings, town hall and the Alameda with its array of statues to modern and ancient heroes of España. Here also we find the ruins of the 13th century Igrexa de Santo Domingo – now a national monument. Head back towards the old centre down any of the myriad narrow paved streets back to the Praza das Cinco Ruas with its tempting Taperías offering a local speciality *Zamburiñas* (scallops in garlic) and all watched over, in case you had forgotten, by the cross of temptation and a direct route to the heavenly Parador down rua do Barón *or* turn right and pick up the waymarks to the camino down rua Isabel.

**If you want to become full, let yourself be empty.
If you want to be reborn, let yourself die.** *Lao Tzu*

21 66.1 km (41.1 miles) – Santiago

PONTEVEDRA – CALDAS DE REIS

		7.6			33%
		14.1			61%
		1.4			6%
Total km		**23.1 km** (14.4 ml)			

23.9 km (+^ 160 m = 0.8 km)
Alto ▲ San Amaro 135 m (443 ft)
< A H > Portela 11.5 km (+ 0.5) / Briallos 18.0 km (+ 0.7)

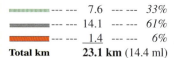
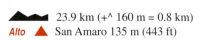

The Practical Path: One third of this stage is along natural pathways through woodland along gentle river valleys which we share with the rail line. We have good shade and several drinking fonts to quench our thirst. Approaching Caldas de Reis we hop on and off the N-550 but the stretches are short and level with good sight lines. However, there are only a few small bars or cafés so it is well to buy some food in Pontevedra to fuel the body through the day and to make a meal if you intend to stay in either of the 2 isolated albergues *off* route – so the choice is lively town or quiet countryside.

0.0 km **Pontevedra Albergue** continue over the roundabout in front of the rail station and take the secondary road *rua do Gorgullón* parallel and below the main road *Avenida Eduardo Pombal* which we cross later into *rua Virxen do Camiño* (Galician spelling) past the hotel Virgen del Camino to continue past the *Glorieta de Compostela* into rua de Peregrina to:

1.5 km **Santuario de la Peregrina**. The camino now continues through the *praza de Ourense* down the arcaded *rua dos Soportais* into the evocative *rua Real* passing the *praza do Teucro* to veer left into the *rua da Ponte* and emerging from the old quarter at the **río Lérez [0.6 km]**. *Here we can see the excavations of the foundations of the original Roman bridge and a replica miliário.* Cross over the busy city ring road [!] over the río Lérez across the Ponte do Burgo into Av. do Coruña and turn <left at the **Banco de Galicia [0.2 km]** into rua Da Santiña, winding our  way through the city suburbs and Pontecabras past a welcome •*fonte* erected by the *Communidades Montes* onto a **track [1.7 km]** Via Romana XIX and under rail **bridge [0.6 km]**. The route now runs parallel to the rail line through the hamlet of Pontecabras for **[0.6 km]** to:

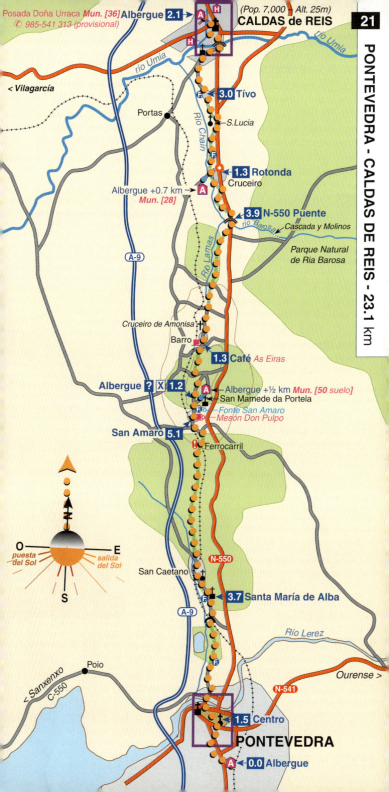

3.7 km Alba / San Caetano •*fonte* Iglesia Santa de María de Alba and pilgrim monument. Continue up past wayside cross and turn <left onto the busy main **road [0.4 km] [!]** with very narrow verge [!] under rail bridge and through Caetano with *Capela San Caetano (right)* veering right> off main road by factory **[0.6 km]** onto country lane turning <left just before railway to pick up the **path [1.2 km]** for a lovely stretch that runs alongside the rail line through eucalyptus woods. In the low-lying sections the path can be wet and the otherwise tranquil setting is somewhat disturbed by the proximity of the A-9 motorway, thankfully out of sight over to our left. We now cross over **rail line [!] [2.3 km]** and up into **San Amaro [0.6 km]**:

5.1 km San Amaro •*Café-Meson Pulpo* small hamlet in the concello de Barro. Just behind the cafe we pass a rest area and •*fonte* **[0.1 km]** continue s/o passing cruceiro de Parada **[0.6 km]** to junction and option **[0.5 km].**

1.2 km Barro / Portela / Option (½ km detour to albergue):

Detour ● ● ● ● ● turn up sharp right> and <left at the Iglesia de San Mamede da Portela and continue to •**Albergue** **[0.5 km]** © 986 711 616 renovated school building with up to 50 mattresses *colchonetas* available in 2 rooms with ample shower and toilet facilities and kitchen / lounge area. This is a quiet location with no nearby shops – the nearest place for food is •Meson Pulpo in San Amaro (1.2 km) or Restaurant •A Eira in Barro (1.3 km).

From the detour junction continue s/o and turn <left on road **[0.5 km]** and right> onto track through woodland and up to road turn right to A Eira **[0.8 km]**.

1.3 km Barro •*Meson A Eira* continue pat the ancient Cruceiro de Amonisa set at a jaunty angle with St. James replete with staff looking towards Compostela *(a mere 52.024 kilometres according to the adjacent wayside marker).* Veer <left by granite blocks and <left again to follow the new railway and turn right> at T-**junction [1.9 km]** over river and <left onto path **[0.3 km]** before emerging onto the **main road [1.7 km]**:

3.9 km N-550 / Option [*Detour* ½ km ● ● ● ● ● *Parque Natural de Río Barossa. To visit the impressive cascades and mill buildings cross the main road and head up directly for ½ km to viewpoint].* To continue along the camino turn <left along the N-550 over the river Barossa turning <left onto one of several short (but welcome) sections of path through vineyards that run parallel to the road. Continue to junction with signpost for detour to the albergue in Briallos just short of the major road roundabout.

1.3 km Rotonda / Option (¾ km detour to •**Albergue**):

Detour ¾ km ● ● ● ● ● •**Albergue**
Follow the signs along a quiet country road to this excellent modern albergue with the welcoming Pilar. 28 bed spaces in 2 rooms with extensive modern showers and toilet accommodation and large kitchen and dining area and upstairs lounge. Note: Caldas de Reis is 5 km further on and there are no shops or restaurants in the immediate area.

Continue on a track (left) alongside the main road, past •*fonte* to join the main road again for a short but busy stretch before turning off <left onto a path by the **capela Santa Lucia [0.6 km]** the path meanders into the río Chaín valley into the delightful hamlet of **Tívo [2.2 km]** where we can refresh at:

3.0 km **Tívo** •*fonte* At the far end of this peaceful hamlet we find a welcome drinking font watched over by a wayside cross •*café* (50m off route). Continue along quiet country road onto an asphalt path to rejoin the main road veering off <left immediately beyond the roadside church Iglesia de Santa Maria into rua Santa Marta to rejoin the N-550 to the **bridge [1.6 km]** over the río Umia into Caldas de Reis with hotel and spa *balneario* •**Acuña** (left) opposite the Ayuntamiento and Policía Local. Cross the stone bridge with the entrance to the renowned •*Taberna O Muiño* (right – below the arches). The waymarked camino now turns <left at Banco Pastor into rua Laureano Salgado to the *balneario* •**Hotel Dávila** which has a public fountain in front **fonte caldas [0.1 km]** where the famous hot waters pour out so you can soothe your feet (for free – see photo) and the

extensive park overlooked by the impressive parish church of St. Thomas à Becket *Iglesia parroquial de Santo Tomás de Canterbury*! which marks the historic and commercial ● **centre of town**. To continue to the new pilgrim hostel proceed along the principal pedestrian street with its granite colonades (part of the original camino) *rua Real* to cross [!] the busy calle de Juan Fuentes Echvarria **[0.2 km]** and cross the emblematic medieval stone bridge •*fonte* over the rio Bermaña with several pleasant •*cafés* and bars overlooking the river and surrounding the square to the adjacent new pilgrim hostel (left) **[0.2 km]**:

2.1 km **Caldas de Reis** •**Albergue** *Posada Doña Urraca* © 986-541 313 provisional municipal hostel opened in 2010 with 36 places and all facilities immediately over Bermaña bridge (back left) close to all amenities.

Caldas de Reis (Reyes) with a population of 10,000 is neatly contained between the ríos Umia and Bermaña. The history of Caldas is inextricably linked to its thermal waters that have gushed from its ground source at a constant 40 degrees for millennia. Inhabited by early Celtic tribes it became a major spa *Aquae Celenae* on the Via Romana XIX. Under Christian authority it became the bishopric of Celenis, transforming itself into Rex Calda during the Reconquest *Reconquista*. King Alfonso VII, son of Queen Doña Urraca was born here – it was later to become the birthplace of hydro electricity in Galicia during the industrial era. Today Caldas de Reis continues to benefit from its waters as a major health spa. It also has delightful botanical gardens *xardín botánicas* planted along the shaded banks of the river Umia located just beyond the Library *Turismo* off Av. Román López. The parish church *igrexa parroquial Sto. Tomás* commands a central position in town and was built in 1890 from the stone salvaged from the medieval castle where Alphonso VII was born. Rest your feet in the hot spring •*fonte* drink the cool waters in the •*fonte* on the Ponte Romano – or if

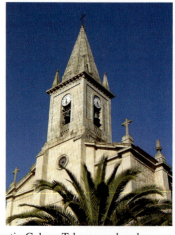

you want something stronger try an authentic Galego Taberna and make your way to •*Taberna O'Muiño* © 986 540 225 by the bridge on the way in to town where you can eat inexpensively with the locals down by the river.

❏ **Alternative Accommodation:** *Turismo* © 986 539 025 (summer only) Av. Román López. •**Hostal Lotus** © 986 540 602 Av. Dolores Mosquera 27 (the main street) 31 rooms from €25 – rooms at the back have balconies overlooking the Ponte Romano (reception in Café Lotus opposite). •**Hotel O Cruceiro** © 986 540 165 west of the main square, just over the rio Bermaña on rua Juan Fuentes 44 – welcoming hotel with 30 rooms from €20. Close by at number 99 is the more expensive •**Hotel Sena** © 986 540 596. Amongst the centrally located spa hotels *balneario* are: •**Dávila** © 986 540 012 rua Laureano Salgado 12. Founded in 1780 but recently modernised with gardens to the rear and offering 27 rooms from €40. • **Acuña** © 986 540 010 rua Herrería 2 (by the bridge on the way in) also recently refurbished. A wide choice of Bars, cafes and restaurants sprawl out along the town pavements and along the riverbanks.

CALDAS DE REIS

❏ Emptiness which is conceptually liable to be mistaken for nothingness is in fact the reservoir of infinite possibilities. *Daisetz Teitaro Suzuki*

22 *43.0 km (26.7 miles) – Santiago*

CALDAS DE REIS – PADRÓN

▬▬▬▬ --- ---	9.1 --- ---	49%
▬▬▬▬ --- ---	8.7 --- ---	49%
▬▬▬▬ --- ---	0.3 --- ---	2%
Total km	**18.1 km** (11.2 ml)	

19.4 km (+^ 260 m = 1.3 km)
Alto ▲ Cortiñas 160 m (525 ft)
<🅰 🅷> Carracedo 4.9 km (+100m)

The Practical Path: Half of this stage is on natural pathways through mature woodland. Facilities are limited on this relatively short stage but there is a choice of pensions and cafes just *off* route – fill up with water as you pass the few drinking fonts. The route takes us along two river valleys, firstly the Bermaña and then a gentle climb up Cortiñas (the high point of this stage) before dropping down sharply into the Valga valley. From there we have another gentle climb up to a viewing point above the industrial suburbs of Pontecesures before dropping down finally to cross the río Ulla to pick up its small tributary the río Sar into Padrón. There are only two short stretches of main road, firstly leaving Caldas de Reis and as we enter Padrón over the bridge at Pontecesures. Otherwise the route is split between natural pathways and quiet country roads – enjoy.

0.0 km **Caldas de Reis** Leaving the albergue in the centre of town pass the *Capilla de San Roque* turn up <left on the main road and down right> onto path where we head along the gentle Bermaña river valley under viaduct **[1.0]** through woodland to crossroads on the busy **[!]** N-550 in **Carracedo [3.9].**

4.9 km **Cruce/N-550**•*Café Esperon* with •*Parrillada Antonio* and •**Habitaciones** ⓒ 986 534 260 with 11 rooms up to the left (100m *off* route). Continue s/o the N-550 **[!]** to iglesia Santa Mariña de Carrecedo with adjoining cruceiro and extensive plaza with bandstand **[0.5 km]** and •*fonte* (often dry in summer). Continue up through *As Cortiñas* and over **[!]** **N-550 [1.3 km]** onto pathway running alongside the motorway, which we cross after **[1.2 km]**:

3.0 km **A-9 Puente** (•*Café Pardal s/o 70m off route*) turn right> immediately

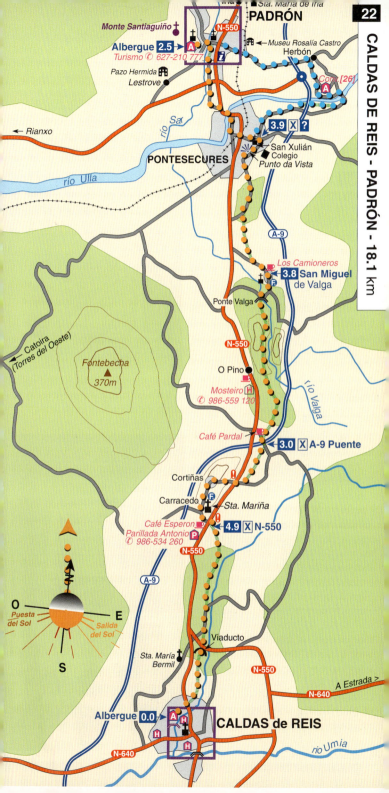

over motorway down onto path between the N-550 and the A-9 through woodland passing sign to hotel Mosteiro climbing to the rear of the small hamlet *O Pino* on the **N-550 [1.3 km]** (•*Bar Los Camioneros on main road 100m off route and* •**Hotel Mosteiro** © 986 559 120 *with 16 rooms from €20.*) This is the high point of this stage at 160m and the camino now descends a steep path passing rest area with pond **[0.4 km]** through dense woodland with the río Valga down to our right to **bridge [1.4 km]** with resting platform over the river to join the country lane into the village of San Miguel •*fonte* (right) **[0.5 km]** passing the parish church of San Miguel and up to shop and bar **[0.2 km]**.

3.8 km **San Miguel de Valga** •*Café-Autoservicío San Miguel* (right) before turning <left onto path after which we cross and re-cross a series of country roads through the hamlets of Pedreira, Cimadevila •*fonte* **[0.6 km]** and Fontela but the camino is well signposted and finally we start to climb to a viewpoint adjoining a school and sports hall *escuela y polideportiva* **[2.7 km]**. Here we have a good view over the industrial area and harbour of Pontesecures on the río Ulla with the town of Padrón built along the banks of the río Sar (a tributary of the Ulla) just beyond. We now continue down the rua Coengos to pass the 12th century Romanesque church of San Xulián •*fonte* to T-junction **[0.6 km]**.

3.9 km **Cruce Opción** Turn <left for the main waymarked route directly to Padrón or turn right> for an alternative route to the monastery in Herbón.

The alternative route to •**Albergue** in the ancient and peaceful surroundings of the Convento de Herbón (3.1 km) is for individual pilgrims seeking a more contemplative time under the care and hospitality of this originally Franciscan monastery. Communal dinner following mass at 20:00. Breakfast at 07:30 with mass at 08:00. The hostel is run by volunteers from the Galician pilgrim society (AGACS) and is temporarily housed in a block at the rear with entrance from a discreet door in the top terrace. 22 individual bunk spaces (no groups) in one dormitory with basic facilities. ***Directions***: Follow *red* arrows to Cortiñas and turn back sharp left **[1.0 km]** onto overgrown path down to and along river to cross bridge **[1.4 km]** back along far side of river up to monastery **[0.7 km]**. Yellow arrows mark the way back to Padrón by road to the town centre a distance of 2.6 km.

To continue on the waymarked route turn <left cross railway and take tunnel under main road and proceed to the bridge with statue of Santiago leaning on his staff and •*Café la Marina* and the recently restored •**Casa do Rio** (50m left). Cross the río Ulla in Pontesecures and at the far end of the **bridge [0.4 km]** veer <left (don't stay on the main road which is narrow and busy). We now make our way up a quiet country lane turning right> along the banks of the **río Sar [0.6 km]** under C-550 ring road and into the outskirts of Padrón at the main market square **[0.9 km]** public toilets (left). Waymarks now split and point either along the rua de Castelao but you can avoid the traffic by continuing s/o along the river Sar (replica Padron on the far bank) by shaded *paseo* lined with plane trees to the heart of Padrón with the handsome statue of her most famous daughter and illustrious poetess, Rosalía de Castro with the church of St. James behind *Igrexa de Santiago* **[0.4 km]**. To make your way to the pilgrim hostel turn <left over the bridge **[!]** (narrow medieval bridge also used by traffic). Cross over the road **[!]** (blind bend) and the hostel is just behind the *fuente del Carmen* just below the Convento do Carmen perched on its rocky promontory above **[0.2 km]**.

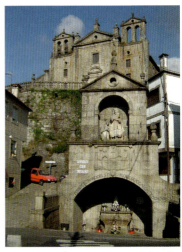

Fuente del Carmen Convento (above)

2.5 km Padrón •**Albergue** ✆ 666 202 863 here below the convent is the pilgrim hostel with 48 bunk bed spaces in one large dormitory with separate room for invalid use. There are ample male and female shower and toilet facilities and a small kitchen area with patio off. The impressive edifice of the adjacent 18th century Carmelite monastery lie above and the climb up offers good views over the river Sar and town.

❏ **Turismo:** ✆ 981 811 550 Av. Compostela. ❏ **Hoteles:** (from €20+ single) •**Hostal Turnes** ✆ 981 810 726 on upper floors of modern apartment block adjacent to the market *mercado* in Campo do Souto adjacent to •**Hostal Flavia** ✆ 981 810 455. •**Hostal Grilo** ✆ 981 810 607 Av. Camilo José Cela. (From €30+ single) •**Hostal Jardín** ✆ 081 810 950 period town house Av. da Estación opposite the Botanical gardens. •**Hostal Cuco** ✆ 981 810 511 modern building on Av. de Compostela. •**Hotel Chef Rivera** ✆ 981 811 454 Travesia Enlace Parque opposite the tourist office (good restaurant). •**Hotel Rosalía** ✆ 981 812 490 modern hotel just past the Rosalía museum by the rail station. Beyond Iria Flavia in Pazos •**Hotel Scala** ✆ 981 811 500. ❏ **Restaurantes:** •*O'Pementeiro* in Praza do Castro (specialising in the Padrón peppers *Pimientos*). •*O Santiaguiño* Praza de Macias (pulpo and mariscos). Wide selection of cafés and bares.

Padrón Town: 20 kilometres South of Santiago is where we find the legendary starting point of James ministry in Spain and also the subsequent return of his mortal remains following his martyrdom in Jerusalem that are considered to lie in the reliquary at the heart of Santiago cathedral. Padrón is a delightful town built along the banks of the rivers Sar and Ulla and essentially an 'extension' of Iria Flavia. The latter being the original seat of the bishops of Galicia before it was transferred to Santiago de Compostela. The varied attractions of this historical town include: ❶ **Igrexa de Santiago.** This Romanesque church dates back to the time of Bishop Xelmírez but has been extended many times since and the present structure is rather sombre in appearance. Inside is one of the great Jacobean treasures for here, below the altar, is the original stone *O Pedrón* from which the town takes its name. You may need to ask for the partition to be rolled back and the light switched on for you to see the stone itself. While legends abound, the most consistent is that this is the mooring post to which the boat carrying

James the Apostle tied up to the quayside along the river bank here. And, just as St. James relics in Santiago were covered over with the basilica church, so too this sacred spot is covered over with the present church. The stone was, allegedly, also a Roman altar dedicated to Neptune. A handsome replica is built alongside the river on the opposite side of the bridge and may evoke a somewhat more authentic response to the legend. It is certainly easier to imagine a boat coming alongside here to tie up with its sacred cargo. Inside the church we also find a fine 16th century Gothic pulpit with an image of Santiago Peregrino, while a glass case houses the image of Santiago Matamoros, slaying the Moors as the spearhead of the Reconquista. A recently restored 18th century oil painting has a more peaceful image of St. James body being carried across the sea accompanied by his faithful disciples.

Immediately over the bridge on the western bank (on the way to the pilgrim hostel) we pass the emblematic drinking font and roadside monument ❷ **Fonte do Carme XVI**[th]c displaying the arrival of the sarcophagus of St. James with his disciples Theodore and Athanasius and the scene of the conversion and baptism of the pagan Queen Lupa. And standing prominently above is the imposing facade of ❸ **Convento do Carme XVIII**[th]c

PADRÓN   187

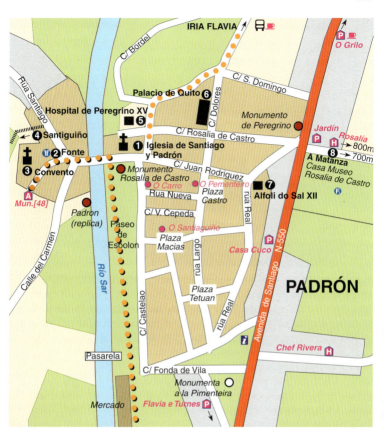

with its extensive balcony in front with fine views over the town. Nearby is one of the best kept Santiago secrets and little visited ❹ **Monte Santiaguiño** here, legend tells us, is where St. James first preached the gospel message. Standing imposingly above the river it is not difficult to envisage him delivering Christ's message of unconditional love and forgiveness from this remote and peaceful place. It is accessed, somewhat inconspicuously, between two houses on the road to Noia (just beyond the Fonte do Carme). Adjoining Santiaguiño Mount is the small chapel of Santiaguiño with a stone motif of the apostle baptising a

pilgrim with water poured from a scallop shell. While it is located less than a kilometre from the town centre it is a very steep climb up the stone steps along the Stations of the Cross but well worth the effort to this most significant of Jacobean sites that forms the front cover of this guide. Just as the vast majority of pilgrims (as well as the population at large) believe there is only one camino de Santiago they also mistakenly believe that St. James arrived in Spain dead – not alive. They therefore miss, perhaps, the most important part of the Santiago story – his life and teaching rather than his death and burial. ❺ **Hospital de**

Peregrinos XVth c. The medieval pilgrim hostal adjoining the church of St. James. ❻ **Palacio de Quito XVIII**th century Palace of the Bishop of Quito. *(see next stage for* **Colegiata de Santa María de Iria Flavia** *and* **Museo de Cela**). ❼ **Alfoli do Sal XII**th century former salt depot and one of the oldest extant building in Padrón (now a café). While not connected directly with the Santiago story, don't miss the most visited museum in Galicia ❽ **A Matanza** – Casa Museo *Rosalía de Castro* (1837 – 1885) is the house where she lived, wrote some of her exceptionally beautiful prose and died. It is lovingly maintained in its original condition and set in peaceful and delightfully shaded gardens. Some of her works are available from the museum shop (with translations from Gallego into Castellano and English). The house is situated just outside the town centre 700 meters from the main road. *Directions:* Take the Calle Salgado Araujo between the Botanical Gardens and the Pensión Jardín, continue over the river cutting (connecting the río Sar and río Ulla) and immediately over the railway turn left and the museum is on your right after 100 meters.

And don't miss sampling a plate of the famous Padrón Peppers *Pemento de Padrón* cultivated exclusively in nearby Herbón a delicious combination of sweet and piquant flesh with only one in every 30 or so being chilli-hot – The added fun is you never know which one! •*Restaurante O'Pementeiro* in Plaza do Castro specialises in them and you can order as a *tapa* from the bar without having to wait for the excellent restaurant (upstairs) to open. Many cafés and restaurants in the area offer this local speciality. The seeds were imported by the Franciscan monks of Herbón during their missionary work in Central and South America which adapted to the soil conditions found locally.

PADRÓN

The eye with which I see God, is the same eye with which God sees me.
Meister Eckhart.

23 | 24.9 km (15.5 miles) – Santiago

PADRÓN – SANTIAGO

--- ---	7.5 --- ---	30%
--- ---	13.8 --- ---	55%
--- ---	3.6 --- ---	15%
Total km	**24.9 km** (15.5 ml)	

26.6 km (+^340m=1.7 km)
Alto ▲ Monte Agro 260m (853 ft)
<A H> Areal 8.5 km / Teo 10.4 km

The Practical Path: This final stage into Santiago provides us with a varied day's walking and the inevitable stretches of main road that gets increasingly busy as we near the city. However, we still manage 30% on natural pathways through oak, pine and eucalyptus woodlands offering shade and respite from the traffic. There are also several cafés and alternative accommodation along the N-550, and drinking fonts at regular intervals. This stage also has the detour to Castro Lupario, so if you want to hack your way through the undergrowth and sit atop the pile of stones (all that remains of Lupa's hill fortress) allow yourself an extra two hours. Alternatively stay at the nearby pilgrim hostel in Teo or the casa rural in Parada de Francos and make your way into Santiago at a leisurely pace in the morning to make the pilgrim mass at noon.

0.0 km **Padrón Albergue** Leaving the hostel cross back over the river Sar via the medieval bridge turning <left past the church of Santiago **[0.2 km]** and make your way through the streets of the old quarter of Padrón along rua Dolores with the 18th century Palace of the Bishop of Quito *Palacio de Quito* (left) emerging onto open ground with the river on your (left) and the main road over to your (right). We pass the bus station **[0.4 km]** with regular services to Santiago throughout the day and •*café* (opens early). Next we cross a channel connecting the rivers Sar and Ulla and cross the main road N-550 **[!] [0.4 km]** with several •*cafés* in the modern buildings on either side that open early for breakfast and we now enter into the ancient bishopric of Iria Flavia **[0.1 km]**.

1.1 km **Colegiata de Iria Flavia** Colegiate church of Santa María de Iria and the adjacent cemetery of Adina mentioned in Rosalía de Castro's melancholy poetry. It was here in 1885 that, as she had wished, Rosalía de Castro

was buried. You can see her gravestone along the wall adjoining the main road (see photo right). In a cruel twist of fate, her body was exhumed and moved to the Pantheon in Santo Domingo de Bonaval in Santiago. The medieval church was originally dedicated to Santa Eulalia and was ransacked by Almanzor in 997. It was later reconstructed and re-dedicated to the Virgin Mary, a sign of increasing Marian
devotion along the Camino at this time. Xelmírez of Santiago further embellished the church in the Romanesque style in the 12th century and accorded it collegiate status. During the 13th century it was expanded along the lines of a basilica and was changed again during the Baroque period by the munificence of the Bishop of Quito (who was born in Padrón) and who commissioned the architect Melchor de Velasco to build the chapel of San Ildefonso. Open sarcophagi, reputedly from the 6th century, line the wall of the church and provides the whole with a final flourish of morbidity. There is some shade by the entrance with •*fonte*.

On the opposite side of the main road is the house of the cannons now principally the museum and office of the Camilo José Cela Foundation. Like Rosalía de Castro, he lived in Padrón and wrote some of his famous works here. He was awarded the Nobel Prize for Literature in 1989, *'for a rich and intensive prose, which with restrained compassion forms a*
challenging vision of man's vulnerability.' He died in 2002. Adjoining is the Cela Railway Museum also housed in this fine 18th century terrace. Cela's maternal grandfather, John Trulock, was a Scot and built the first railway in Galicia.

We now pass to the rear of the church and make our way over the railway line **[0.5 km]** emerging back onto the N-550 for one kilometre passing the modern •**Hotel Scala** *Café* **[1.0 km]** © 981 811 312 before turning off <left by a small garage *Talleres Casal* **[0.3 km]** to take a quiet road *(that runs between the railway and N-550)* part of which has overhanging vines and granite horreos as we pass through a collection of small hamlets Quintáns, Rueiro over stream **[0.8 km]** and thence through Cambela and Vilar. We now take a short stretch of track by the rail line to emerge back onto the **N-550 [1.6 km] [!]** in Loureiro •*Café Rianxeira* for a noisy but brief stretch to **A Escravitude [0.4 km]**:

4.6 km **A Escravitude** •*fonte* Here we have another famous Marian shrine built in the early 18th century over a fountain, site of a miracle that took place here in 1732. It is an enormous Baroque sanctuary, and like the church at Iria, has the N-550 built hard up against both the fountain and the church. Not a peaceful place to pray or slake the thirst but •*Café-*

bar Anaga nearby has refreshments and also •*Restaurante La Marmita*. Just *off* route is hotel •**Casa Grande da Capellanía** © 981 509 854 (from €40) and casa rural •**Casa da Meixida** © 981 811 113 (from €50) in Muiños. Proceed around the small park at the side of the sanctuary and up a steep country lane past the Romanesque church of **Sta. María de Cruces [0.3 km]** and up along an asphalt road to turn off <left onto **path [0.7 km]** through peaceful pine woods over rail line at **Picaraña Abaixo [0.8 km]** and through the village of Anguería de Suso and back down to the N-550 at Areal **[1.0 km]**.

2.8 km Areal (Picaraña/ A Gandaría) with choice of inexpensive Pensiónes (from €15) and restaurants along the main road opposite the industrial estate. •**A Milagrosa** © 981 803 108 •**Hospedaje Glorioso** © 981 803 181 above restaurant of the same name and •**Alfonso** adjoining restaurant Alfonso. We have another one kilometre stretch of main road up to a steep bend where we need to cross over **[!]** at sign for Faramello **[1.0 km]** passing the ancient Pazo do Faramello (down left) and •*fonte* (right) in the small hamlet of Faramello and shortly afterwards we reach a junction ❖ and sign for albergue **[0.8 km]** 100m *off* route up to the right in Teo **[0.1 km]**.

1.9 km Teo •**Albergue** modern pilgrim hostel with 24 spaces in bunk beds and good shower and toilet facilities. Also kitchen and extensive lounge/ dining area. 200m further up on the main road is •*Café-bar Casa Javier* which serves a pilgrim menu and there are several other bars along the main road.

At the junction ❖ The camino continues downhill to the río Tinto valley and then up sharply to the ermita de San Martiño and the cruceiro do Francos **[0.6 km]** one of the oldest wayside crosses in Galicia (see photo right). It is here we also join the ancient pilgrim way, which still retains its original name *rua de Francos* that leads us to the wide and shaded village green with casa rural and optional detour **[0.4 km]**.

1.0 km Cruce/Option ❖ •**Parada de Francos** © 902 200 432 casa rural in tranquil location amongst the ancient oaks directly on the camino with rooms from €45 with adjacent •*Restaurant* and detour to the little visited *Castro Lupario* one of the legendary sites of the fortress of this infamous pagan queen.

Detour 1.1 km ● ● ● ● ● ● **Castro Lupario** (one of the sites associated with the legendary queen Lupa and central to the Santiago story): Round trip of 2.2 kilometres (ruins only – no standing buildings). Access has recently been improved but you may have to push through the undergrowth. Allow around 2 hours to give yourself some time for reflection amongst the ancient stones and to admire the view. This route is not waymarked but a sign on the road now points to the start of the track and indicates the hill fort. ***Directions***: To take this detour, make your way diagonally over to the far side of the square and take the asphalt road by the modern house (no. 56). As you turn the corner, a distant view of Castro Lupario opens up in front of you. Proceed down to the río Tinto (a tributary of the Sar which in turn flows into the Ulla at Padrón) and cross over on the original and beautifully preserved Roman bridge **[400m]**. Continue up the asphalt road into the Concello de Brión and proceed to the top of the short incline and just where the road begins to drop down again over on the left hand side of the road is a rough lay-by **[200m]**. Proceed along the track and after another **[150m]** turn up right onto the ancient stone access route that winds its way up around the hill for **[350m]**. The fort

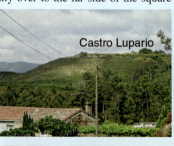

Castro Lupario

extends over the entire hilltop which is surprisingly level (see photo) and has a diameter of 100m. Make your way to the stand of stunted oak trees that struggle for a root hold amidst the ruins and let your imagination loose. It certainly evokes a greater sense of mystery than the alternative site at Castro de Lobeira overlooking the ria Arousa and the Pico Santo. From the ancient ruins here it is not difficult to imagine the pagan rituals, wild bulls and wolves which are all intimately connected with the fabled story of Queen Lupa and Sant Iago's faithful disciples searching for a site in which to bury his mortal remains.

❖ From the option point in the Village square take the road between the casa rural and restaurant and head down the narrow track to a short stretch of path before turning right> over rail bridge **[0.9 km]** into Osebe (O Seve) turning right> and then <left *(just before the N-550 with •café 200m off route)* past Casalonga school to cross the medieval bridge over the río Tinto **[1.1 km]** where you can (perhaps) observe the red on the rocks providing us with the key to its name •*fonte*. Continue s/o over crossroads onto delightful woodland path **[0.3 km]** crossing road **[1.0 km]** (•*Casa do Cruceiro* Ⓒ 981-548 596 off *route left 400m)*. Continue along path onto wide forest track before emerging onto road by factory and continue to new roundabout on the N-550 in A Grela **[1.3 km]** and take the pilgrim track to join a quiet lane and take the 2nd turn <left up to the main road **[0.6 km]** and turn right> to climb steeply up to Novo Milladoiro **[0.7 km]** (the tiny chapel *Capela de María Magdalena* looks somewhat out of place amongst the towering modern luxury apartment blocks right). Continue along the main road for **[0.2 km]** to:

STAGE 23: **195**

6.1 km Milladoiro *Polideportivo •café* modern sports complex with welcome café (left). *(Milladoiro is an exclusive new suburb of Santiago).* Continue s/o to the junction at the far end (radio mast) and onto a narrow asphalt track through eucalyptus passing the gates of the electricity utility *Union Fenosa* **[1.1 km]** to the high point of the day *Agro dos Monteiros* 260m and the Camino Portugués version of *Monte Gozo* with the spires of Santiago cathedral now visible just below the north / east horizon. Cross the AG-56 motorway turning <left onto woodland path that winds its way down to emerge between 2 houses in *A Rocha Vella*. Turn right> along the railway to bridge **[1.6 km]**. ❖¹ ● ● ● ● ● *(200m) on the far side of the crash barrier is a path alongside the railway leading to Castelo de Rocha Vella site of the city's ancient fortified bishops residence- head towards the electric pylon in the centre of the ruins. This historical area is presently undergoing excavation but the site is very accessible and has not (yet) been closed off to the public. If you visit be aware this is private land and take care not to disturb the ruins or fall into any of the open stone stairwells.* ❖¹ Proceed over the railway bridge down a very steep lane turning >right at T- junction **[0.2 km]**. ❖² ● ● ● ● ● *(100m) to medieval fonte left and then down right to this delightfully shaded drinking font on the banks of the river Sarela.* ❖² continue to bridge over the río Sarela and option point **[0.3 km]**:

3.2 km Option *Ponte río Sarela* a new route now enters Santiago via **Conxo**. This adds 0.7 km to the original road route but it is quieter and well waymarked. [● ● ● *for the road route proceed up (left) under city bypass past Universitario/ Hospital and down to a small park in A **Choupana**. Continue up to a modern block of apartments at Campo and turn <left along the main road into the city (church of Santa Marta opposite) merging into rua Rosalía de Castro to rejoin the recommended route].* For the new route take the path up right> under bridge **[0.7 km]** taking a series of turns into rua da benéfica de Conxo up past Televés over roundabout into rua de Sanchez Freiré crossing the busy Av. Romero Donallo and rejoining the road route in rua Rosalía de Castro **[2.4 km]** Here we turn up right over Av. Coruña into Av. Xoán Carlos I turning <left up into the city park *Alameda* by Capilla del Pilar through the park passing over the busy ring road and the traditional Portuguese entrance *Porta Faxeira* **[0.7 km]** (The historic gate no longer exists). We now take our final steps towards the fabled cathedral down the narrow rua Franco, lined with bars and restaurants and pause, perhaps, at another of the little known gems of the caminos and one of the most historic of all the buildings in Santiago associated with St. James *Capela de Santiago (this tiny chapel is the place where, by tradition, the cart carrying the body of St. James from Finisterre came to a halt and the body was laid out awaiting its final resting place – No.5 it is easily bypassed).* We have taken our weary body on the self-same road and now we take our last few steps towards the cathedral. By tradition the pilgrim from Portugal turns up right into rua Fonseca into the *Praza das Praterías* to enter the cathedral by the south door. This was the particular entrance used by the medieval pilgrim travelling the Camino Portugués and remains the oldest doorway to the Cathedral dating back to the 11th century (1078). The magnificent stone carvings surrounding this portal show hardly a hint of the intervening 900 years. St. James is represented in the centre between 2 cypress tress next to Christ **[0.4 km]**.

4.2 km Santiago Cathedral. Take time to just 'arrive'. We each feel different emotions on arriving at our destination after weeks of physical, emotional and spiritual challenges. Entering the cathedral can bring tears of joy… or disappointment. Whatever our individual reaction it is absolutely valid in that moment so honour it. Gratitude for our safe arrival is a universally appropriate response. However, if you are overwhelmed by the crowds why not return later when you might feel more composed and the cathedral is, perhaps, quieter. Whether now or later and whichever door you entered by, you might like to follow the timeworn pilgrim ritual as follows:

[1] Stand before the Tree of Jesse, the central column of Master Mateo's masterpiece: the Entrance of Glory *Pórtico da Gloria*. Millions of pilgrims, over the millennia, have worn finger holes in the solid marble as they placed their hands there as a mark of gratitude for their safe arrival (a barrier was placed here in 2007 to prevent further wear) but we can breathe in the beauty of this inner portico fashioned by Mateo in the 12th century (the outer porch was added in 1750). The Bible and its main characters come alive in this remarkable marble façade. The central column has Christ in Glory, flanked by the apostles and, directly underneath, St. James sits as intercessor between Christ and the pilgrim. Proceed to the other side and **[2]** touch your brow to that of Maestro Mateo, whose kneeling figure is carved into the back of the central column (facing the altar), and receive some of his artistic genius in the ritual known as the head-butting saint *santo dos croques*. Proceed to the High Altar (right hand side) to ascend the stairs and **[3]** hug the Apostle. Perhaps lay your forehead on his broad shoulders and say what you came here to say. Whatever your motivation and beliefs you have arrived here in one piece because, on some level, of the call of St. James. Proceed down the steps to the far side to the crypt and the reliquary chapel under the altar. **[4]** Here, you can kneel before the casket containing the relics of the great Saint and offer your prayer. A Pilgrim mass takes place every day at 12-noon. The swinging of the giant incense burner *Botafumeiro* was originally used to fumigate the sweaty (and possibly disease ridden) pilgrims. Requiring half a dozen assistants known as *Tiraboleiros* it became a rare occurrence, but it is used increasingly during mass these days. It is certainly a very moving and unique experience despite the constant sound and sight of flashlights. Perhaps the photo in this guide will suffice for your own memories so you can enter the whole experience more fully without having to think of composing your own shot.

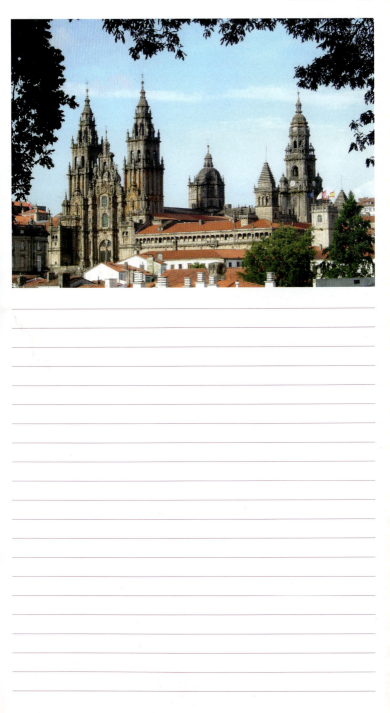

❏ Before a new chapter is begun, the old one has to be finished. Stop being who you were and change into who you are. *Paulo Coelho*

❏ **Historical Monuments:** ❶ Convento de Santo Domingo de Bonaval XIII[th]c *panteón y museo do Pobo Galego* (Galician ethnography). ❷ Casa Gótica XIV[th]c *museo das Peregrinacións* ❸ Mosteiro de San Martín Pinario XVI[th]c ❹ Arco y Pazo de Xelmirez XII[th]c ❺ Catedral y Portica de Gloria XII[th]c *claustro, museo e Tesouro* (treasury) *da Catedral* ❻ Hostal dos Reis Católicos XV[th]c *Parador* ❼ Pazo de Raxoi XVIII[th]c *Presendencia da Xunta* ❽ Colexio de Fonseca y claustro XVI[th]c *universidade.* ❾ Casa do Deán XVIII[th]c *Oficina do Peregrino* ❿ Mosteiro e Igrexa de San Paio de Antealtares XV[th]c *Museo de Arte Sacra.*

❏ **Turismo:** **[1]** Rua do Vilar, 63 ✆ 981-555 129 **[2]** Kiosco Plaza do Galicia **[3]** *Turgalicia* *Galicia regiao* rua do Vilar, 43 ✆ 981-584 081.
❏ **Albergues de Peregrinos:** ❶ **Monte del Gozo** *Xunta.*[500+] ✆ 981-558 942. ❷ **Residencia de Peregrinos San Lázaro** *Xunta.*[80] rua de San Lázaro 981-571 488. ❸ **Final del Camino** *Xunta.*[176] C/Moscú (behind Policia Autonomica) ❹ **Santo Santiago** *Priv.*[30] rua do Valiña,3 ✆ 606 437 437. ❺ **Acuario** *Priv.*[58] rua Estocolmo, 2-b. ✆ 981-575 438 ❻ **Seminario Menor La Ascunción** *Par.*[177] rua de Belvis (via rua de Trompas). ✆ 881-031 768. ❼ **Fogar de Teodomiro** *Priv.*[20] Plaza de Algalia de Arriba,3. ✆ 981-582 920 and its sister albergue ❽ **Roots & Boots** *Priv.*[48] 7 Rua do Campo Cruceiro do Galo. ✆ 699 631 594 (with garden)
❏ **Hoteles:** ■ €30 – €60 individual: •**La Salle** ✆ 981-585 667 Tras de Sta. Clara. •**Hostal Moure** ✆ 981-583 637 rua dos Loureiros / Laureles, 6 y •**Hostal Moure 2** Laureles 12. •**Hotel Fonte de San Roque** ✆ 981-554 447 rua do Hospitallilo, 8. •**La Campana** ✆ 981-584 850 Campanas de San Juan, 4. •**Estrela** ✆ 981-576 924 Plazuela de San Martín Pinario, 5-2° •**Hospedería San Martín Pinario Seminario Mayor** ✆ 981-583 009 Praza da Inmaculada. •**Pico Sacro** ✆ 981-584 466 rua San Francisco, 22 y •**Pico Sacro II.** •**La Estela** ✆ 981-582 796 rua Raxoi, 1. •**Hostal Barbantes** ✆ 981-581 077 rua do Franco, 3. •**Santa Cruz** ✆ 981-582 362 rua do Vilar, 42. •**Hostal Suso** ✆ 981-586 611 rua do Vilar, 65. •**San Jaime** ✆ 981-583 134 rua do Vilar, 12-2°. •**A Nosa Casa** ✆ 981-585 926 rua Entremuralles, 9 y •**Hostal Mapoula** ✆ 981-580 124 rua Entremuralles, 10. •**Hostal Alameda** ✆ 981-588 100 San Clemente, 32 *Alameda.* ■ €60+ individual: •**Hotel Rua Vilar** ✆ 981-557 102 rua Vilar, 12-2° •**Hotel Airas Nunes** ✆ 902-405 858 rua do Vilar, 17 *(opp. pilgrim office)* •**Entrecercas** ✆ 981-571 151 rua Entrecercas. •**Costa Vella** ✆ 981-569 530 Porta de Pena, 17. •**MV Algalia** ✆ 981-558 111 Praziña da Algalia de Arriba, 5. •**Hostal de los Reyes Católicos** Plaza Obradoiro ✆ 981-582 200.

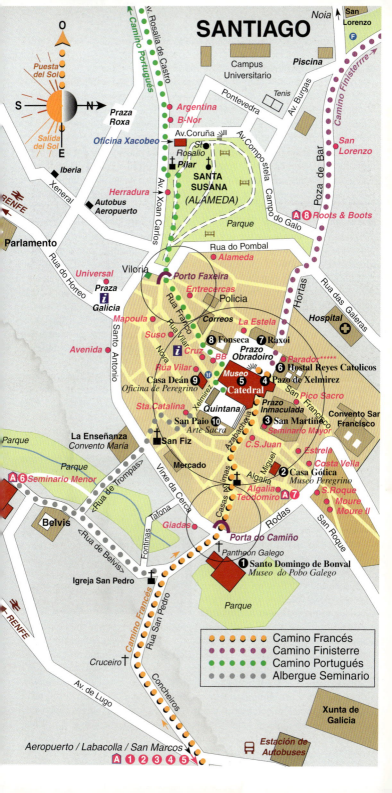

The four squares surrounding the cathedral, and providing access to it, are:

■ **Praza das Praterías**. The most intimate of the squares with its lovely centrepiece, an ornate statue of horses leaping out of the water. On one corner is the Dean's House *Casa do Deán*, now the pilgrim office. *(Providing you have fulfilled the criteria of a bona-fide pilgrim and have walked at least the last 100 kilometres, you will be awarded a certificate of completion* Compostela*)*. Along the walls of the cathedral are the silversmith's shops that give the square its name. Up the steep flight of steps we come to the magnificent southern door to the cathedral, traditionally the entrance taken by pilgrims coming from Portugal. Amongst the many sculptured figures portrayed here is one of St. James between two cypresses. The quality of the carvings and their arrangement is remarkable.

■ **Praza da Quintana.** This wide square is readily identified by the broad sweep of steps separating the lower part *Quintana of the dead* from the upper *Quintana of the living*. Opposite the cathedral is the high blank wall of the *Mosteiro de San Paio de Antealtares* (with museum of sacred art). The square provides the eastern entrance to the cathedral via the Holy Door *Porta Santa*, sometime referred to as the Door of Pardon *O Perdón*, which is only opened during Holy Years (any year when St. James Day, 25th July, falls on a Sunday). Adjoining it is the main entrance to the cathedral shop, which has several guidebooks with details of the cathedral's many chapels and their interesting carvings and statuary and the priceless artefacts and treasures in the museum.

■ **Praza da Inmaculada.** Here we have the north facing Azabachería façade, with the least well-known doorway and the only one that descends to enter the cathedral. It certainly has the most weathered aspect, with moss and lichen covering its bleak exterior. Opposite is the imposing edifice of the Mosteiro de San Martiño Pinario while below is Bishop's Arch *Arco Arzobispal* into:

■ **Praza do Obradoiro**. The golden square of Santiago is usually thronged with pilgrims and tourists admiring the dramatic west facing façade of the *cathedral*, universal symbol of Santiago, with St. James looking down on all the activity from his niche in the central tower (see photos right). This provides the main entrance to the cathedral and the *Pórtico da Gloria*. To the right of the steps is the discrete entrance to the museum. A combined  ticket will provide access to all rooms including the crypt and the cloisters and also to the palace of Archbishop Xelmírez *Pazo de Xelmírez* on the opposite side of the cathedral steps. A separate ticket gives access to the roof terraces. In this square we also find the Renaissance façade of the Parador named after the Catholic monarchs Ferdinand and Isabel *Hostal dos Reis Católicos* on whose orders in 1498 work commenced on its construction as a pilgrim hostel making it the oldest 'hotel' in continuous use in the world. At right angles (opposite the cathedral) is the more austere neoclassical town hall *Pazo de Raxoi*. Finally, making up the fourth side of the square is the gable end of the *Colexio de S. Xerónimo*, part of the university.

Museums and Parks: The crowds head for the Museo da Catedral but try and make time for the Pilgrim museum *Museo das Peregrinacións* in the Casa Gótica on rua de San Miguel dos Agros (behind Praza de S. Martiño Pinario). Further away at the Porta do Camiño (where the Camino Francés first enters the old city) is the Galician museum *Museo do Pobo Galego* housed in the Convento do Bonaval with artefacts and displays of Galician culture. The adjoining church has the relics of some of the illustrious sons (Castelao) and daughters (Rosalía de Castro) of Galicia *Panteón dos Galegos Ilustres.* To the rear of the church is a pleasant park, a good place for quiet reflection. At the other end of town are the delightful shaded city gardens, the *Alameda*. Take a stroll up the Avenue of the Lions *Paseo dos Leóns* to a handsome statue of Rosalía de Castro where a viewing gallery looks out westwards towards Finisterre. Opposite the statue are steps up to the semi-abandoned Igrexa de Santa Susana hidden amongst the trees. Santiago is a wonderful destination, full of vibrancy and colour. Stay awhile and soak up some of the culture and atmosphere of this fabled city. The official literature for the last jubilee year *año jubilar compostelano* stated boldly on the front cover: 'a road with an END *camino que tiene META*. That may be so, but it is not the end of the road.

Finisterre. Before you leave this corner of the peninsular why not visit the end of it at *Finis terrae*. '…Finisterre is one of the great hidden treasures amongst the many Caminos de Santiago. Only a tiny proportion of pilgrims arriving at Santiago continue by foot to the end of the road. The way to Finisterre truly follows *the road less travelled* and that may make all the difference. We need to search out the waymarks to the source of our own inner knowing. The light, while obscured by the dense materialism in our secular lives, lies hidden in our memory. It is no coincidence that the path to Finisterre ends at a lighthouse and the Ara Solis.' From *A Pilgrim's Guide to the Camino Finisterre* (new bi-lingual edition published in 2011).

You can obtain a pilgrim record or *credencial*, subject to membership, from one of the organisations listed below. The various Portuguese associations are currently in a flux with the pilgrim office in Porto now closed and information on the Camino Portugués still very limited. However, new associations are currently being discussed with the promise of more active engagement in the immediate future. In the meantime the following contacts may be of help.

UK: The Confraternity of St. James *www.csj.org.uk* the pre-eminent site in English with an on-line bookshop.

IRELAND: The Irish Society of the Friends of St. James based in Dublin, contact through their web site: *www.st.jamesirl.com*

U.S.A. American Pilgrims on the Camino. *www.americanpilgrims.com*

CANADA: Canadian Company of Pilgrims Canada. *www.santiago.ca*

SOUTH AFRICA: Confraternity of St. James of SA *www.csjofsa.za.org*

PORTUGAL: *www.caminhoportuguesdesantiago.com*

GALICIA: The Galician association AGACS *www.amigosdelcamino.com*

GENERAL: (latest news formerly Santiago-Today) *www.caminodesantiago.me*

There are a number of additional web sites connected with the Way of St. James or with the theme of pilgrimage in general. These sites provide links with other organisations so you can explore and find information that resonates with you:

Alternatives of St. James *www.alternatives.org.uk* exploration of ways of living that honour all spiritual traditions. Based at St. James Church, London.

The Gatekeeper Trust. Devoted to personal and planetary healing through pilgrimage. *www.gatekeeper.org.uk*

The Beloved Community *www.emissaryoflight.com* on-line courses in spiritual peacemaking and peace pilgrimages based in the USA.

Findhorn Foundation dedicated to personal and planetary transformation *www.findhorn.org* with daily reflections from 'Opening Doors Within.'

Lucis Trust incorporating the Arcane School of spiritual education, meditation and World Goodwill *www.alicebailey.org*

Paulo Coelho *www.paulocoelho.com.br* also *www.warrioroflight.com* with on-line news and reflections from Brazilian author of 'The Pilgrimage.'

Peace Pilgrim *www.peacepilgrim.com* reflections on her life and work.

The Quest A Guide to the Spiritual Journey. A practical home-study course for personal and spiritual discovery *www.nvo.com/thequest*

BIBLIOGRAPHY: Some reading with waymarks to the inner path include:

A Course In Miracles (A.C.I.M.) *Text, Workbook for Students and Manual for Teachers*. Foundation for Inner Peace.

Art of Pilgrimage *The Seeker's Guide to Making Travel Sacred*, Phil Cousineau.

Anam Cara *Spiritual wisdom from the Celtic world,* John O'Donohue. Bantam.

A New Earth *Awakening to Your Life's Purpose*, Eckhart Tolle. Penguin

Loving What Is *Four Questions That Can Change Your Life*, Byron Katie. Rider Books.

Handbook for the Soul *A collection of wisdom from over 30 celebrated spiritual writers*. Piatkus

How to Know God *The Soul's Journey into the Mystery of Mysteries*, Deepak Chopra. Rider Books.

The Journey Home *The Obstacles to Peace*, Kenneth Wapnick. Foundation for a Course In Miracles

No Destination *Autobiography (of a pilgrimage), Satish Kumar*. Green Books

Pilgrimage *Adventures of the Spirit*, Various Authors. Travellers' Tales

The Pilgrimage *A Contemporary Quest for Ancient Wisdom*. Paulo Coelho

Peace Pilgrim *Her Life and Work in Her Own Words*, Friends of Peace Pilgrim.

Pilgrim Stories *On and Off the Road to Santiago.* Nancy Louise Frey.

Peace is Every Step *The path of mindfulness in everyday life*, Thich Nhat Hanh. Rider

Sacred Contracts *Awakening Your Divine Potential*, Caroline Myss. Bantam

Sacred Roads *Adventures from the Pilgrimage Trail*, Nicholas Shrady. Viking

Secrets of God *Writings of Hildegard of Bingen*. Shambhala

Silence of the Heart *Dialogues with Robert Adams*. Acropolis Books

The Road Less Travelled *A new Psychology of Love,* M. Scott Peck. Arrow

The Soul's Code *In Search of Character and Calling,* James Hillman. Bantam

Wandering Joy *Meister Eckhart's Mystical Philosophy*. Lindisfarne Press

Wanderlust *A history of Walking*. Rebecca Solnit. Verso

Returning Home: These guidebooks are dedicated to the awakening of human consciousness. They arose out of an existential crisis and the perceived need for time to reflect on the purpose of life and its direction. Collectively we live in a spiritual vacuum of our own making where the mystical and sacred have been relegated to the delusional or escapist. Accordingly, we live in a three-dimensional world and refuse to open the door to higher dimensions of reality. We have impoverished ourselves in the process, severely limiting our potential. Terrorised by the chaotic world we have manifested around us we fail to notice that we hold the key to the door of our self-made prison – we can walk out any time we choose.

Whatever our individual experience it is likely that we will be in a heightened state of sensitivity after walking the camino. Be careful with whom you share your experiences and stay in contact with fellow pilgrims who can share or support any new understanding. This is a delicate moment when fear and doubt can easily creep in from a sceptical audience and dissipate our resolve. We are embarking on a journey of re-discovery of our true nature and opening to knowledge of Higher Worlds. Remember that we have, collectively, been asleep a long time and while change can happen in the twinkling of an eye it is often experienced as a slow and challenging process. It is never easy to let go of the familiar and to step into the new but all the help we need awaits but our asking.

The journey is not over and continues, as we will have it be. Dedicated to waking or sleeping, to the sacred or the mundane. As fellow pilgrims we tread both the physical and mystical paths together for there is a continuum that connects us with some larger way. This common purpose is encapsulated in the words of Peter Millar from *Our Hearts Still Sing:*

> A community of pilgrims needs to abandon clutter and to recover fundamentals. It needs to be set free from the obsession with trivia, to discriminate between things that abide, and passing fashions and fads. The sacraments of the pilgrim church deal with basic things – bread, water, oil, and the clasp of our sisters and brothers hand. They are the food, provisions and resources for people on the move.

Stay in Touch: The evolution of human consciousness is gathering apace, one manifestation of this is the increasing interest in taking time to go on pilgrimage and nowhere is this more apparent than along the camino where facilities struggle to keep up with demand. Information garnered in one month may be out of date the next as old hostels fall prey to new building regulations while new ones open up. Paths are realigned to make way for new motorways and budget airlines suddenly announce new routes (or with the advent of 'peak oil' – closing some). Whilst great care has been taken in gathering the information for this guide it also requires feedback from pilgrims who have recently walked the route to enable it to stay fresh and relevant to those who will follow on after us. Your comments and suggestions will be gratefully received and used to provide up-to-date advice on the free 'updates' page on **www.caminoguides.com** so if you would like to offer something back to the route or simply stay in touch please e-mail me at:
jb@caminoguides.com

A tithe of all royalties from the sale of this guidebook will be distributed to individuals and organisations seeking to preserve the integrity of this route.

Name *Nombre:* _____

Nationality *Nacionalidad:* _____

Passport No: *Número de Pasaporte:* _____

You are encouraged to join your local confraternity who may provide an official pilgrim record *credencial do peregrino*. This is essential if you intend to apply for a Compostela in Santiago. You can also obtain one at the commencement of your journey in either Lisbon or Porto. Apart from establishing your pilgrim status (essential when staying in hostels within Spain) they make an interesting record of your travels. The Galician Government *Xunta de Galicia* published a *Pilgrim's Rights* guide in 2008 which states 'if for whatever reason you cannot get a credencial you can use a route diary.' A pilgrim stamp *sello* (in Spanish) *carimbo* (in Portuguese) can readily be obtained from cathedrals, churches, hotels, tourist offices and pilgrim hostels.

Date *Fecha:*	Date *Fecha:*
Date *Fecha:*	Date *Fecha:*
Date *Fecha:*	Date *Fecha:*
Date *Fecha:*	Date *Fecha:*

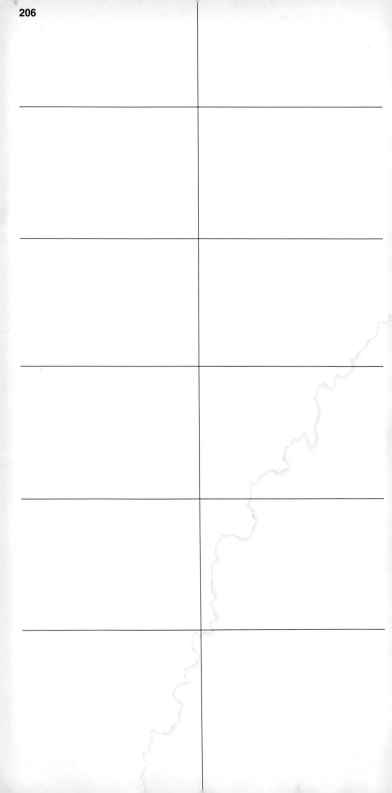

207

12 • Ways of St. James – Weeks [#]
12 • Caminos de Santiago

① • **Camino Francés** 800km [5 #]
  St. Jean / Roncesvalles – Santiago

② • **Chemin de Paris** 1000km [6 #]
  *Paris – St. Jean via Orléans & Tours
  Alt. route from Chartres - also:
  Soulac – Tarnos 170km [1 week]*

③ • **Chemin de Vézelay** 900km [5 #]
  *Vezélay – St. Jean via Bazas
  Alt. routes via Nevers and Bergerac
  Ext. to Namur (B) & Maastricht (NL)*

④ • **Chemin de Le Puy** 740km [4 #]
  *Le Puy-en-Velay – St. Jean
  Ext. to Geneva, Konstanz, Prague*

⑤ • **Chemin d'Arles** 750km [4 #]
  *Arles – Somport Pass
  (Ext. to via Francigena, Italy)*
  Camino Aragonés 160km [1 #]
  Somport Pass – Óbanos
  Cami *Catalán* 305km [2 #]
  *Barcelona (Montserrat) – Jaca
  Alt. via Zaragoza – Logroño (Ebro)*

⑥ • **Camino de Levante** 900km [5 #]
  *Valencia (Alicante) – Zamora
  Alt. route via Cuenca – Burgos*
  Camino de Madrid 320km [2 #]
  Madrid – Sahagún

⑦ • **Camino Mozárabe** 390km [2 #]
  *Granada – Mérida
  (Málaga alternative via Baena)*

⑧ • **Via de la Plata** 1,000km [6 #]
  *Seville – Santiago (Cadiz +175km)
  Huelva – Zafra 180km*

⑨ • **Camino Portugués** 240km [1½ #]
  Oporto – Santiago
  Camino Portugués 376km [2 #]
  Lisbon – Oporto

⑩ • **Camino Finisterre** 87km [½ #]
  Santiago – Finisterre
  Return via Muxía 114km [½ #]

⑪ • **Camino Inglés** 110km [5 #]
  Ferrol – Santiago

⑫ • **Camino del Norte** 830km [5 #]
  Irún – Santiago via Gijón
  Camino Primitivo 320km [2 #]